PRAISE FOR

WOMEN TALK MONEY

"These riveting essays will inspire, challenge, and force you to confront and reimagine your relationship with money. I cannot recommend it enough."
—Rachel Rodgers, Esq., author of *We Should All Be Millionaires*

"This book reads like lightning and works like a floodlight. A page-turner filled with enlightening. If you want to feel rich, read this book!"
—Susan Cheever, Guggenheim fellow and bestselling author of *Home Before Dark*

"This book is a gift I wish my younger self could have read as I worked to discover a healthy relationship with money. Each essay here, each secret told, helps anchor our money stories in values, based on a beautiful dance between power and love."
—Zainab Salbi, author of *Freedom is an Inside Job,* and founder of Women for Women International

"*Women Talk Money* is required reading. I didn't realize how alone I was feeling, and now, like with most great books, I feel held."
—Noor Tagouri, podcast producer of *Sold in America*

"The road to financial competence can be complex, scary, and seemingly impossible. This book let's you know that you're not alone."
—Tiffany "The Budgetnista" Aliche, *New York Times* bestselling author of *Get Good with Money*

"This powerful book helps us navigate our narratives around lack, abundance, well-being, privilege, oppression, suffering, and joy. We are reminded that money isn't everything and money impacts everything."

—Layla F. Saad, *New York Times* bestselling author of
Me and White Supremacy

"The collection contains universal truths as well as uniquely American ones. Thoughtful and expansive . . . A worthy read."

—*Kirkus Reviews*

ALSO BY REBECCA WALKER

Black, White, and Jewish: Autobiography of a Shifting Self

Baby Love: Choosing Motherhood After a Lifetime of Ambivalence

Adé: A Love Story

What's Your Story? A Journal for Everyday Evolution (with Lily Diamond)

ALSO EDITED BY REBECCA WALKER

To Be Real: Telling the Truth and Changing the Face of Feminism

What Makes A Man: 22 Writers Imagine the Future

One Big Happy Family: 18 Writers Talk About Polyamory, Open Adoption, Mixed Marriage, Househusbandry, Single Motherhood, and Other Realities of Truly Modern Love

Black Cool: One Thousand Streams of Blackness

WOMEN
TALK
MONEY

BREAKING THE TABOO

EDITED BY

REBECCA WALKER

SIMON & SCHUSTER PAPERBACKS

NEW YORK   LONDON   TORONTO   SYDNEY   NEW DELHI

Simon & Schuster Paperbacks
An Imprint of Simon & Schuster, Inc.
1230 Avenue of the Americas
New York, NY 10020

Tressie McMillan Cottom's essay "The Price of Fabulousness" was first published in her own essay collection, *Thick: And Other Essays* (New York: The New Press, 2019).

Daisy Hernandez's essay "Only Ricos Have Credit" was first published in her memoir, *A Cup of Water Under My Bed* (Boston, MA: Beacon Press, 2014).

And an excerpt of Alice Walker's foreword, "Counting My Eggs," was first published in Jonathan K. DeYoe's book, *Mindful Money: Simple Practices for Reaching Your Financial Goals and Increasing Your Happiness Dividend* (Novato, CA: New World Library, 2017).

Names and identifying characteristics of some individuals and places have been changed.

First Simon & Schuster trade paperback edition March 2023

For information about special discounts for bulk purchases, please contact Simon & Schuster Special Sales at 1-866-506-1949 or business@simonandschuster.com.

The Simon & Schuster Speakers Bureau can bring authors to your live event. For more information or to book an event, contact the Simon & Schuster Speakers Bureau at 1-866-248-3049 or visit our website at www.simonspeakers.com.

Interior design by Ruth Lee-Mui

Manufactured in the United States of America

1   3   5   7   9   10   8   6   4   2

Library of Congress Cataloging-in-Publication Data

Names: Walker, Rebecca, editor.
Title: Women talk money : breaking the last taboo / edited by Rebecca Walker.
Description: First Simon & Schuster hardcover edition. | New York, NY : Simon & Schuster, 2022. | Summary: "A searing and fearless anthology of essays exploring the profound impact of money on women's lives, edited by prominent feminist and writer Rebecca Walker"—Provided by publisher.
Identifiers: LCCN 2021042302 | ISBN 9781501154324 (hardcover) | ISBN 9781501154348 (ebook)
Subjects: LCSH: Women—Finance, Personal. | Sex workers. | Money.
Classification: LCC HG179 .W5767 2022 | DDC 332.0240082—dc23/eng/20211013
LC record available at https://lccn.loc.gov/2021042302

ISBN 978-1-5011-5432-4
ISBN 978-1-5011-5433-1 (pbk)
ISBN 978-1-5011-5434-8 (ebook)

For all of us who struggle to make sense of money:
how to earn it honestly and spend it well,
to respect its power and transform it for good,
to say no to business as usual and survive what comes next.

Contents

x   CONTENTS

COUNTING MY EGGS

ALICE WALKER

I HAD my first paying job when I was seven. My two older brothers and I were hired to pick daffodils for the wife of the man who owned the land our parents worked. In this part of middle Georgia there are thousands of gigantic pecan trees, and it was under such trees that the three of us set to work. There were deep-yellow and pale-yellow daffodils (which our boss, in a strong Southern accent, referred to as "jon'quils") almost as far as the eye could see. To a child it seemed a fairyland, and I set to picking daffodils with delight. We were paid a nickel a bunch (our boss lady sold them in town for a quarter a bunch, which we didn't know and didn't care about), and I proved to be a speedy and efficient picker. I might have earned as much as half a dollar each day.

This went into a piggy bank that was shaped like an actual pig. My hardworking parents instilled in all their children, early on, that saving was to be a habit that would mean we could afford to buy presents for ourselves as well as for others at Christmas.

A few years later, when I wanted desperately to learn to play the piano, my mother decided to let me have all the eggs laid by our chickens. I sold these to a market in town and was able to pay the fifty cents per lesson my teacher required. In winter, though, the hens laid less, and eventually I had to give this up.

Not until fifty years later would I circle back to this dream, hire a piano teacher, and learn to play six songs, among them James Weldon Johnson's "Lift Ev'ry Voice and Sing" (commonly known as "The Negro National Anthem") and Beethoven's "Ode to Joy." Having learned these six songs, I promptly forgot how to play the piano, which is one of those mysterious happenings in life that makes you wonder.

But the egg experiment taught me something that put me at odds with the endless-growth idea of classic capitalism and made me a budding socialist. I could see that the number of eggs required to fund my musical expansion was finite. I could also see that the eggs my passion for music was taking from my protein-deficient family would, in the end, undermine the health and stability of all of us. The experience taught me that I needed to develop a keener sense of planning and a deeper understanding of the means and reliability of production.

One of my father's biggest dreams was to own a car. When my older brothers grew skilled enough to keep one running, my father bought one. It was not the little red sports car of his dreams, but it was roomy and rugged, and he could get almost all of his large family inside it. In this car the two of us, when I was thirteen or so, rode off to his lodge meetings, where I was designated secretary and took notes, or "minutes," as they were called. We also rode into town to visit the bank. If the family had accumulated even ten dollars above the month's expenses, into the passbook of the Farmers & Merchants Bank it went.

Many years after I, the youngest, had left home, it was a joy to learn that my mother, who had always stayed home after getting everyone else dressed and ready to leave the house, learned to drive a car and at some point found her way to the ocean, which she had never seen. Not even bothering to take off her stockings, she plunged in, as if she could swim. There is a wonderful photograph of her beaming and sopping wet, as if she'd just met her own mother. (And of course she had!)

But how clever it was of my father to take me with him to his boring (to me) lodge meetings, where I was to take down information that had zero meaning to me. I see it now as preparation for the writing life that has been mine since I was in my teens. And how positively resolute it was of him to take me with him to make deposits in the Farmers & Merchants Bank, the only unsegregated establishment in the county and the only place white people seemed almost happy to see him.

I somehow developed, with the guidance of my parents and the love of my community, a sense that I could learn the mechanics of life: find work, do it well, enjoy it as much as possible, and use my earnings to support the yearnings that sprang, apparently, from my soul. Babysitting, waiting tables, and working as a "salad girl" at a local 4-H retreat for white youth all meant I could, by the time I was a junior in high school, take care of all my clothing, hair, health, and dental needs. This was fortunate because, after raising eight children, my parents were exhausted and struggling with their own health.

Right up to my forties, I made a monthly list of every purchase and every anticipated expense and measured it against what income I might expect to receive. I had a profound sense of my indebtedness to both my parents on the day that I knew I could singlehandedly pay all my daughter's expenses as she went off to Yale.

As a woman I was always aware that unless I wanted to be someone else's dependent throughout my life, I must become, myself, my own breadwinner and independent person, and that the freedom this assured meant I could speak my mind and share my thoughts and resources in any way I choose. A woman afraid to speak her mind is usually a woman who depends for her upkeep on someone else. This would have been intolerable for me, though I might have adored the person who "kept" me.

Learning about money is as important, perhaps more important, than any other subject. I recommend finding a teacher, or teachers, who can help navigate the world of saving, and of spending, wisely. It is crucial that women have shelter, for instance, listed in their names. Otherwise, they and their children can be held hostage as they were for hundreds of years during which only the man "owned" the house, as, by marriage, he "owned" his children.

If individual ownership is impossible, then by all means form collectives with other women that will allow for the acquiring of property together. This can strengthen one's own stability as well as ease the burden on everyone. I have not myself been able to do this, but it has always seemed to me to be both extremely logical as well as a way to foster well-being and community in a country rarely supportive of independence of this kind and magnitude.

Attempt to find a system of saving and increasing one's wealth that is ethical in its concern for the planet and for other creatures, as well as humans. Witnessing school closures, widespread food anxiety and homelessness, and the lack of access to basic health care in our country and beyond, I am reminded of what was important in my community and in my family as I was growing up: learning how to earn money, how to use it for good purposes, and to save whatever you could of it, in anticipation of one's most cherished desires. All with the understanding that if there is to be a future at all, it is best to be able to support it in a style that one wants, rather than one that is imposed.

WOMEN TALK MONEY

An Introduction

REBECCA WALKER

THOUGH WOMEN'S bodies, labor, and very existence have always been interchangeable with money itself, their lived experiences of this reality are often unspoken, silenced, or forced into incoherence. Women's stories of their struggles with money are shrouded in secrecy and shame, and frequently marked by paralysis and disenfranchisement. Women's domestic labor is still undervalued to the tune of almost $11 trillion a year; the wealth of twenty-two men in the world is equal to, or surpasses, the wealth of all African women; and the mass exodus of women from the workforce during the Covid pandemic is set to reverse a decade of progress toward global gender equity. To paraphrase Audre Lorde, our silence is clearly not protecting us.

Until women begin to talk freely about money, to amass information about money, to reflect critically on how money works in our society and strategize how to change it, until we put as much thought into negotiating our money as we do into maintaining our relationships, plotting our careers, or raising our children, we are at an even greater risk of remaining victims of a predatory financial system. Our contributions will continue to be unrecognized and undervalued, and our compensation will continue to pale in comparison to our male counterparts'. We will remain ignorant where we should be informed, silent where we could be loud, and weak where we must be strong.

This book is about forwarding this critical and essential work, with the intention of supporting the radical shifts necessary to bring more women into positions of financial power, even (and perhaps especially) if those positions are used to dismantle the structures that brought them there in the first place. This collection did not emerge from a vacuum, but rather from the years following the Great Recession in America, when I became acutely aware of how little women spoke honestly with one another about money.

My circle of friends at the time—mostly women artists, writers, doctors, lawyers, academics, nonprofit directors, researchers, entrepreneurs, and consultants of all stripes—were socioeconomically displaced. Mostly middle-class, with outliers on each end of the spectrum, we felt the same economic winds that bore down on our working-class and working-poor counterparts, and struggled with many of the same outcomes: upside-down mortgages, sudden and unfathomable debt of the sort our parents warned us about, growing financial anxiety about health care, tuition, food. Mainstays of our privileged lives, like a trip to another country, a meal at a favorite restaurant, a random theater performance, were now expenditures to be carefully considered. Whole neighborhoods were abruptly beyond our means.

Talking to the women in my life during that period, hearing their stories, and commiserating with their stress, it occurred to me that we were all, in our own similar but separate ways, going through a collective and distinctively gendered Class Crash. Even though we had not caused the economic crisis—not by a long shot—still, we asked ourselves what we had done wrong and what we could do to fix it. We took every gig we could get, pushed ourselves harder than ever, and contemplated our deepening fatigue. *Is this the new normal?* we wondered. *And if it is, how will we survive it?*

Swept along with the crowd, child underfoot, and living on Maui where one bag of groceries might cost a hundred dollars, I tried hard to stay calm and carry on. I pitched projects and took on speaking gigs and writing assignments in far-flung places like Estonia and Bulgaria, grateful that my son's father still cared for our son while I was gone. While I was privileged most of my life—private high school, Ivy League college, international travel, and the like—I wasn't always, and, unlike many of my peers who were second- and third- and fourth-generation middle or upper-middle class, I felt the specter of poverty keenly. I knew how a culture punished single mothers by depriving them of respect and financial support. I knew how an economic system built around slave labor treated Black women, limiting their opportunities to backbreaking work, paying them just enough—not even that, sometimes—to survive.

My father's mother was a bookkeeper who worked several jobs to feed and house her three sons in Brighton Beach, Brooklyn, after the Second World War. My mother's mother worked as a sharecropper in Georgia, and then as a domestic, cleaning the homes of white people and caring for their children more than she was able to take care of her own. By comparison, we had plenty and then some, but I still noticed the differences. When I was a child, we lived in a beautiful but dilapidated brownstone that needed, literally, everything. I liked my public school but loved the private school across the park: its stately Victorian limestone building, language and music classes, and attentive teachers. But even though my father often worked sixteen-hour days arguing civil rights cases on behalf of people who needed and deserved his help, my parents could not afford the tuition. After they divorced, I moved into a two-and-a-half-room apartment with my mother and watched her track her income and expenses to the dollar.

I also made a few financial mistakes in my life before the Recession, decisions that haunted me decades later and left me too close to the edge. I bought expensive sweaters and boots at a high-end department store on Madison Avenue—itself no longer standing, a victim of its own excess—when perhaps I should have put my money in a high-yield savings account or prevailed upon my father to teach me to navigate the wilds of the stock market. I sold my first apartment—bought with an advance from my second book and the help of my mother—impulsively, in a fugue state of infatuation. Perhaps because the object of my romantic fixation was a woman, I conveniently forgot the teachings of Virginia Woolf and glossed the wise words from the women in my life who taught me to hold on to that which was hard earned and hard won, to remember the generations of toil that brought me to my own bought and paid-for doorstep.

But by the so-called end of the Recession, the specifics were no longer relevant; only shame remained, feelings of failure and irresponsibility, a nagging sense that I squandered my financial foundation. I had made a lot of the money back by then, yes, and I bought new dresses, and life insurance, and put money into my son's 529 account even though he was only in second grade; I donated to organizations that supported women's entrepreneurship around the world, to politicians I thought could make a difference, to the fund I had cofounded for young women and trans youth working for social justice, but it was never enough. I would never catch up to where I should be. I was tortured by this thought, and yet I spoke of it to no one. Until I did, and it changed my life.

As my women friends and I stood squarely in the wreckage of our newfound reality, the effects of the global economic crisis around us as if sticks of dynamite had been hurled through each of our siloed existences, I spoke of my shame, and they spoke of theirs. Really, at that point, what else was there to talk about? And then we were off and running and speaking about what we had not spoken about for decades, for centuries, forever: money. And what it was doing to us. Money. And what we had done with it. Money. And how it had been used to control us. Money. And how the workings of it had been kept from us. Money. And what our parents taught us about it. Money. And what we had learned about it ourselves. Money. And how it shaped our lives. And our parents' lives. And their parents' lives. Money. And what we needed to change—or not—in how we thought about it. Money. And what we wanted our children to know about it. So that they would live their lives with money thoughtfully. Out loud. Without shame. Like we planned to.

It was extraordinary. I found myself in a netherworld with one, twelve, a hundred other women, letting my proverbial hair down, eventually unfurling stories not just of financial missteps and miscalculations, but also of savvy decisions and calculated windfalls and fiercely negotiated paydays well above the norm. I was far from alone. One friend was getting one meal a week from a food bank, while another had gotten a small business loan and opened a restaurant that was barely breaking even. A colleague was on the precipice of eviction, and another had just flipped a house and cleared $200,000 for her efforts but lost her partner in the process. A classmate from college had filed for bankruptcy not once, but twice, and another, who always looked perfectly turned out with fashionably dressed kids in tow, waited for child support payments that never came. Our money stories revolved around everything under the sun: marriage and divorce, aging parents and ailing children, the fight for tenure before a committee that was entirely male, the fight for a promotion under a team leader who preferred his assistant keep assisting.

For me, these conversations were catharsis ripped straight from Greek drama. Medea. Iphigenia. Antigone. And we were the choir. It was similar to talking about any other collective cataclysmic event, the fall of the World Trade towers, for instance, or the attack on the Capitol. Except that we had never approached our experiences with money in this way, as something that was happening to all of us, that was connected to a system designed to keep us all separate, in our respective places. We had thought that telling the truth about money might divide us by revealing how different we were; we had not considered that the same honesty might unite us against whatever forces still kept us apart. The disclosure of my sliver of shame, the ejection of this tiniest morsel of my potential undoing, was liberating beyond expectation. I had shared myself free. Not free from bad decisions or patriarchal, white supremacist capitalism, but free from thinking that its machinations and mutilations, its structurally maintained inequality and callous disregard for life, the earth, the future, was somehow my fault, my crime, my cross to bear. Free from thinking I was alone in it, this story of money and how it shaped my life. I was not.

The writers in this book are here to help you find the same freedom. They are, collectively, some of the most brave and wonderful women I've had the good fortune to work with, and I applaud and bow in gratitude to each and every one of them for the pain and struggle and wisdom they spilled onto these pages in the name of sisterhood and reclamation. For what I know now is that it is extremely difficult for women to talk honestly about how money works in our lives; it is in fact quite nearly the last taboo. The way money moves in women's lives, mysterious and mystified, shuts us down just as we begin to speak. Our money stories resist their own telling, as if the revelations might bring down an empire, starting with us, those who dare to look.

I won't list all the stories told here, all the burdens laid down, but I will say that they span the gamut from the perils of technocracy to the financial implications of transgender identity, from the loss of material inheritance to the discovery of spiritual wealth, from fat as a financial issue to foster parenting as an act of resistance. It is a wonderful and inspiring collection, and I love it more, now that it is finished, than I ever thought I could. I am heartened to imagine how these stories might impact the global discussion of women and money in the shadow of a global pandemic that has hit women, and especially women of color, extraordinarily hard.

To all who find themselves here I say: may these essays, these voices, help you write your own story of money, and put to rest forever the thought that you have to carry it alone.

REBECCA WALKER
Los Angeles, California
April 2021

ONLY RICOS HAVE CREDIT

DAISY HERNÁNDEZ

AT FIFTEEN, I land my first job. At McDonald's.

Learning the register's grid with its Big Macs and Value Meals is easy, like picking up the mechanics of playing Pac-Man. My fingers memorize the grid so that in a few weeks I am considered what the managers call "one of our fast cashiers." At the end of my shift, I feed my card into the time clock, and then stand next to the manager's desk to hear how much money is in my till from the day's orders, hopeful that it will be higher than the white girl who has been here longer and can handle more customers.

I love my job. I love that it's not a job. It's the start of something, not the American Dream exactly, because I am an American, so what other kind of dream would I have? No, this job at McDonald's is the start of the rest of my life. It is the first stop on my way to that country where rich people live and don't worry about money or being treated badly when they don't know all the English words or behave *como una india*.

A man shuffles up to my register at McDonald's one day. He's old and his voice is muddled, as if his mouth were full of marbles. When I ask him to repeat his order, he snaps, "What's the matter? You don't know English?"

Without thinking, I twirl around and walk away, past the fry machine with its crackling oil and into the kitchen, where the guys are peeling slices of cheese and tossing them on burger patties, then wiping their foreheads with the back of their hands. I stop at the freezer. I'm not breathing right. My hands are shaking, and a minute later, the manager wants to know why I left the register and he ended up having to take the gringo's order. But I don't know how to say that I didn't trust myself to be polite, and I can't lose this job.

When my first paycheck from McD's lands in my hand, it is for a total of about $71 and change. I cash the check and take it to the beauty store on Anderson Avenue. There I spend close to an hour, inspecting rows of matte lipsticks and lip glosses and lip liners with names the colors of precious stones and wild flowers and sand dunes. The price tags are glued to the front of the display case, the numbers in thick block print: $3.99, $4.99.

The women in my family buy 99-cent lipstick. The women in my family are their lipsticks. My mother is a pale strawberry. Tía Dora, a warm peach. Tía Chuchi, a pomegranate. Tía Rosa, a plum. And I am a black raspberry. The fruit never lasts. It smudges. It hardly sticks. It vanishes when you take a sip of soda. Tía Chuchi, who knows everything, schools me in how to eat a meal without losing your *pintalabios*. "You put your tongue out like this," she says, and then she sticks her *lengua* out at me and maneuvers the spoon's contents onto it (some melon, a *pedazo* of yuca), careful to not touch the edge of her lips. "See?" she says, chewing. "I knew a woman who did that. She kept her lipstick on the whole day."

Sometimes, Tía Dora splurges on a $3.99 tube. Sometimes, a friend gives her a makeup bag from the mall, the kind they include as a freebie after you've spent $75. The color from those lipsticks is thicker, like hand cream.

Now at the beauty store, I choose the items I could never ask my mother to buy, because a $4.99 lipstick would make her shake her head and ask, "What's wrong with the ninety-nine-cent one?"

It is a question I never know how to answer because I don't know that what I am trying to say is this: "I'm buying lipstick to make myself feel better about the classist, racial, and sexual oppressions in our lives. The ninety-nine-cent lipstick ain't gonna cut it." Instead, I roll my eyes at the suggestion. "Mami, *por fa*. It's ugly."

With my own paycheck, I buy the lipstick I want, which with tax turns out to cost something like $5.07. I also pick up face powder and eyeliner and mascara. In a single hour, half of my paycheck is gone. Back at McD's, I plead to work more hours, and when I get longer shifts and more pay, I am earning almost as much as my mother does in a week at the factory. Close to $200.

In her book *Where We Stand*, bell hooks writes about a time in American life, or at least in Kentucky where she grew up, when people did not spend their earnings on lipstick, face creams, or even television. People valued what they had. They enjoyed homemade fruit jams, scraps of fabric, and each other's stories. They didn't even blame the poor for being poor.

If a Black person was poor back then it was because the white man was keeping them down. The day would come when racism would be wiped out and every Black man, woman, and child would eat with only fine linen napkins and not worry about their lipstick smudging. Class wasn't the problem; race was.

Unfortunately, when the lunch counters and the schools were integrated, the wealthy Black families got out of town, the white activists went back home, and the rest of the country turned around to look at poor and working-class Black people and found them to blame for not having the good napkins.

A manager at McD's approaches me one day.

"I've got a proposition for you," she starts and explains how we can make money from the till, how easy it is, how you can pretend to ring up an order but not really do it, how, you see, it isn't a big deal. We'll split the money. It'll be cool. And I say, "Sure," not because I want to steal, not because I understand that she's asking me to do that, but because I'm afraid that if I say no, she'll be angry with me. I'm a teenager. She's in her twenties. I want her to like me.

At the end of the shift, she finds me in the break room. She has light brown eyes and a wide forehead. She grins at me, places a small bundle in my hand, and walks away. I shove the money in my pocket, and, alone in the McDonald's bathroom, I count the bills.

$20. $40. $60 . . . $300.

That's the number that stays with me decades later. It might have been less or more, but what I remember is $300 and that I had never held so much money in my hands, never seen so many twenties all at once, not even in the envelope my mother got at the bank when she cashed her paycheck.

I know exactly what to do with the money, too. Or at least a part of it. I take it to the dentist on Bergenline Avenue.

Fragoso is a crabby old Cuban who works out of a back room in his apartment. We owe him hundreds of dollars for filling the holes in my mouth. Now, however, I enter his apartment the way rich people must feel all of the time—on top of things. Here I am, with hundreds of dollars to put toward the bill, hundreds of dollars my parents won't have to worry about. I am singlehandedly taking care of business.

Among the drills and jars of cotton balls, Fragoso counts the twenties. "That's it?" he asks, looking over at me.

My face freezes. The room grows smaller, suffocating. I nod my head, bite my naked lip, the shame running through me like a live wire, and I promise to bring more next time.

What I knew back then about money was that you could work for it or you could take it. In college, I found out people I had never met would also give it to you.

He's wearing a business suit. A dark suit. The tie is some brilliant color, a red perhaps. He smiles at me the way men do on television, warm and confident, but this man is younger. He can't be much older than me, twenty-five at most, and he is white or Italian or maybe Latino. He calls out from beside a folding table at my college campus. The sun is bright and the man is offering free mugs, free keychains, free T-shirts. All I have to do is apply for a credit card.

I fill out the form the way you would enter your name into a raffle. It is all a matter of luck. I am eighteen and I don't know about credit scores. My parents pay in cash for everything. Credit cards are a phenomenon that happens to other people, rich people.

When the credit card comes in the mail, however, I know exactly what to do. I march into a shoe store in Englewood and ask to see a pair of dark-brown Timberlands, size seven. It's the early '90s, and everyone is parading around school in that brand. You wear them with baggy Tommy Hilfiger jeans and dark lipstick, and when people dress that way, they look special, like the white plates with gray flowers my mother brings out for Thanksgiving.

The shoes cost close to $100, a little more than half of my weekly pay from my two part-time jobs. But I don't have to give cash now. I hand the woman the plastic card the way I have seen other women do in stores, as if the price doesn't matter, and I'm grateful that my hand doesn't shake, even though I'm outrageously nervous.

She hands me the receipt, a slip of paper that fits in my palm like a secret note a girl has passed to me in class. Just sign here. That's all. My signature. My promise to pay.

Back home, my mother stares at my feet. "One hundred dollars?"

The question hovers at her lips, as if she has come across a cubist painting and is trying to untangle the parts.

First *pintalabios*, now shoes. Tía Chuchi doesn't know how I turned out to be such a materialist. "No one in our family is like that," she insists, and I would like to believe her.

It is a strange comfort to think that some aspect of being raised among strangers brought out the worst in me, that if I had been born and raised in my mother's native land, I would have known the Kentucky that bell hooks writes about.

But this is an illusion. Colombia is where I sometimes think it began.

• • •

I am walking down the street in Bogotá, holding my mother's hand. We are visiting for a few weeks, spending days with my grandmother and enough cousins to fill up two of my classrooms in New Jersey. The civil war reveals itself here and there, mostly in the rifles of the security guards at the airport.

As we stroll down the street, a boy my age, about six or seven, his arm thin as a twig, his lips cracked, extends a hand toward me. Our eyes meet, the same eyes I have, the same small voice except his pleads, "A few coins please, to buy a little milk."

His hand is a tiny version of my father's. It is dirty and scarred. I cringe, afraid of something I cannot name.

My mother snaps me close to her and quickens her pace, my head close to the fat on her hip.

"Why is that boy asking for money?" I ask.

"To buy *leche*."

"But why?"

"That's what children here have to do."

Language is a rubber band. It bends and stretches and tries to hold in place our mothers and the street in Bogotá and the boy asking for milk.

In English, they are street children. Abandoned children. Neglected children. Thrown-away children. The adjectives expand to make sense of little boys having to ask strangers for the first taste we are entitled to in this life: milk at the tit.

In Spanish, though, in Bogotá, there is no need for extras or explanation. These boys are everywhere. They are *gamines*, a word borrowed from the French and meaning "to steal." A boy who steals.

"You were so afraid of the street kids," Tía Chuchi remembers now, fondly, as if, as a girl, I had been frightened by spiders or ladybugs or wingless birds.

After my first credit card, an offer arrives in the mail for another one. I call the 800 number nervously, as if I were asking someone on a date who has shown a bit of interest. When the person says, "You've been approved," I feel it in my body, an elation like warm water.

The offers continue to come in the mail, and I buy a large, red fake-leather wallet and fill each pocket with a credit card: Discover, Visa, MasterCard, Macy's, J. C. Penney, Victoria's Secret. I sit in my bedroom, admiring the little plastic rectangles and feeling genuinely accomplished, because in my home, in my community, people do not have credit cards. "*Nada de deudas*," my father declares, and my mother agrees—no debts.

Down on Bergenline Avenue, storeowners are used to people buying even large purchases like refrigerators with cash. Only *ricos* have credit. My mother doesn't even believe in layaway plans.

At the Valley Fair department store, she explains, "It's better to wait until you have all the money."

"The dress will be gone by then," I argue, to which she gives me her maddening standard answer: "There will be another one."

During my last semester of college, I study abroad in England with a group of students from private schools. I am there on a scholarship with a $5,000 student loan and a wallet full of Visas and MasterCards. With every purchase, I tell myself why it's necessary.

When will I be in London again? Never!

You can't find sweaters like these back home.

What would people say if I returned without souvenirs?

This is my only chance to see a real Oscar Wilde play.

And the classic: *All the other kids are going.*

None of this is to say that I don't keep track of my spending. I do. I review my new credit card charges, mentally checking off why each one was required. I monitor my bank account frequently, careful to slowly chip away at the student loan.

One night, standing in line to use the phone in our student house, I overhear one of my classmates, a tall girl from a state I've only seen on maps. She's going through her own list of justifications for charges on her father's credit card. "I had to buy the boots, Daddy." A pause. "I know they were expensive, but I needed them. It's so cold here."

I shake my head, quite smug that I would never do anything like that to my own parents. My credit card bills, and I am very pleased to say this, are my responsibility. So caught up in this perverse pride, I fail to see that I am a college student with two part-time jobs back home and a student loan here, trying to pay off the kind of credit-card balances a grown white man in the Midwest is struggling to handle.

My mother is pleased that I traveled to England. She knows it's a good place. It's like here. Children have *camitas* and *leche*, and they don't wake up in the middle of the night with hurting bellies or have to steal. When I remind her that children *are* homeless in the United States, she sighs. "It's not the same."

Over the years, her sisters board airplanes for Colombia, like migratory birds. Once a year, twice a year, every other year. They hear an echo of their homeland, and suddenly, they are spending weeks packing suitcases and shopping for jackets and medications and *chanclas* for their brothers and nieces and nephews. On the day of departure, they dress in matching skirts and blazers and *tacones*, like women who are traveling on business. They wear their 99-cent lipstick and take pictures at the airport.

My mother does not hear the echo of Colombia. In fact, she has not been back in more than twenty years. "What would be the point?" she says. "To see all that *pobreza*?" My father agrees. He also hasn't returned to Cuba in two decades.

But it's not poverty that scares my mother.

"It's so sad to see the children," she murmurs.

The street children, the ones with hungry hands and lips that never quite close.

The easy part is getting the job after college. The hard part is having the money to keep the job. To go out for drinks, dinner, and brunch. To pay for a subscription to the *New York Times*, the *New Yorker*, and *New York* magazine. To buy wine, even cheap wine, for yet another party, and clothes for it as well. The hard part is listening to middle-class, white coworkers talk about the poor and the working class, because it's the '90s and the headline is welfare reform. The hard part is nodding numbly when they say, "Isn't that awful?" and not telling them that Mami can't find work right now and neither can Tía Chuchi, and Papi only has a part-time job. The hard part is pretending you know what a 401(k) is, and then buying a MAC lipstick, believing it will make you more comfortable about who you are and where you come from and the things you don't have words for.

The bills arrive each month. Discover, Visa, MasterCard, American Express. Numbers have stopped being numbers. They are hieroglyphs. The due date, the interest rates, the account numbers—all these curves and slants on the page belong to a language I am failing to learn.

My mother doesn't understand how my wallet is so full of plastic instead of dollars, but the white girls at work are sympathetic.

"I try not to think about it," a coworker says about her debt.

"It's depressing," agrees another.

"I owe thirty thousand dollars just in school loans," one confides.

It's the day before Halloween. The supermarket is selling mini chocolates in bulk. The party stores are peddling temporary selves: angels, devils, pirates, and princesses. Pumpkins are perched on windowsills, candles balancing on their tongues. And I am at the kitchen sink, wishing I could fit myself into a new life.

I have consolidated the debt, so that now instead of having a lot of bad little dreams, I have one giant nightmare, and it's in my hands: the new credit card bill. It doesn't matter that I have been sending more than three hundred dollars a month in payments. The total due does not budge.

A thread in me, a piece of *hilo* that has thinned over the years, snaps.

I pull every single credit card from my wallet and throw them in the freezer. I look up the support group a friend recommended, and when I show up at the meeting, I take my place in a folding chair and vow to myself that I will sit in this exact chair every week even if doing so will kill me.

And I do believe it will kill me to spend an hour listening to people talk about not having the money to pay the dentist, the paycheck being short this week, losing their jobs, and the humiliation of not being able to buy a friend a gift as expensive as the one she gave you.

There are other stories in the group, of course—positive tales about people negotiating job salaries, setting up debt-repayment plans, planning weddings without credit cards—but all I hear are the stories that scare me. I sit there, and sometimes I daydream and don't listen, and other times I tell myself that I am not like these people. I am still going to turn out rich and confident and not worried about money.

But I do what the people at the meeting tell me to do. I buy a notebook and start writing down how much I spend and on what. A woman from the group helps me identify my slippery places, the bookstores and clothing stores where I am most likely to use a credit card. I employ the forty-eight-hour rule, waiting two days before making a purchase I haven't planned. I even start depositing a few dollars into a savings account. Someone from the group says it doesn't matter if all I put in there is one single dollar.

After a year, my savings total a little more than one thousand dollars. I sit at my computer, dazed. For so many years, my mother urged me to save, and my father would ask me how much I had saved, and I always insisted, at least to myself: *I don't earn enough to save it.* But now, here is proof that I can do it. I have done it.

I shut my laptop and declare myself cured.

What I loved as a child about rich people on television was that they didn't need help. They never had to stick their hand out for charity or even ask a question about what someone said in English.

We were always needing help, always needing a health clinic or a dental clinic or a women's clinic. We were always needing someone to translate for us or give us a ride somewhere because we didn't own a car. We were, I thought naïvely as a child, always waiting.

I was too young then to understand that health care was privatized, that factories needed people like my mother and my father and my *tía*, that rich people especially needed us. It was our work that made their days possible.

It takes thirty-seven days, about five weeks, for me to charge $1,003.28 on my credit cards, and for this, I blame the man at Amtrak.

Sure, I had signed up for a new credit card, telling myself that this one would be different. It wasn't like the other cards. This was an airline credit card. I would be charging, yes, but paying it off at the end of the month, while accumulating points for a free flight. I told myself, I'll be getting one over on the airline companies.

Instead, I find myself at Union Station in Washington, DC. I am in line behind business suits, waiting to get my electronic Amtrak ticket and feeling annoyed that I will have to wait a few hours at the station. When I reach the self-service computer monitor, an Amtrak customer representative is there (in theory) to field any questions I may have. A tall man, he is a bit older, smiling and friendly, and offers to help me locate my ticket.

He blinks at the monitor. "Your train isn't leaving until eight o'clock."

"I know." I pout.

He taps the computer screen. "There's a five o'clock train. Why don't you take that?"

An earlier train? I look at him and find myself staring into a fatherly face. Why don't you take the earlier train? You're tired. You deserve it.

"How much is it?" I ask, dubious.

"It's just another twenty-one dollars," he says, adding, "It's not that much. You'll be home in no time."

I look at the monitor and the Amtrak worker with those father-knows-best eyes and think about the guava pastry waiting for me at my auntie's apartment in Jersey. I hand the man my credit card. He swipes it for me, and in less than a second, my reality has changed. I will not have to eat a cold sandwich at the train station and arrive in the city at midnight. I can now board the train, nap, and when I wake up, I will be home.

A month later, when I open the bill and see the amount due, I review every charge. New tires ($232.76), contact lenses ($209.51), a purchase at the Hello Kitty store ($25.05), and a few other small necessities. Important stuff, I tell myself. But still. I add up the charges, confident that the company has made a mistake. It cannot be $1,003.28. It just can't. But it is. And the $21 for the Amtrak ticket sits there on the page, as if it were blameless.

Back to my little support group I fly, this time in tears. "This is just money," I keep repeating. "How can it affect me like this? It's ridiculous."

The group meets in a church room that has fraying carpet and thin, plastic chairs. Through the windows, the morning sky is gray and dull. About twenty people have gathered to talk about the same things: money, credit cards, unsecured loans. When the meeting pauses for a break, four or five people rush to my side. They want to help.

I wish I could be like bell hooks.

She has written that because she was never accepted in white or Black middle-class circles as a young woman, she didn't try to belong. She didn't try to dress like she had money she didn't have; she didn't enjoy the illusion that material goods would make her feel better. She found that she liked to live simply, and she hated the hedonistic consumer culture that is American life.

I wish I could be like that, but I'm not. I love the iPhones and iPads, the hybrid cars and hybrid bikes, the leather shoes made in Israel, the $22.50 lipstick, the Coach handbags, the hotel rooms with flat-screen televisions in the bathrooms, the $10 herbal teas, the $3.99 a bag organic lettuce, the Kindles, the hardcover books with their deckled edges, even the $3,000 bred-to-size lapdogs.

When I create a spending plan that includes only the organic lettuce, and no fantasy that I will ever use a credit card to buy that or anything else, I am heartbroken. And embarrassed. I'm a feminist. I write about social justice issues. How can I want any of these things? I berate myself, and before that gets out of hand, I call a friend because by now I know that blaming myself for what I feel only makes me think that buying a mocha-scented soy candle for $21 will make me feel better. It doesn't.

I wake up one morning and reach for my cell phone. I turn it on and hit a speed-dial button, but an automated voice answers me instead.

It has happened exactly as the customer-service representative said it would: a Sprint computer has shut off my phone. I can't place another call until I have paid the bill, a little more than $200, which I will in about two days when my paycheck appears in my Washington Mutual checking account. In the meantime, I have consulted with my support team, reviewed my options, and concluded that I can live without a cell phone for three days.

The hard part is telling my mother.

I have decided to be honest, which benefits my spiritual practice but bruises my ego and worries Mami.

"What do you mean you can't pay the phone bill?" she asks.

Not being able to pay a bill in my family means a person is close to financial ruin, about to apply for welfare or, worse, about to be thrown out of their home and forced to live on the street like *gamines*.

"I mishandled things," I tell her. "But I'll pay it on Friday."

She grows silent, furrows her eyebrows. She's worried and confused, because my mother is familiar with the likes of bell hooks. She can walk through the shopping mall in Paramus and feel rich from the looking.

The street children.

It's their hands that haunt me. Little brown hands. The fingers stretched out like the basket for *limosna* in church on Sundays. The baskets were made of wicker, and we dropped our alms (four quarters) into them when I was a child, and the baskets ate the coins and I worried that we wouldn't have enough to feed them. They looked like open hands to me, those baskets. Open hands and terror.

AMERICANA: A MEMOIR OF MONEY

VICTORIA PATTERSON

LAST YEAR, a friend of mine called panicked about a fancy event she had to attend in New York. Struggling to find the right attire, she asked if I might go shopping with her. This friend thinks of me as her peer, another woman writer who works to get by. She knows me as the person I present myself to be—a former waitress, a working mother who lives in low-income housing with her family.

This is all true. But that afternoon, whirling through Nordstrom with her, I felt the hidden Self come alive the way it does sometimes—the self I'm always unsuccessfully trying to kill off for good. She was still alive in me, this girl I've been running from for years. I knew the bag my friend should carry and what dress to match it. I knew which shoes she would wear and what color to adorn her nails. I chose the scarf and coat she should add at the end.

At the cash register, my friend, laughing, thanked me for my help. She asked where I'd learned to shop like that. I laughed and looked out at the bright gilded tacky splendor of the Americana mall and told her the truth: "You can take the rich white girl out of Newport Beach, but you can't take the Newport Beach out of the girl."

It's true I have been posing as poor for years. But it's also true that, relatively speaking, and in relation to my birth family, I am poor. Like a thousand heroines of a thousand movies and novels: I am the rich girl who forsakes everything she's been promised for love.

But love wasn't the only reason that I left my family. It was hate. And greed. And the sense, which I had somehow even as a young woman, that to allow myself to love them would kill me. That to stay inside their tacky splendor would be the death of all I believed in and hoped for myself.

My family's religion is money. From the beginning, it has been their greatest preoccupation, the source of their grandest fights. Money is the thing that has made us—and destroyed us—as a family. Money is the direct source of divorces and betrayals, and it was why my mother and her brother became estranged, spending millions on lawyers in a prolonged financial feud; and why, though I'm not my mother, I've been disowned by my uncle, aunt, and cousins as well.

Money is what made my grandfather capitalize on the Korean and Vietnam Wars. And money is what made him sell his plane parts business and start Maple Brothers, a crown molding business, where most of the adults in my family worked, including my mother's cousin Tommy. Tommy's own brother fired him when a larger company made his absence a deal point in their partial buyout. Soon after, Tommy parked in front of the local fire station and put a towel to one side of his head and a gun to the other, in what I've come to think of as a thoughtful suicide.

Money is what my grandfather used to control and torture his wife (my grandmother) and children (my mother and uncle), and what my mother now uses to control and torture me.

At the moment, I'm trying to convince my mother to buy my shares of the family business. If I sell the 14 percent of stocks I own, I'd have economic freedom. I could buy a home and invest money. This is why I play tennis with her every Sunday, even though my ambivalence about the sport is unnerving, to say the least. Whether rich or poor, my hidden self feels like a fraud. My predicament is navigating the privilege that I both want and don't want as a member of a tribe to which I never belonged.

Early on, I tried to free myself. My childhood was spent as an unwilling participant. Not because of money, necessarily, but because of my racism, and all of the other heinous values and politics that came with a family life centered on the attainment of wealth.

I am six years old, in a party dress at my grandparents' house. My mother has insisted that I have a Dorothy Hamill haircut, short and wedged in the back. She nudges me into the middle of the living room to tell a joke. This has long been our routine. My father and mother teach me a joke, and I perform it for my grandparents, whom everyone in our family tries to impress. I'm pretty, sweet, and earnest, which I suppose adds a certain piquancy to what I now recognize as the rank racism of the jokes. Up until this moment, I have not understood the jokes or why they are funny. Today is no different. I don't "get" this one either, but this is the last one I will tell for my parents. A Jew, a Black person (this is not the word I used), and a Catholic are on an airplane that's going to crash . . . I struggle to get the words out, eager to please. They open the door and jump. Which one hits the ground first?

I have no idea why these particular people are in an airplane together, and I certainly can't tell you what their labels mean. But the punch line— "Who cares?"—makes me burst into tears. It suddenly occurs to me that I've professed humans worthless, their deaths funny. My grandfather, a self-made multimillionaire, laughs out loud at the joke and at me, while my grandmother, laughing too, rubs my back in a gesture of consolation.

Two years later, I'm eight years old, and my older brother whispers to me in a movie theater, "You are adopted." He intends it to be cruel, but instead of shock or sadness, I'm jubilant. It explains so much. Now that I'm not blood-locked, not truly one of them, I can love my family. We are about to see *The Sound of Music*. In the flickering of the movie trailer, I peer at my parents a few seats over. I have the same sloping nose and angular cheekbones as my mother, and the same flat, skinny face shape as my father. Our facial features are nearly identical, and I know my brother is lying. I begin to cry.

Soon enough, The Big Feeling and The Family Weirdo become my nicknames, and I begin to see more and more how little I share with these people I call family. Sure, my proficiency at sports and physical appearance provide the illusion of fitting in, but deep down I know I am not one of them. Still, my life is a steady flow of tennis lessons and clinics as my mother dreams of my becoming a professional tennis player. I'm gifted a light blue Honda Civic bedecked with a giant red bow on my six-teenth birthday (license plate Tory16). There's also the country club: the kowtowing to men, the learning to please, the training to be a trophy wife. There are all the trappings of privilege: the bank card that spits out twen-ties whenever I want; the peers with eating disorders, plastic surgeons, and homes with elevators.

There's one Black person at my high school, and when he asks my ten-nis doubles' partner to prom, I'm pleased for her. But she declines, telling me later, "I like him, but my parents would kill me." At the sole football game I attend, the cheerleaders direct us to cheer at our less affluent op-ponents: "It's all right, it's okay, you're going to work for us someday."

In my sophomore civics class, our teacher asks, "How many of you are Republicans?" All the hands rise, except mine. My best friend, three desks over, sends a warning stare: Don't do it. Don't raise your hand when he asks. But when he does—"How many Democrats?"—my hand goes up. I am taking steps away from my tribe, to define myself in opposition to them.

When I turn eighteen, my grandfather hands me a list of who (George H. W. Bush) and what (a straight Republican ticket) I should vote for in the upcoming election. He also gives the list to my mother and grand-mother (only the women in the family receive it). I vote for Michael Du-kakis and for a straight Democratic ticket, and then I let him know it.

"There must've been someone," I ask him, a pleading desperation in my voice, "somewhere, at some point in our family, who wasn't a Repub-lican? Who felt like I do?"

"Nope," he says, dead-eyed.

Our love is wretched and ridiculous, but I keep both feet in my tribe for security even if they are pivoted in the opposite direction. No matter that I'm ridiculed as The Big Feeling and Weirdo, I'm not ready to leave. Besides, what would it be like to exit? A stepping-off into space.

In my early twenties I meet Chris—older, half-Mexican, middle-class, an artist. He and his family revere art and culture, not financial success, and he likes to say, "Money solves money problems." We take in Vincent van Gogh's *The Mulberry Tree* at the Norton Simon Museum, and talk about literature, paintings, and movies. I read poetry aloud to him, and he doesn't make fun of me.

A few months in, my phone rings as I am in the next room and I ask Chris to answer. It is my brother, who I know is saying "Hey, Weirdo," his standard greeting, thinking it's me on the line.

As I walk into the room where Chris is, I hear him respond: "Don't call your sister that. It's demeaning."

I step off into space. I marry for love.

Chris was the opposite of what my family wanted and expected of me. His mother was a high school Spanish teacher, his father an author and professor at the local community college. His father passed away before I met Chris but left copious journals, which I voraciously read and admired, and I felt close to him. I began to flesh out my own possibilities as an artist, something I'd never dared imagine before. Sensing that I belonged in his family more than my own, when I married Chris, I chose and sealed my fate.

I knew that my family wouldn't approve of my choice, but I hoped that they'd nevertheless help launch me into my new married life. After all, there was plenty of money. My grandfather had bought various homes for my parents, both as newlyweds and later, and he'd always financially assisted them. But financial support, I learned, was a by-product of living my life as they imagined, and I had not complied. My parents had always told me that they'd happily pay for my wedding; the sky was the limit, especially since I was their only daughter. But not this one, though my parents and grandparents begrudgingly attended, cautiously eating the homemade tamales and frijoles that Chris's mother prepared.

I discovered quickly that I had no support, financial or otherwise. They believed Chris an opportunist, marrying me for their wealth. (Twenty-four years later, he's yet to hit that financial jackpot.) Fine, I decided, I didn't want my family's money and all the pain that came with it anyway. My husband would become a famous painter. I'd make it as a writer. Now, I know that it's more complicated. Only someone growing up as privileged as I had could be this naïve.

I quickly learned the value of having money. We moved into a small apartment above a dry cleaner and struggled to make ends meet. Chris went to art college, and I found a job as a waitress and a caterer at a high-end restaurant, soon learning what it was like to serve, rather than to be served, and remained the server for the next fifteen-plus years. Being served, as it turns out, is more satisfying.

Chris's widowed mother had limited means but was always generous ("What's mine is yours"), though her badly concealed contempt for my family was a big source of friction between us. She found them snobby, vain, shallow, and ridiculous. My family's lack of generosity proved her point. I didn't ask for my mother-in-law's help, either, because, while I valued her opinions, I also held them against her. I can now say with experience that familial loyalty is real, and the adage is true: it's fine to disparage or joke about your loved ones, but the second someone else does, it's not okay.

Perhaps if Chris and I had chosen professions other than artists, we'd have had an easier ride. Truthfully, we're both not that interested in money, and while we're not extravagant or careless, we'd rather the other take care of the financial duties. My friend once told me: "You chose a bohemian lifestyle, but the problem is that you also decided to have kids." And it's true: my children are what made my exodus complicated.

After my first son's birth, I craved financial security. I wanted to own a home. I wanted my son to attend the best preschools. Maids had done the difficult child-rearing tasks for my parents, who hadn't changed diapers or potty-trained my brother and me. My mother and father weren't parenting examples, but at least they could assist financially, I thought. But my family didn't offer to help, and I didn't ask. I had my pride. Besides, my disconnection from the greed, stultifying comfort, entitlement, and insulation that accompanies my family's wealth made me feel superior to them. I sensed their vindictive pleasure in my financial travails, knowing that at the same time, they were clueless. People with money, I've learned, have no idea what it's like not to have money, and they indulge their ignorance every day.

By the time my second son was born (on Medi-Cal), I had started living off my family's scraps and it shamed me. My grandfather would occasionally, erratically, gift us money, based on tax breaks rather than generosity or need, and I'd come to rely on these financial reprieves. My mother might take me on shopping sprees, advantageous around Christmas, so that I could strategically have gifts for my sons and husband. "Get whatever you want," she'd say, encouraging me to buy more. "Go on, get it. It's fine." But I'd restrain myself. Like going from an anorexic spender to a bingeing one: it sickened me.

She'd give me her old purses, which smelled like the interiors of her perpetually new luxury cars. She'd also take me to her hairdresser, since looking good is important, rich or poor. I was gifted her reward cards (for being such a good shopper!) from Saks Fifth Avenue and Bloomingdale's (which usually amounted to around sixty dollars' credit), and the perfume and makeup samples that came with her extravagant purchases.

Only once, when my sons were toddlers, did I ask my mother for help. Chris had been in the county hospital after a near-fatal accident, and we couldn't afford health insurance. I hadn't told my family, sensing we'd be judged. He was home now, but his hospitalization had rattled me: crossing through a metal detector to visit him, the subpar care. Living hand to mouth with two young sons had worn me down, and I wanted health insurance with a burning passion.

Parked in my mother's giant SUV after a Target shopping spree where I'd bought my sons clothes and shoes, and stored up on essentials like dish soap and toilet paper, I said, "I need money."

"That's Chris's job," she said. "The husband is the provider."

I explained how Chris cooked. How we shared parenting responsibilities; how he was emotionally supportive; how, compared to my friends' husbands, he was amazing; how we strove not to give up on our art; and how I loved him.

When she didn't respond, I said, "We're struggling. I can't make it work. The boys are insured through Healthy Families, but we're not. I'm scared something bad will happen. We're both working, but the restaurant and the stained glass studio where Chris works won't provide health insurance."

There was a long pause. Turning the air conditioner down a notch, she said, "Have you considered welfare?"

My forehead and cheeks hot, I looked out the window at the cars in the parking lot. My silence shamed me further. I realized I was alone, that I'd cemented my isolation from my tribe, and that I couldn't turn to them for help ever again, and I never have. We were quiet, and then she drove me home. I opened the car door, and then I dragged my bags from her SUV. She didn't come inside.

In fact, not long after, she stopped visiting altogether. It's been close to twenty years now. Recently she explained: "It makes me too sad to see the way that you live."

Her visits make me feel bad, too. Though I know better, it doesn't matter. No matter how many books I write, no matter how much critical acclaim, no matter how good I am as a mother, a daughter, a wife, deep inside of me I've failed my tribe: I'm supposed to be rich. For my family, being poor is a moral failing.

While my mother no longer comes to me, I still go to her. Tennis is her drug, and I play with her each Sunday. But it's not just about my being a good daughter. I think about how I can bring up money, because, you see, now I want my share. I do favors for her, like fishing her lipstick pencil from between the car seat and the front console of her Jaguar, resetting her Netflix, fixing the ice cube maker on her deluxe freezer, and explain-demonstrating how to forward texts and photographs on her iPhone, all while trying to convince her to buy the small percentage of shares of Maple Brothers that I own, willed to me by my grandfather.

Only three members are left in the family business: my mother, my brother, and me. My mother bought out everyone else. As the majority stockholder, she makes all the decisions. My brother and I have no power.

No third party will buy my shares, since it's a family business. My title, in name only, since I have no agency, is treasurer, the same position that Tommy held before he parked in front of the fire station and shot himself in the head.

As a shareholder, I receive a monthly check, the entirety of which is spent on rent, bills, and responsibilities. My mother likes to remind me that I'm indebted to my tribe for providing this income, and my ambivalence makes me feel callow, ungrateful, and like the very entitled and spoiled person that I've fought not to become.

My longing to be bought out of the family business—to be more aggressive about my financial well-being and demand what is mine— happened over time. I used to worry that by caring about money, I'd become like my family, my values aligned. But after twenty years of living free of them, I know I'm not, and I won't. This realization came partially from witnessing the yearslong battle between my mother and her brother over my grandfather's will. Millions of dollars sucked into lawyers' fees, and it made no sense. So much money. Why fight? There was enough for everyone and more. Just a portion, I'd think, not a million, just a fraction, say a hundred thousand or so, could have changed our lives so much for the better. But the two continued to fight, the money drained away, and in a fury, my uncle, aunt, and cousins disappeared from my life.

I don't want that life. I don't want those problems. I will never choose them.

My husband, our sons, and I live in a small house owned by the California Department of Transportation, one of the homes rented out to non-profits and low-income families in the continuing battle over the dreaded 710 freeway. Some of the Caltrans houses have already sold to the lower-income families at a price they can afford; ours will come up for sale someday. We've been waiting for more than twenty years now, stuck in a kind of economic limbo, relying on Caltrans to determine our future: a bureaucratic nightmare. But now that I'm a member of Maple Brothers, and my mother uses the company for tax purposes (it appears as though I'm receiving money I'm not), I'm screwed. On paper I'm wealthier than I am in life.

Now that I no longer qualify as low income, I'm trying to full-heartedly claim my privilege, without full-heartedly returning to my tribe. I want what is mine, so that my sons and husband will benefit, and so that we can finally own a home.

Last Sunday on the tennis court, as I gave my mother lobs and volleys, I said, "Buy me out."

She said she'd check with her "financial people," and I knew nothing would change.

"Do you think," I asked, hitting her a forehand, "that if I don't depend on you financially, I'll stop visiting? Are you afraid I won't take care of you? Are you still punishing me for my marriage?"

We switched sides, hitting backhands, and I said, "I don't want to destroy our relationship."

I'm not my birth family, and yet I've needed—and still need—their money. The emotional bonds are financial. A vocal tribe dissenter, I haven't freed myself, and I've learned from repeated, continuing, and endless trials that you can't fully extract the girl from Newport Beach, just like you can't marry for love and assume that money won't matter.

In my long reckoning, I've struggled with my bondage to my tribe, my inability to escape, my humiliation, and the benefits, too—the entire scrappy mess. This coming Sunday, I'll play tennis with my mother, compelling her between shots—with unlikely success—to buy me out. My internal dialogue, as I try to summon perspective, will go something like this: Spoiled brat. Lighten up. Complaining about tennis at an exclusive club in Newport Beach. Most people would appreciate the extravagance.

Dressing in tennis gear and pretending to be someone I'm not feels torturous, and also natural. After all, I'm good at the sport, from the years and years of lessons. And what I'll ask myself for the thousandth time, and what I ask you now, is this: Can we ever really be free from the tribe to which we were born?

Can we ever really find a way to reject the world that gave us life?

STAY.

JEN/ELEANA HOFER

conversation // about mother tongues versus foster-languages, how to forge belonging.

—Layli Long Soldier

I'VE ONLY ever lived in one spot in Los Angeles. I moved to the Northeast LA neighborhood of Cypress Park from Mexico City's Centro Histórico in 2002. For Sale By Owner: *AS IS!!!!!*—the sign on the shipwreck foundering in its own history that was to become my house was barely readable beneath exuberantly overgrown trees and weeds. The house, which we bought from the only living son of the couple who built it in 1920, was beyond a fixer-upper. It was a tear-it-down-to-the-studs skeleton where it rained in the living room. Termites were both visible and audible along the entire dry-rot-compromised north side of the house. Dozens of stray cats, fed by the elderly Cuban sisters across the street, nested under the house and in the attic crawl space, easily accessible through gaping holes in the roof. The pipes were so rusted that a mere touch would dissipate them into billowing blood-colored clouds.

Realizing it would be quite some time before we could do anything there other than demolition, and the occasional dance party atop the exposed subfloor, my then-girlfriend and I bought a 1974 Airstream Argosy—the same make, model, and color my maternal grandparents hitched to their avocado-green sedan to travel the country when they retired—and lived in sixteen-foot-by-six-foot not-so-blissfully close quarters in a fake-wood won-derland parked among the eucalyptus in our backyard for a little over a year while we unbuilt and then rebuilt the house. Our imaginations billowed, yet we could never have envisioned, even in our wildest unleashings, what and who we might encounter—and how—as we made this unlivable house and our trailer perched on the dollop of land behind it—soil the consistency of stone and seeded with rusted nails and broken glass—into a home.

I don't believe in possession of much of anything—other than our words, our actions, our mistakes, and other inter-personal–inter-political accountabilities. Without the spark provided by a girlfriend whose family life was marked by a level of post-carceral instability that led her to want to grow enduring roots, it wouldn't have been my impulse to purchase a small sliver of Tongva territory not far from the confluence of the Arroyo Seco and the Los Angeles River, where the so-called *pobladores* first staked their erroneous claim on this land. The irony of the fact that in the end it is I who have lived in this home for nearly two decades is not lost on me.

I take as a given that we exist in a context of white supremacist set-tler colonialism and voracious capitalism. It is in the heavy atmosphere of these oppressive forces that I feel responsible to enact a model of caretaking, stewardship, and gardening—in the literal and metaphorical sense—tending to the seeds, blooms, and fruits that provide me and oth-ers sustenance. I strive and sometimes struggle to enact a spirit of porosity where my openness is grounded in both intention and intuition. I work toward a horizontalist practice of deep listening and deep expression, walking as lightly as possible on ground that does not belong to me but to which I feel intensely accountable, offering, as much as I'm able, welcome and sanctuary—in the literal and metaphorical sense.

I want to live within my means and with meaning and without ex-cess except where gratitude and other joyous emotions can exceed despair and distress, to identify the level of comfort I and others need in order to thrive, and the level of discomfort I can embrace in the effort to navi-gate and wherever possible right the imbalances that are the foundation for the structures of scarcity that delimit so many people's living. Good gardening practices produce enough abundance to share widely; as I grew comfortably uncomfortable with the reality of "owning" my house "alone," it became clear that my charge was, and is, to find ways to make a meaningful home for myself and for more than just myself.

I want to live within my means and with meaning and without excess except where gratitude and other joyous emotions can exceed despair and distress. I actively work to identify the level of comfort I and others need in order to thrive, and the level of discomfort I can embrace in the effort to navigate and wherever possible right the imbalances that are the foundation for the structures of scarcity that delimit so many people's living.

I take inventory as honestly as I can:

What do I have?

What do I need?

What can I offer?

I locate myself within an intersecting web of privilege and invisibility. I read as white and come from a background of forced and chosen diaspora rooted in economic distress and also economic mobility, racist genocide, and race privilege. I am a queer person in an open relationship with a cisgendered man who is also queer, and it would be easy to mistake our relationship for heteronormative. I don't feel misgendered when people defer to *she* as my pronoun, though I do tend to feel somewhere to the left of binary and prefer the potentialities of the pronoun *they*. I speak English fluently and without an accent (okay, with a California accent, some might argue!) and am the child of accented non-native English. As a half-Latinx white-privileged Ashkenazi Jewish person whose paternal family consists of just a few survivors of the Holocaust, and for whom being Jewish represents a cellular understanding of ethnic persecution that requires support of BDS and Palestinian self-determination, my relationship to whiteness and white supremacy is especially fraught.

In trying to understand and inhabit the particular kind of diasporic whiteness I've been thinking through lately as "off-white," I have acted out of self-hatred and hatred of whiteness, out of debilitating guilt and regret that stem from visceral and violent rejection of race privilege and class privilege, though manifesting those as guilt is damaging and use-less, out of corrosive self-doubt and the paralysis that comes from feeling that my responsibility is much greater than my capacity, and my silence can perhaps do more good than my speech. These not-so-strategic cop-ing strategies can also be viewed as a kind of protection: protection from vulnerability, from exposure, from my own and others' humanness, from having to show up and be myself and speak honestly and listen genuinely, ready to be challenged, ready to be changed.

> *This is collaboration in zero gravity democracy*
> *—blurry violet lights and no clear answer*
> *This is a nuclear glow in the dark so we can start over*
> *We board planes to Mars and six engines fire*

> *You spin away.*
> —Vickie Vértiz

I dropped out of college in 1990 to walk across the United States with a group of activists advocating for environmental justice, Native American land rights, and an end to nuclear testing and development. It was on this slow, attentive journey through vast landscapes and endless fields and tiny towns that I first encountered a person who dedicated her maternal en-ergies to foster parenting: a sixty-something Mexican American woman from Los Angeles who had fostered and/or adopted a dozen kids of vary-ing ages at varying stages of their lives. A seed was planted: I knew in my bones that fostering was something I wanted to do, though I was far from ready and it would be decades before I moved forward in any concrete way. I know now that I had absolutely no idea then what fostering actually entails, what that experience would require of me and invite me to release.

Many adventures later, I found a person whose definition of family is as elastic as mine and who could share my enthusiasm for biking through the city to return home to a forever-partially-broken-down house with its always-overgrown garden. On our first anniversary, he adorned the front porch, which doubles as a haven for street cats, with a doormat that reads: COME BACK WITH A WARRANT. Twenty-five years after I walked across the US, my current sweetheart and I became certified as a "resource family"—bureaucracy-speak for foster-adopt parents.

In 2016, we welcomed tiny newborn P into our home and hearts. We didn't know which was rounder: his gorgeous snoozing face, the tightly coiled black curls that grew in about a week after we brought him home, or his forever-surprised-looking eyes that blossomed with curiosity as soon as he could focus. We still have the clear glass bottles from the Jarritos Mineragua we bought at a quesadilla stand in South Central on our way to the hospital to meet him. Memories held by objects held by houses held by the memory-laden land that cradles them, and us. An artist friend and her family were staying in the Airstream that summer. Her three-year-old son, dreadlocks haloed around his dazzling smile, danced circles around us holding P for the very first time at the house, then ran out the door shouting for nine-day-old P to follow him—"Come on! Let's run!" At P's first court date three months later, with no advance warning and no sense whatsoever of what it might entail for P, a judge ordered reunification for P and his birth father the following morning. We walked to the river to watch the sunset with P wrapped in my green-striped rebozo, spent one last night with him, and have not seen him since.

The stars recall what they have always known: heat
and how the body opens   quite suddenly
to the universe's black tongue

                                    I

See a night rashed with constellations and consider
      ways the body breaks
      publicly

how we carry our shattered selves
into all spaces

—Ashaki M. Jackson

My practice of resource sharing stems from my thinking about and within privilege, and from a desire to deconstruct unjust systems and build a wildly different constellation for sustainable coexistence. I've thought a lot about reparations as one model for that unbuilding and wonder how fostering might land within that model. To give without expecting anything in return other than the flourishing of those who have not historically been offered the opportunity to flourish or who have flourished despite society's every roadblock to the contrary. There are certainly contexts where acting in solidarity means I step up by stepping back, removing myself from a position of leadership or spotlight. I do my best to do so when it's called for. In a reality where there are more kids in the foster system than families willing to foster, and where there are more Black kids in the system than Black foster families, I am well aware of all the ways, categorically speaking, that we as white people are less than ideal caregivers for kids of African descent like the ones we've nurtured. I am thinking about models of solidarity that involve stepping in and staying in. No matter the cost.

And what does it cost us to stay? To offer solidarity—real, concrete, material solidarity? To share resources and dismantle systems of privilege decision by decision, micro and macro? What do I have? What do I need? What can I offer?

> *don't climb the ladder burn it down*
> —Uhuru Moor and Jasmine Nyende,
> FUPU (Fuck U Pay Us)

P's mom never trusted us. To her, we represented the system that had taken her child away, and nothing more. One of my greatest fears about becoming a foster parent was that we would not be able to build a relationship with the birth family of a child we welcomed, that the very fact of our being willing to receive a child who was being removed from their birth family would irrevocably position us as part of the system, and nothing more. And perhaps in the end, we are irrevocably part of that system.

Perhaps to a mom like P's, who felt her child had been stolen from her, my desire to be seen beyond my role in that theft was not only impossible to fulfill but also irrelevant. But being a foster parent does not by any means imply that I believe in the systems that land so many kids—and especially so many kids of color—in the foster system to begin with. In fact, part of the reason I'm a foster parent is precisely because I want to approach the task of fostering—of loving and nurturing the child of a parent who is experiencing challenges that erode their capacity to do that labor—as part of the work of racial justice, as part of the work of living a life grounded in solidarity and the redistribution of wealth and resources. I have the luxury of not interacting with the child welfare system if I choose not to do so; the families ensnared in that system do not, even if they are there in part because of choices they made.

My sweetheart and I went into this form of family-making with as much critical consciousness as possible in a context of wild unpredictability and multiplying uncertainties, with the intention of intervening in the lives of the families with which we'd intersect through this process with as much empathy, love, and political awareness as possible. We were hoping to make a family, yes, but our definition of family does not include rooting for anyone else's failure to thrive and does not include parenting at the expense of anyone else's well-being. And that approach carries risk. It costs us. It costs us in ways that have absolutely nothing to do with money. And that cost—that priceless, immeasurable cost—is the heart of what we are willing to give. And is the heart—that priceless, immeasurable heart— of what these experiences and relationships give to us.

About six weeks after P left to live with his dad, fortunately while we still remembered everything we needed to keep a newborn moderately happy and in clean diapers, Z came into our lives; he was ten days old and tiny, just four pounds. My cousin and his family were visiting at the time and we came home to delicious Thai takeout, a bottle of champagne, and a tres leches cake from the Super A down the street with bright red cursive lettering: *Bienvenido Cuzzy*. My eight-month-old cuzlet looked like a giant next to Z; though they had baldness in common—his fuzz black, hers blond—it was hard to believe you could use the word *baby* to describe them both. We settled into a rhythm. Z came with me almost everywhere: I wore him in a sling against my chest when I interpreted for tenants on rent strike and Puerto Rican revolutionaries, at poetry readings and book fairs. He taught my classes with me, snoozing on his back on the seminar table. We spent hours in parks lying on a giant "IMAGINE PEACE" towel designed by Yoko Ono, a gift from a Brazilian performance artist who had spent a week in the Airstream, gazing up at the sky with our faces side by side.

Z and his mother had court-mandated monitored visits twice a week. We were the monitors, so the four of us spent many hours together over the next two years. As the weeks stretched into months and then years, we realized we were spending more time with Z's mom than with any other friend in our lives. She had given him his name, and she asked us to give him a nickname. We became a family and called ourselves that explicitly; we talked all the time about coparenting Z together no matter what happened. When he learned to talk, Z learned names for each of his three parents: Emaye ("mom" in Amharic, the language of his birth mother's education in Ethiopia), Mamá ("mom" in Spanish, the language he shared with me and the Mexican side of his family), and "Rorray" (a version of my sweetheart's name, as he can't stomach any of the standard parental monikers).

For a while, our little nonofficial family was gathering weekly at the central branch of the LA Public Library—the only governmental institution I can celebrate without reservation (if only we could earmark our taxes!). Z and his birth mom would play wild games of chase among the stacks; he would shout with laughter, eliciting a pointedly raised eyebrow from the children's librarian. I think all the time about the micro and the macro. I think about specific, singular, unique people: each born somewhere, each raised by someone, each finding or not finding the chosen family that will become our compass. Z would share snacks with K, a girl about a year older whose mom was eternally impatient with her toddler demands. K would beg to come to the bathroom when Z's mom and I would go to change his diaper together; she didn't want to let us out of her sight.

And I think about systems: constructing molds, infrastructures, and transitways that extend far beyond what any one single person's experience can encapsulate or address. I urgently desire to live in a world where the foster system doesn't need to exist because all people have the resources of shelter and nourishment, education and conflict resolution, health care and physical-spiritual well-being they need to flourish. In this world, there are networks of care and interdependence that can catch us when we falter and can provide alternatives to the kinds of violent undermining of well-being that are all too common and all too understandable within structures based in scarcity, bigotry, lack, and disrespect—in short, within a future of no future bound by imperialist settler colonial capitalism and all its damaged interpersonal manifestations.

The public library became our home base, our playground on cold days, our space for conversation and weeping and laughter and naps and surreptitious snacks (technically not allowed; please take note). It was at the library, almost a year and half after Z and his mom came into our lives, the three of us sitting in a circle on the floor in an empty auditorium to one side of the Spanish-language children's book section while Z napped, that Z's mom once asked us to adopt Z. She wanted to draft a letter to the judge requesting that her parental rights be terminated so we could adopt her son—our son, collectively. We said we would adopt him gladly, astonished she'd proposed it, half-hoping she'd change her mind and keep trying to get him back, half-hoping she wouldn't.

As we discussed possibilities, we agreed that no matter what, we'd remain a family: if we adopted Z, we would continue to nurture our relationship with his mom; if she reunified with him, she would always want Z to know us, to love us, to have our love. We all agreed: more love is better. Not long after this conversation, on another visit to the library, Z took his first steps, having waited, or so we suspected, until we were all together—his mom, my sweetheart, my parents, and me. He walked for the first time at the library, lurching across the rug patterned with jungle animals from me to his mom and back again, tracing a path I hoped he might walk for many years to come.

On the day she was planning to give the judge her letter, Z's mom changed her mind about asking the judge to terminate her parental rights so we could adopt Z, and five months later, a couple of weeks before Z turned two, he and his birth mom reunified. At first, we were seeing each other a few times a week, and then we settled into our regular pattern of visits on weekends. After a couple of months, weekend visits reduced to once-a-week visits, then every other week, and then Z's mom asked us to give her space to explore parenting entirely on her own. Throughout this time, we were exchanging dozens of texts every day, checking in, making each other laugh, comparing notes, sending pictures and videos, marveling at the child who'd brought us together. Soon, however, her texts became fewer and further between, and then, four and a half months after reunification, she went completely silent. As I write this, it's been a month since the communication blackout began; during the editing process, that month stretched into seven months with no contact. I have no idea where things will stand as you read this.

The pain is unbearable, and there is no option other than to bear it. And it is not more unbearable than the pain Z's birth mother experienced when she had to let go of her son just a few days after he was born. Not more so than the pain it would have caused her and us and Z if she had failed to reunify with him, with all that would represent. What we possess, ultimately, is our responsibility and our ability to enact intentional response. And the unpossessable: each other. This web of intentionality and connection, even in moments of distance or disconnect. What it costs me to share the resources I have is not monetary. It is emotional. It costs me irrevocable and irreparable grief. It costs me fear, uncertainty, the constant in-the-marrow ache of missing, of devastating grief for which no language is adequate. The fear that the memories of Z I have now are the only memories I'll have of him. And it costs me the work it takes to show up 1,000 percent, regardless of what I receive in return, or whether I receive anything at all. Being a foster parent requires me to put my politics into practice like no other experience I've ever had; it invites and demands that I enact the world I imagine rather than the one I inherited.

Part of what we open ourselves up to when we open to radical resource sharing—to being changed by the act of giving and being given—is the potential for experiencing pain, loss, grief, lack of mutuality. There are all kinds of reasons, some imaginable and some unimaginable, some concrete and some entirely ephemeral, why mutuality might not be possible. Why showing up might become a unidirectional experience or might simply look like showing up for someone else's absence. It is beyond my capacity for me to welcome a context—which is my current context as I write this essay—where the very real possibility exists that Z's birth mom will decide she doesn't want to continue a relationship with us, and she doesn't want us to have an ongoing relationship with Z.

I cannot welcome that loss, that grief, that searing impossible pain. But I can accept it, and if I have to, I will. I can understand it. I can respect the autonomy of my sister-in-parenting even as she decides, at least for now, that parenting with me is not what she needs, and hence not what her child needs. I can support her autonomy even if the result of that autonomy is my broken heartedness.

> We've all been through a lot we don't understand in a world made
> to either break us or make us so hard we can't break even when it's
> what we need most to do.
>
> —Tommy Orange

Two days after Z moved to his birth mom's house, I got an urgent text from a friend whose organization cosponsored the caravan of refugees who crossed into the US in April 2018: a mom and her two kids needed immediate emergency housing. Did I know anywhere they could spend a night or two? The Airstream Argosy has been many things: my home, a source of support for me in paying my mortgage, an inexpensive rent for artist and activist friends over the years, a guesthouse, and, more recently, as my own working life became relatively more stable via a combination of part-time jobs and freelance work, a sanctuary for folks who need a place to land for a few days, weeks, or months.

I felt depleted, hollow, incapable. And at the same time, I was aware of having a resource I did not need to use for myself, a resource I could share. How could I know this family needed space and not offer what I had? The feeling that I had nothing to offer is not the same as the reality of what I could offer. The feeling that I will never recover from the grief of potentially losing contact with the small person I love beyond all love is not the same as the reality of being able to go on living through and within grief. A and her kids arrived with the clothes on their backs and one package of diapers and a collection of narratives, experiences, curiosities, and affections that have been as important and healing for me as any balm my home has provided for them.

I have not started over, and yet I will keep going. No one is replaceable: the space in my heart labeled Z or labeled P cannot be filled by any other shape. Our hearts are immense: more love makes space for more love. I don't want to sight translate *The Grouchy Ladybug* into Spanish for A's kids the way I did for Z because it's too wrenching, but they adore the book so I do, and I can feel the rust-colored cloud of pain shifting just the tiniest bit. Not dissipating, but making space for something else to circulate. I give in order to give more in order to receive the gift of giving and receiving. I offer what I can and then a little bit more. I am willing to be vulnerable, willing to be exposed. I am fallible and broken beyond repair but not beyond forgiveness. I can provide sanctuary because I need sanctuary.

"You're an angel," "You're such an amazing person," "You're so noble," "That baby and his mom are so lucky to have you," people would often say while cooing over Z. I believe in spirits more than angels and that we all have access to that, regardless of what we'd call it or whether we'd even use language to recognize it. I believe each person is capable of amazingness and amazement. I believe that everyone has the capacity to understand right action and move toward it. The term *nobility* makes me think of hierarchy and fiefdoms and inappropriate hero worship—the only kinds of kings and queens I'm willing to bow down to are the ones in drag, thank you very much. And as far as luck goes, it's not luck that brings us into relationship with one another. It's openness, preparation even when we know we can't prepare for something, and damn hard work. And if anyone is lucky, it's us, to have been blessed to share time with Z, and to have gotten to know his fiercely beautiful mom and her capacity to shine in a landscape of struggle.

That shine is our beacon, and will be Z's as well, as he grows. To call us "angelic" or "amazing" or "noble" or any of the other at-arm's-length objectifying praise terms people with a more philanthropic view tend to use is to somehow remain removed from the possibility of being genuinely impacted by the ways we engage with others. What we're enacting is not benevolence; it's the most human form of being human, in a body intertwined with other bodies. It's the irreplaceable memory of carrying Z out of the hospital after he was born, the way his head felt, a tiny interplanetary sun in the crook of my arm, his entire body fitting against my forearm. To hold a person that completely, be trusted that completely, and to give yourself over to a person that completely and be willing—just as completely—to let go because someone else's needs and perspective and framework must be prioritized over our own.

Deep caretaking of the radically vulnerable—newborns, the ill, the very elderly—is inherently about prioritizing someone else's needs over our own, at least for a time. And more so when that deep caretaking involves fostering—the care for a stranger who will become familiar, if not family. But what is family if not wholehearted offering of care across divides of difference with no control over outcomes or futures, the ultimate manifestation of process over product? The question *staying* constructs for us—for those who stay in and with, the difficulty—is how to remain breakable even when we have been broken and might continue to break. How to stay anyway when it is too difficult to stay. How to keep staying even when the other person leaves. How to stay no matter what it costs.

. . . Charting northward
to make a lapse where someone will want

to explain. North, a door opens toward
the hole of the capacious. No word but
a blade to shudder at blade. Halfway
across the radius one more descends
toward the ocean bowing into blow as
in prayer. Records make themselves known
by what is raised. Interior of my interior.
That which gave us name for impossible devotion.

—Maryam Ivette Parhizkar

All parenting entails such intensely loving, heartful giving without expectation or control. Fostering is the extreme-sport version of parenting, with all that parenting entails yet in a context of infinitely refracting uncertainty, every decision we make just a breath away from loss, the potential for intense grief as present as the potential for intense connection. *The ultimate manifestation of process over product:* the most nontransactional, anticapitalist activism there is, at the most intimate, cellular, one-to-one level with very real ramifications for the collectivity. It is here, in the prioritizing of someone else's needs and frameworks and desires over our own—the key element of parenting, after all—that we can build our own vision of economies of exchange, engagement, and interdependence.

It's only capitalism that would say that the home I own and can offer to share is more valuable than the things Z has taught us about parenting or the things his mom has taught us about communication and making amends. We can decide, autonomously and situationally, which kinds of exchange are commensurate, equitable, livable, transformational.

"Is he yours?" people would often ask upon seeing me in a clearly intimate relationship with a baby who is not visibly related to me, as we don't share a racial or ethnic background.

"No," I'd respond, "I'm his."

THE PRICE OF AIR

NINA REVOYR

IT STARTED in March of 2017, when I had an asthma attack so severe that my wife rushed me down from a remote mountain cabin to the closest emergency room—where, for several hours, neither of us thought I'd make it through the night. Or it started a few weeks before that, when I came in from exercising out on our deck, where dust and chemicals floated over from the construction site next door, and I began to cough up blood. Actually, it started in December 2016, when a fellow passenger's fragrant lotion triggered an asthma attack on a plane. Or maybe it started earlier that year, when I began a new job and walked past three massive construction sites between the parking structure and our office in downtown Los Angeles every day. Or maybe the summer before that, in 2015, when construction began on five properties next door to our house. Or in the summer of 2014, when I was diagnosed with adult-onset asthma. Or maybe it was the previous October, when a mysterious illness—typhus? Lyme disease?—sent me into a nine-day fever and left me, when it passed, with shortness of breath. Or in the spring of 2011, when the nonprofit I worked for moved into its new headquarters, a block from the 101 Freeway. It's also possible it really started years before that, in 1999, when I moved to Glassell Park—my beloved neighborhood of rugged hills and mountain views, of hawks and owls and coyotes, but also an area bounded by four busy freeways and a railroad line to the south. Or maybe it really started when my dad and I first moved to LA, way back in 1978. The truth is, I'll never know exactly when it started. I just know that it got worse, and then critical.

This is a story of illness, but it's also a story of money. It's a story of how closely one is linked to the other, how those lucky enough to be financially secure might find a path back to relative wellness, while others continue to wander without a map.

On Friday, June 2, 2017—three months after the asthma attack in the mountains—I left my house in Glassell Park and never went back there to live. Earlier that week, on Memorial Day, we had ended up in urgent care—again. The next day I'd flown up to Seattle for work. In the previous few months, Seattle had been an escape—a place where the dramatically cleaner air and abundance of green gave my respiratory system a break. But on this particular trip, I was already so sick that Seattle didn't help. Then Thursday evening I flew back into Burbank, descending through a visible layer of brown smog. For years, like so many LA residents, I hadn't really noticed the dirty air; I'd come to think of it as normal. But that day, landing in Burbank, I was struck by the contrast between the pristine air I'd just left and the pollution to which I'd now returned. I couldn't catch my breath between the airport and the house, and as soon as I got home it was worse.

In the morning, exhausted after a sleepless night and too sick to go into the office, I arranged for a colleague to meet me at a coffee shop in my neighborhood so we could touch base on our various projects. I'd left a message for my pulmonologist, Dr. Robert Wolfe, on the way down the hill. (A few years before, I couldn't have conceived of knowing someone I'd refer to as "my pulmonologist.") He'd been watching my condition worsen with growing alarm over the last several months, had adjusted my medications and introduced new ones, and had put me on several rounds of prednisone when I was especially struggling. He had also encouraged me to move out of our neighborhood of unhealthful air and get closer to the beach, where it was cleaner. When he called me back at the coffee shop, he was silent for a moment as I told him I couldn't breathe at my house. Then he said, "You have to get out of there, you have to get out of there *now*."

I was a week short of forty-eight when this happened. I had always been healthy. A basketball player in high school and part of college, I'd stayed fit in the years since, working out and lifting weights regularly. In my thirties, I fell in love with the Sierras, and so I started hiking seriously, graduating to backpacking at high elevation and to the occasional mountain climb. I summited Mount Whitney and Mount Shasta in my forties and came close on Mount Rainier. My hardest mountain adventure had come *after* my asthma diagnosis, which, until late 2016, had been so mild that it hadn't slowed me down. I was confident to the point of cocky about my health. A friend who'd had serious health problems once warned, "You have too much faith in your body." So confident was I that the novel I published in 2015, *Lost Canyon*, was—among other things—a celebration of physical strength and resilience in the face of adversity. I even chose an epigraph that underscored that idea, from *Deliverance*: "The body is the one thing you can't fake; it's just got to be there."

Suddenly, dramatically, my body wasn't there. Its most fundamental action—breathing—seemed impossible. The results of my spirometry tests—which measure lung function—were steadily getting worse. I'd have so much trouble breathing that I'd grow light-headed and unable to think, go into a panic, and on a couple of occasions, pass out. Needless to say, I couldn't exercise, and so I felt physically weaker, which in turn probably worsened the asthma.

My decline accelerated over a period of months, but it happened so gradually that I didn't fully register that something was wrong—or at least I didn't want to acknowledge it. The asthma attack on the plane—the worst since my diagnosis—was the first sign that things were amiss, but I dismissed it as an anomaly until I started to have other problems: coughing and burning lungs after using my exercise bike, spitting up blood after the workout on my deck, more bloody coughing when I'd walk past the construction sites downtown.

One clear factor was that I'd been developing an allergy to dust.

Having never had allergies, I didn't recognize the signs—I just knew that I'd get stuffed up at night, which in turn led to my lungs constricting. My pulmonologist referred me to a doctor he described as "the best allergist in town"—but given there was a two-month wait for that doctor and that he was out of network, I got a referral to someone in-network who could see me much sooner. That doctor's testing revealed that I was allergic to cockroaches, hemp, and most severely, dust mites—but his schedule was so full that he couldn't meet to discuss next steps for another six weeks.

But what was happening went far beyond allergies or asthma. Something had caused damage to my lungs—most likely, I learned later, the ingestion of chemicals, gas, or particulates, probably through some combination of long-term exposure to air pollution and then the intense impact of construction detritus both at home and at work. It's also possible that I'd been affected by a onetime blast of gas or chemicals; we'll never really know. Thankfully, Felicia, my wife, was very healthy—while her sinuses acted up on extremely smoggy days, she had no issues with her lungs. But mine had weakened to the point that things that might not have impacted someone with normal lungs—construction dust, the air at the Burbank airport—rendered me totally unable to breathe.

During this time, I discovered two separate, interactive measures of air pollution—the *Los Angeles Times* Pollution Map, and CalEnviro-Screen. Both measures painted a daunting picture of our neighborhood, but CalEnviroScreen—a tool created by the State Office of Environmental Health Hazard Assessment to identify areas disproportionately burdened by pollution—was particularly startling. It showed that our neighborhood census tract—in the midst of a working-class, predominantly Latino area that had started to gentrify—was heavily impacted by multiple sources of pollution: ozone, diesel, particulate matter, and toxic releases. While our immediate block ranked "only" in the bottom 75th percentile for bad air pollution, parts of our neighborhood ranked in the 95th percentile—that is, in the lowest 5 percent for air quality in the state. (And California, in turn, has seven of the ten smoggiest cities in the country.) Not surprisingly, asthma rates were high—higher than in 78 percent of counties in

California. Our lovely hill retreat with a view of the mountains sat near the nexus of two intersecting freeways, with two others to the north and the east. There was also the railroad line just down the hill to the south, as well as Taylor Yards—an old freight-switching facility that *Los Angeles* magazine recently described as "polluted to high hell." All of these sent toxic pollutants into the air, where they were trapped by the San Gabriel Mountains, and where the heat converted them into lung-searing ozone. I had not only been breathing in pollutants but baking in them for the better part of twenty years. It's likely that this had contributed to the development of my asthma. And it weakened my system enough that the pile-on of construction, chemicals, and dust was like a final knockout punch.

But we couldn't control the air outside of the house, so we tried to control it inside—where, at least, we could manage the dust. Our 800-square-foot house had always been clean, even with dogs. Because dust mites burrow into upholstered furniture and leave their waste, which is the actual allergen, we gave away all our upholstered furniture except the new couch. We encased the mattress and pillows. We got rid of our rugs. We used dust-mite-killing laundry additives to wash our bedding, towels, and clothes. We bought HEPA air filters. We decided to pare down on dust-collecting books—a painful exercise for two writers—and Felicia boxed up dozens and dozens of them when I was out of town for work. We Marie Kondo'd before Marie Kondo was a thing. And still nothing helped.

That Friday, June 2, I left my home of eighteen years and walked out of my life. I never moved back, and besides a brief pit stop two weeks later, I did not step foot in my own house for more than a year. For the next two nights, I stayed in a quirky old hotel in Santa Monica—the only place I could find on such short notice, which, despite its two-and-a-half-star rating, ran me four hundred dollars a night. Then I started to look for a place to rent in better air. On Saturday, we visited apartments in Playa Vista and Marina del Rey, all of them depressing and expensive. We wanted to find a place that Felicia and Ariat, our Border collie, could eventually move into, and so a townhouse or small house with some outside space would be preferable to an apartment. Finally, I found a small rental house in tony, mostly white Manhattan Beach—CalEnviroScreen top 5 percent in air quality—newly remodeled, with a yard for the dog. At \$3,900 a month, it was just slightly more expensive than the apartments we'd seen and cheaper than rental houses in Santa Monica, Venice, or Westchester. The difference in air quality was obvious—even two miles from the ocean, we could feel the ocean breeze, and the temperature was fifteen degrees cooler than at home.

Suddenly, over a weekend, I'd gone from living at home with my spouse and dog to living alone in a strange, empty house. I'd left my wonderfully diverse neighborhood for a homogenous part of town where we—a same-sex, Mexican American (Felicia) and Japanese American (me) couple—felt completely out of place. While I wasn't allergic to my dog per se, I *was* allergic to the dust mites she carried, and we realized that, despite the comfort she gave me, I couldn't be around her. And so, Felicia would come down in the afternoons, and then go home at night to care for Ariat. It was miserable, of course, but we didn't have time to ponder it; we were just doing what had to be done. We figured it would be a short-term arrangement. And we were both optimistic that, soon, between the move to the beach and the intense new medication that Dr. Wolfe had put me on, I'd start to feel better.

Except I did not feel better. As we shopped at the local Target for household supplies; as we ate burgers at a place near the beach; as we drove around with the windows down to take in the air, I still struggled and struggled to breathe.

Because I did not yet have furniture, I'd settle down on the floor at night on an exercise mat, with a comforter wrapped around me, and try to sleep. But then, on the third or fourth night, I woke gasping for breath. This was a new feeling: not the usual tightening in my chest, but complete suffocation—as if someone had placed an invisible hand over my nose and mouth; as if my lungs were being squeezed from the inside. I went to the window, opened it, and sucked in the air. Finally, I burst through the back door and out to the yard—it was like breaking through the surface of water. I filled my lungs, desperate for oxygen. Whatever was causing this misery was inside the house, and it wasn't dust.

I did some research online and discovered that new construction or remodels often cause problems for people with asthma, because of the off-gassing of volatile organic compounds (VOCs)—such as formaldehyde—from composite flooring and cabinetry, from glue, from paint, from carpet. And gas ovens and washing machines—both of which we had in the rental's kitchen—can also be culprits. We shut off the gas to the stove and washing machine, but that didn't help. We bought two heavy-duty air purifiers at over six hundred dollars a pop that were designed to help with VOCs and filled the house with air-cleaning plants—to no avail. Whatever toxic mix was coming from the floors, the cabinetry, and the walls was making my eyes burn, my head spin with dizziness, and my lungs clench and close.

When I realized this, a week and a half after we'd rented the place, I tried to go home. I couldn't be inside the house, where the dog and dust mites were, so I set up a backpacking tent on our deck. But I couldn't breathe for the pollution, and when I looked out over Eagle Rock and toward the 134 Freeway, I could see, even at night, the brown layer of heavy air obscuring the mountains—smog so thick I could have chewed on it. I had to get to better air. So, I drove the twenty-four miles to Manhattan Beach, went straight through the house, and set up my tent again in the backyard. And that is where I slept for the next four and a half months.

Those summer and fall months of 2017, I tried to keep as much of a normal routine as I could. Every morning, I would break down my tent, go inside, take a shower (where I'd often get light-headed from whatever was coming off of the building materials), eat my breakfast on the back steps, and drive an hour to my downtown office—where I generally felt a bit better. (I worked for a new philanthropic organization, and we'd moved offices by then, away from construction.) Every evening, I'd drive back to the little house in Manhattan Beach, where Felicia would be waiting—she headed down before me to beat the traffic. On days when I was up to it, we would drive to the beach and slowly do a three-mile walk along the Strand from the pier to El Segundo and back. The ocean air felt great and was easier to breathe, but I was so sensitive that dust blowing from gardens or construction sites would set me off, creating a chain reaction, first making my head stuff up, then causing my lungs to constrict. From the Strand we would go to Whole Foods, where the employees quickly came to know us, sensed that we—like they—were not of the neighborhood, and treated us kindly. Almost always we got food from the food bar, since our stove was disconnected. We'd sit there in the store or take the food to the little house, where—because I couldn't be inside for more than a few minutes—we'd eat in the backyard. We spent our wedding anniversary and my birthday sitting on an exercise mat, eating takeout from the Whole Foods food bar.

When Felicia left, I would set up my tent, put in the exercise mat, and pile on a comforter and pillow. I usually waited until well after dark, self-conscious that the neighbors would see me. I'd sleep with a paper mask on, since the slightest stirring of the comforter would cause my allergies to flare and make my throat and chest tighten. I would read or surf the internet on my phone, anything to keep myself occupied, to keep from falling into despair. Never a meditation person—I was generally too high-octane to sit still for very long—I tried a meditation app in an attempt to control my fear. But the woman's calm, steady voice would tell me to focus on my breathing—the very thing that was so fraught and difficult—so I had to stop. There were a few particularly bad nights—the night a rat fell from a tree right onto my tent; July Fourth, when the fireworks going off in the neighborhood kept me up until dawn; the nights when the neighbor's dogs would bark at me through the fence. But mostly it was a mundane kind of awful. I couldn't believe this was my life. I knew exactly how far the urgent care and the ERs were, as well as their hours of operation. Every night I prayed that I'd make it until morning. Then I'd fall into a fitful sleep, wake up at 5:30, and start all over again.

I hated being alone, but it eased my mind to know that Felicia was caring for Ariat. I loved my dogs, so much so that I'd written about both Ariat and our English springer spaniel—who'd passed a couple of years before—in different books, and there was no way that we were giving her up, especially since she was older. So, Felicia would come see me for several hours each day and then go home at night. We both assumed that the two of them would be able to join me shortly, or that maybe, in a few months, I might even be able to return home.

Once I realized the little house was making me sicker, I started looking for another place. But summer in the beach cities is a tough time for house hunting. I saw any number of apartments and little houses, and they were either in terrible shape—full of dust and crumbling walls—or brand-new, which might cause the same problems as the little house. Almost all of them were more expensive than the place I had, or similarly priced. Any apartment that could accommodate a lively dog was at least $3,500; small houses ran from $4,500 to $10,000 and above, and places in Venice, Santa Monica, and the once-modest area now known as Silicon Beach were even more expensive. Plus, there was the fact that I'd already signed a lease. Sometimes, as I walked on the Strand with Felicia, past outsize houses, I felt an intense frustration and yearning. All those rooms, all that space, and some of the houses were not even occupied. I did not need or want anything even a quarter as fancy. I just wanted to sleep inside.

In early July—a month after I moved—I finally got an appointment with Dr. Jonathan Corren, the allergy and asthma specialist that Dr. Wolfe had recommended. I'd gotten much worse since the original diagnosis in May. My lung function readings were lower, and I'd grown more reactive to dust. By that time, I couldn't be in a car, fold my clothes, or towel myself off after a shower without wearing a mask; otherwise, the swirling dust would make me congested and cause my throat and my lungs to clench up.

Dr. Corren retested me and found the same results, except that my dust allergy—as I already knew—was more severe. He suggested a course of allergy shots to address the dust mite allergy and adjusted my medications. At first, we tried an accelerated schedule of shots in the hopes that I could improve quickly enough for Felicia and Ariat to join me by fall—but I reacted so badly that we had to slow down. It would take six months of shots to get to "maintenance" level—the maximum state of defense—which I'd have to boost every month for the next five years. All through the rest of the summer and fall, maintenance seemed a long way off.

Dr. Corren also told me about the concept of "toxic load"—the accumulation of toxins, chemicals, and allergens that affect our bodies. If you imagine yourself as a water glass, the "load" would be the level of fullness. Pour in chemicals from the food and liquids you consume, from the plastics you eat off of, from personal care products and home cleaning supplies. Add on top of that particulate matter or nitrogen dioxide from the smog you breathe, from exposure to car exhaust or factories or your living room fireplace, and from construction. Then add allergies: to dust, to pollen or dander. At some point, the water level grows so high that it spills over the edge of the glass: the load becomes too heavy, and you get sick.

My own toxic load was clearly off the charts. Air pollution in our old neighborhood got mixed with exposure to chemicals, gas, and particulate matter from construction at home and work, as well as with other factors we may never really know. Then my dust allergy developed. Then I moved into a house where the off-gassing of new construction materials made me even sicker. And I was now taking more medications than I could count—which helped in some ways but also resulted in the ingesting of more chemicals. By July, I was a walking node of reactivity, unable to do the most common everyday tasks—going for a walk, getting a ride in someone's car—without risking a major allergic response. At one point I was so insanely sensitive to chemicals that I could smell a woman's perfume from across the street, or sense a gas leak that no one else could detect, or walk into a drug store and be able to tell from the entrance which aisles the laundry detergent or cleaning supplies or deodorants were in. It was like a perverse kind of superpower.

The idea with toxic load is to lower the water level so it's not constantly running over the edge. We can't, of course, avoid exposure to chemicals and toxins completely. But we can control some things, and so Felicia and I tried to do so. We switched to scent-free and chemical-free toiletries and cleaning supplies. We bought mostly organic foods. I had always eaten pretty much whatever I wanted, but now I drastically altered my diet—cutting out gluten, soy, dairy, alcohol, and anything else remotely inflammatory—and lost so much weight that I looked like a ghost of myself. I religiously went for my allergy shots, which slowly started to take effect. I reduced the bad things going into my body to try to lower the water level, so that each new irritation wouldn't cause it to run over.

At night, alone in my tent, I would scour the internet for information. I read everything I could find about asthma, toxic load, exposure to gas and chemicals. I read about multiple chemical sensitivity, stories of people who became complete recluses because they could not leave their controlled environments. These stories scared me most of all, because I saw myself in them. Before, with the arrogance of the healthy, I'd largely dismissed such stories—if I noticed them at all—as the complaints of the hypersensitive or the mentally unwell. Now I *was* one of those stories. How could this have happened? I'd always taken care of myself, was happy and energetic; I had a temperament that trended toward optimism. I wasn't yet as bad as some of the people I read about—I could still be in an office or at a restaurant—but for how long?

But there were also stories that gave me hope: those of people who got better. I looked into a health retreat on Vancouver Island, British Columbia, that had successfully helped people detox from chemical exposure. It would cost $4,200 for a week, or $8,400 for two weeks, excluding travel—ridiculously steep prices that didn't, in my desperation, seem unreasonable. Before I got sick, I was so cost-conscious that we hardly ever ate out; that I was reluctant to pay for home repairs we couldn't handle ourselves. Now, I would have spent down my savings and emptied my retirement account for even the slightest chance to feel better. I reached out by email to the health retreat people, but I was afraid of having an asthma attack either there or on the plane, and so reluctantly decided against it. Soon after, I read about another guy who'd had to sleep outside for months, but who slowly improved with a restrictive diet, supplements, attention to his gut health—and of course, removal from the things that made him sick.

One message was clear from all of these sources: it had taken a long time for me to get this sick. It was going to take time to get better.

While the medications kept me alive at my sickest point, they also caused other problems. I'd started using a daily inhaler—QVAR—when I was diagnosed with asthma in 2014, but by the spring of 2017, Dr. Wolfe switched me off of QVAR to the stronger Symbicort, adding Montelukast for good measure. In early summer, with my lung function readings worse, the doctors eventually upped the ante even more to Spiriva, and then Breo. I was also taking over-the-counter Flonase for allergic rhinitis, and a number of supplements that were said to help with asthma. By July of 2017, I was on a regimen of multiple over-the-counter and prescription medications and supplements so complicated that I had to keep a chart:

MORNING	MIDDAY	EVENING
• Symbicort	• omega-3	• Singulair (montelukast)
• Flonase		• Symbicort
• Spiriva		• Flonase
• Xlear		• Xlear
• Rhinocort		• Rhinocort
• Azelastine		• Azelastine
• Zantac		• Zantac
- omega-3		- magnesium
- probiotic		- omega-3
- Emergen-C		

There was also, of course, albuterol—the fast-acting rescue medication that could open up my lungs in the event of an asthma attack. I kept this with me always and used it often. All of these things together did seem to help temporarily, or at least hold the worst at bay. But the Flonase contributed to my superhuman sense of smell, the Spiriva began to damage my vocal cords, and the asthma meds gave me terrible acid reflux. When things were especially bad, they'd put me on another round of prednisone—a steroid that caused its own dangers if used for too long.

Off the prednisone, though, I still wasn't able to breathe any easier, and we were running out of options.

One thing I could not acknowledge at the time—that I couldn't afford even to think about—was the utter loss of having been removed from my house and my neighborhood, the only home I'd known for two decades. One day I left my house and I never went back to live there. I did not pack my bags; I did not prepare; I did not plan for the transition. I just left. My walk through the neighborhood with the dogs every morning and evening— gone. The view of the mountains, how they changed with the shifting light—gone. The hawks circling overhead, the hooting owls, the coyotes crying in the canyon—gone. The vibrant mix of people, the variety of languages and cultures and music and foods—gone. My wonderful neighbors, who always stopped to say hello, who'd welcome us in for a drink or a cup of coffee—gone. Our backyard, with its lemon and avocado trees, where I'd sit with a cold beer after work and play with the dogs—gone. My home, where I had lived and slept, written and loved, dreamed and grieved; my home where I'd made a life and had planned to stay forever—gone, gone, ripped from me, or I from it, without even a chance to say good-bye.

Slowly, through the summer, I began to improve. While I was still insanely allergic to dust, the congestion in my head wouldn't always lead to the tightening in my chest—what had been a chain reaction now stopped short with the first link. Being in better air, and removed from construction, was unmistakably helping my lungs. I still could not be outside in the smog—I had to wear a mask on days of high pollution or stay out of downtown altogether. And I'd developed a new problem—a searing pain in my esophagus with exposure to car exhaust or strong chemicals, which felt like an internal sunburn and which could, when severe, cause an asthma episode. But when I could avoid exposure to burned fuel, when I stayed close to the beach and off the freeway, I could feel the improvement. My toxic load was getting lower, so that every new bit of stimulus didn't cause the cup to flow over. Slowly I scaled back on the medications that caused the worst side effects. By late September, I was able to get through most days without struggling every minute to breathe.

I was feeling marginally better enough that I decided to risk a trip— first to Palo Alto for work, and then on to Seattle, where I'd check in at the office and then take a few days off in a lovely, sustainably built rental home on Bainbridge Island. (Needless to say, we had not taken a vacation that summer.) It was the first time I'd been on a plane since I'd moved; the risk of an asthma attack had been too great.

I can't begin to describe what a luxury it was to sleep inside—in Palo Alto and Seattle, where the carpet-free rooms were fine, and especially in the beautiful rental on Bainbridge, where I felt well inside a living space— where I could just linger in the kitchen or drink coffee at a table—for the first time in months. Felicia joined me for two nights, another luxury. Between the rental, Felicia's flight, and restaurant meals, that short trip put us out more than $1,500. But it was worth it to have even a couple of days of normalcy. And it made me realize that, with my underlying lung health slowly improving, the biggest culprits were whatever chemicals were inside the beach rental, and Los Angeles itself. When I returned to LA, I miserably resumed sleeping outside. Then in early October, I went on a work trip to Detroit—where, again, I felt infinitely better. I had no problems inside the hotel where I stayed, nor did I have any issue walking around outside. For three days, I forgot I had asthma. At the airport in Detroit, I had to run to catch a flight—and the fact that I could take deep breaths and actually *run* filled me with utter joy. I dreaded the return to LA. But after having experienced another three nights of sleeping inside, and the incredible sense of being rested after months of exhaustion, I knew I had to get out of the rental. It was October now, and the weather was changing. I had been sleeping outside for four and a half months. I did not want to be in the tent when the rains came and the weather turned cold.

With the help of a young realtor we'd met the previous summer, we found a lovely furnished cottage in Hermosa Beach, with an owner who would allow a dog, when we were ready. Felicia and I went to see the cottage; it was adorable and impeccably clean. Best of all, it had been remodeled some time ago, so it hit that sweet spot of not too old, yet not recently remodeled. At $5,300 a month, it was significantly more expensive than the rental I was already in. I was still nervous about committing, but I remember the yearning I felt when we first saw the cottage, the desire to have a place where I could stay. The owner—amazingly—suggested that I spend a couple of nights there before signing a lease. So, I did. I slept comfortably in a bed, inside, in the LA area, for the first time since the beginning of June—longer even, since I hadn't been able to sleep well in our home for months before I moved to the beach. I could be indoors—just drinking coffee or watching TV—without feeling like I was suffocating. All summer and fall I had pressed on every day, in pure survival mode, dealing with the challenges of simply trying to breathe. I had not had the space to process or feel. Now, the weight of the last few months finally hit me. The relief I felt at the promise of rest, at having a place to be, moved me to tears.

I was not out of the woods yet. I still had episodes when I'd grab my emergency inhaler and think about heading to urgent care. I still had to avoid downtown LA for days and even weeks at a time, when the air was bad from pollution, or later that year, from catastrophic fires. I was still living separately from my spouse—which lasted another half year—and my dog, whom I hadn't seen in four months. And crucially, I was still having and would continue to have the searing reaction to burned fuels and toxic chemicals, which left me always somewhere on the continuum of mild to severely in pain.

But I was able to breathe, and the move to the cottage was a turning point. It got me away from the VOCs that made me worse at the first rental. And since we did not use the stove and got by with electric space heaters, it also removed me from gas. I was now living on a hill where the ocean breeze came in through the windows. In the months that followed, I began to think that a return to good health, or something close to it, was possible.

This is a story of illness, but it is also a story of money—what financial stability and a bit of cushion made it possible for me to do. One afternoon, during the time I was living in the first rental, I had a meeting with a community organizing group in South LA. I mentioned self-consciously that I was living in Manhattan Beach and why. The woman I was speaking with—the daughter of a Mexican immigrant family who'd grown up in South LA—told me that her mother, who had asthma, was in the hospital that very moment; the relentless smog of that summer had exacerbated her condition. (After a couple of decades of improvement in Los Angeles's air quality, the last three summers had seen worsening smog.) This often happened, she said, during periods of particularly bad air. But there was nothing her mother could do except go to the doctor. What option did she have?

I had never thought of myself as privileged. I was raised by a single father in a small apartment in a gritty part of LA, where gang members congregated in the schoolyard. His parents had worked in a shoe factory and a chicken-slaughtering plant, and he himself had earned a steady but modest living working in collegiate licensing. On the other side of my family, my mother and stepfather, both Japanese immigrants, were an adjunct community college professor and an electrician. In a typical—though increasingly less common—story of upward mobility, I went to fancy East Coast colleges on scholarship, but I still felt drawn to work and live in economically challenged, mixed-race communities like the one where I'd grown up. I'd chosen non-lucrative careers—working for a nonprofit that served low-income kids, writing novels, and occasionally teaching. The nonprofit had offices in Central LA and Watts, both landscapes of disenfranchisement and poverty.

Our neighborhood, Glassell Park, was surrounded by Cypress Park and Highland Park, both low-income immigrant neighborhoods where the Avenues—a Mexican street gang—ruled the streets. While the small house I'd shared with Felicia was up on a hill removed from the main action, we heard gunshots frequently and were often awakened by LAPD helicopters flying overhead. Even as our neighborhood gentrified, the sense of challenge was ever-present. We loved it there, though; it reflected and suited us. We could be comfortable as a gay couple and as people of color, and as writers still connected to our blue-collar roots. We lived simply and humbly, as most of our neighbors did.

But when I got sick, I realized how privileged I truly was. We had money and little debt, and that made all the difference. My story could have played out much differently—and does play out differently, every day, for thousands of people in my city alone.

And when I say we had money, I don't mean we had a ton of it, or that we could turn to our families. I mean that, thanks to the sheer luck of buying a house when I did, coupled with the frugal, cheapskate habits I'd picked up from my family, we had always lived well below our means. We drove modest cars—our Honda CR-V clocked 211,000 miles before we finally traded it in for a Subaru. We did not spend money on travel, pricey clothes, or fancy restaurants. We never bothered to upgrade our simple, small house. As a result, even on a nonprofit salary, I had saved. I had listened to all those financial gurus who preached about paying off debt and building an emergency fund. Having watched both my parents weather separate financial crises and be dependent on their spouses, I had vowed never to be caught off guard. And so, when crisis did hit, we were—at least financially—ready to weather the storm.

Here is what money and relative financial security made possible:

First and foremost, I had good medical care, thanks to the health insurance provided by my job. The testing and treatment I got from Dr. Wolfe, my pulmonologist, and Dr. Corren, my allergist (who was out of network), was first-class and largely covered by my insurance. Insurance also took care of my trips to urgent care and the emergency room, one ambulance ride, two separate hospital stays, and the many medications I was on.

Second, we were able to pay for a rental in an expensive part of town while still carrying our house. This was possible because in 1999 I'd bought a house for $190,000 in a transitioning part of town long before LA real estate got crazy—and had paid the mortgage off in fifteen years. The fact that we did not have monthly mortgage payments freed up money to pay rent, and though we were now double paying on utilities and still covering property taxes and insurance, this was, if a struggle, still doable.

Third, I'd accumulated some savings, which meant we could cover things like deposits and furnishings, dog care, gas, the hotel in Santa Monica, the trip to Bainbridge Island, medical expenses—and for a couple of months, the rents on *two* places, since I had broken my original lease. (The landlords were understanding, but I agreed to extend payments to soften the blow.) It helped ensure that we were able to buy good, organic foods at Whole Foods. It also meant that, for more than a year, Felicia could take a break from teaching while she bore the weight of caring for me, our house, and our dog, and commuted daily from downtown to the beach.

Fourth, I had a well-paying new job, and just as important, an employer who was understanding and flexible, and who made allowances through the worst of my illness. I'd been hired for a significant task: to build out the LA presence of a big new philanthropic venture. But we were still in start-up mode. My bosses were fine with me not flying up to the main office in Seattle through the summer of 2017. They were okay with me working from home—which meant sitting outside in the backyard—for weeks at a time when the air was too polluted downtown. They were all right with me taking meetings in Marina del Rey or the South Bay, where the air was better. Needless to say, this was a tremendous luxury. It's true that work was therapeutic for me—my distraction, my way of not slipping into despair. But regardless, there are countless employers who would not have been nearly so understanding.

Finally, our financial standing—and the fact that our little home had quadrupled in value—put us in a position to buy another house. We thought long and hard about whether to even stay in Los Angeles. But by the summer of 2018, I'd improved enough that we were willing to bet I'd continue to get better. Plus, quite simply, LA is home. We both love it fiercely, despite and maybe because of its complexities and challenges. Desperate to be back on our side of town, we came close to buying a place in Altadena—a beautiful, quiet, diverse community at the foot of the San Gabriel Mountains, where the levels of particulate matter are decent thanks to the greenery and distance from freeways. But the scorching heat also creates high levels of ozone, and after a few days of visiting, I couldn't deny the discomfort I felt in my lungs—so, regretfully, we pulled out of negotiations. A few months later, we found a place in Hermosa Beach, not far from our second rental, on a hill where we catch the ocean breeze. Needless to say, this area was much more expensive than our old neighborhood, and also more expensive than Altadena. But we were able to swing it. And our savings—which had dwindled, but not completely—allowed us to do what we needed to make the house livable: remove the gas range and replace it with an electric one; replace the carpet in the master bedroom with chemical-free wood flooring. We are in debt again—we had to take out an enormous loan for the house—but I am alive. And I've found a way both to stay in Los Angeles, and to breathe.

I have not bounced back completely. But I am better than I could have imagined two years ago. My lungs are 90 percent improved but still sensitive—which means I can carry a thirty-five-pound pack high up in the mountains, where the air is pristine, but can't walk past a tailpipe without coughing. My recovery has come at a high cost—not just the tens of thousands of dollars we spent on my care and the rentals, not just the new mortgage, but the loss of my beloved home, which we ultimately had to sell; my neighborhood, a place I was deeply connected to; and with those things, my sense of who I was. We've also lost the day-to-day comfort of living in a place where neither our race nor our relationship caused any notice. But these losses, in the scheme of things, are relative. And I'm very clear that I would not have recovered at all if I hadn't been able to move to healthier air. There are tens of thousands, hundreds of thousands of people in my city alone who do not have the luxury of those options. And of course, there are tens of thousands of people sleeping in tents every night, not in a safe, suburban backyard, but on sidewalks, and medians, and worse.

In the last few years, I've learned a lot about environmental justice. I've learned about the children and families who live next to oil extraction sites that are right in the midst of neighborhoods; whose housing sits beside freeways or under flight paths or near ports; who live in buildings with crumbling lead paint; who have been poisoned by battery plants; whose proximity to oil refineries and pesticide plants and trash-burning facilities has caused asthma and cancer and brain damage and premature births. I've also learned that Los Angeles ranks highest among US cities for deaths caused by air pollution. Not surprisingly, the deaths and illnesses are disproportionately borne by low-income people of color. Many of the affected people don't know what's making them sick. Most of them cannot afford to live anywhere else.

Of course, all of these realities—which communities are most endangered by pollution and chemicals; who can afford to live in healthier areas—have been underscored and exacerbated by the Covid-19 pandemic. It's no accident that Covid has especially ravaged low-income communities of color, in Los Angeles and elsewhere. The neighborhoods close to oil wells and freeways and trash-burning facilities, the neighborhoods filled with lead or chemicals, are also the ones most likely to be home to essential workers, who have not had the option—as I have—of staying home. When you start with higher rates of preexisting conditions linked to environmental factors, add on overcrowding and poverty, and then send people out into a region where the virus is prevalent, the results are predictable. If you compare a map of Covid infections and deaths in LA County with the CalEnviroScreen map of most polluted communities, the two maps are eerily similar.

I knew about environmental issues before I got sick. But they were not quite real to me. Even though I've spent my entire adult life working to better the lives of low-income kids and families, what I worked on—what I thought about—was early childhood education and public schools, violence prevention and trauma treatment, families having access to parenting classes and job training. I didn't think about the very air that people breathe; I didn't think about contaminants in soil and drinking water, the environmental safety of families' houses and neighborhoods. I understood the challenges of community violence because I'd seen it myself; of single-parent households and immigration and racism because I'd known them myself; of the incredible opportunity of a good education because I'd been blessed with one myself. But I'd been healthy, had never questioned my very ability to live and breathe. Until suddenly I couldn't.

I'm not 100 percent better. But I'm better enough—and in a global pandemic, when no one's ability to breathe can be taken for granted, better enough is just fine. I'm better enough to have resumed the activities that bring me joy, including exercise and backpacking trips. I'm better enough to have reengaged with my work—both job and writing—with a renewed sense of purpose. I'm better enough that I am now completely off of asthma medications—not just the new ones I started to take when I spiraled in 2017, but all of them, every single one. I'm better enough to feel grateful for how much better I've become; to know how lucky I was that my health improved before the coronavirus struck; to think of the events of 2017 to 2018 as part of my past. I'm better enough to feel a sense of responsibility and anger on behalf of the many, many people who've been made sick, as I was, by environmental poisons—but who do not have the options I did; as well as the people who've put themselves in harm's way this last year, in order to take care of the rest of us. I'm better enough to want to use my experience, good fortune, and yes, privilege, to do what I can to help others get better—or to never get sick in the first place. And I'm better enough to see that good air in Los Angeles—like good education and quality housing—is only within the reach of the wealthy.

HAVING PLENTY

SONYA RENEE TAYLOR

IN 1986, my mother, five foot three inches and shrinking in frame daily, stood in the living room of our military housing apartment and handed me a $100 bill, crisp as the first bite of December air. She said, "Sonya, here, take this money and go to the toy store and get you and your brother the presents you want for Christmas." I cannot recall if shame or secrecy tinged her voice, not that it mattered—in those days, both hung in our home like curtains. I looked at the small fortune resting in my ten-year-old palm and considered how I had never seen nor held so many zeros in a solo note—at least, not outside of Monopoly money. The biggest bill ever belonging to me at that point was a twenty-dollar bill, a single two and a single zero, given only on exceptional birthdays from well-to-do aunties and my father's childless workmates. But my mother had just placed what felt like all the world's wealth, a $100 bill in my hand, entrusting the whole of Christmas to me.

Today I know that she had given me only one seventh of the check my father had mailed to her, separate from the monthly bills—from a naval aircraft carrier floating in the Indian Ocean. When I was a child, my parents didn't tell me about the family finances. I didn't need to know. I was a kid. Only decades later would my father share how much money he sent that year. Today I know we were supposed to have seven hundred dollars' worth of Christmas gifts. Today I know seven hundred dollars is the equivalent of $1,603.78 adjusted for thirty-two years' worth of inflation. We were supposed to have plenty. But I was ten years old, old enough to know Santa was made up and young enough to still wish he wasn't. I was old enough to know what "I'm hungry" felt like and to wonder why I was buying Christmas presents when the fridge had little more than an assortment of caked and dried jellies, ketchup, and Miracle Whip, with no bread, meat, or potatoes to put them on. And still, I was ten years old, young enough to be proud of the fact that my mother had given me all our riches and a task of grown-up-sized proportions: make Christmas happen.

The mission was to go to the military base toy store and return with a skull-and-bones skateboard for myself, just like the one Jason, my best friend Rizalynn's boyfriend, rode in the neighborhood on Saturday mornings, and a He-Man Castle Grayskull Slime Pit, the one my brother had been raving about for nearly two months. I made the executive decision that my brother and I would each get a single item from the toy store: the one we desired the most. Not because we were a family prone to modest holidays: historically, we had epic Christmases with racetracks, games, puzzles, bikes, dolls, and clothes galore scattered beneath an enormous tree laden with lights and ornaments.

We were getting only one item each because we were no longer in history.

We were in 1986, in the height of the crack '80s—the days of missing dinners and dirty laundry stacked higher than both my and my brother's bodies. The days of missing school for days and looking at the locked door of my mother's bedroom until late in the afternoon. If we were lucky, her friends would come over at some point, bearing McDonald's Happy Meals for my brother and me. As the adults retreated to the bedroom for hours, my brother and I ate cheeseburgers in front of the television in the living room. This Christmas, we would get only one gift each because I was ten years old—not old enough to know all the costs of the family bills but old enough to know that we were not in times of plenty and that I should probably act like it.

Our small northern California suburb of Alameda seemed to hide a Christmas secret, tucked in a pocket of sunshine and clear skies. I didn't even wear a jacket as I walked to the Toys"R"Us on the naval base, crossing the railroad tracks, walking along empty lots closed off with chain-link fences. Arriving on the base, I eyed a small ice cream shop sandwiched between the Navy Exchange (a Walmart-style military department store) and the toy store. A double scoop of delicious creamy goodness seemed appropriate remuneration for the high level of grown-upping for which I had been tasked. I entered the store, my forehead barely clearing the height of the freezer case, and ordered a double scoop of cookies and cream on a sugar cone. The act seemed simple enough. It was mature of me to order and pay for my own ice cream, but not nearly as adult as Christmas shopping. The detour should have been inconsequential.

Thirty years later, the face behind the counter remains a blur, their gender and age swallowed by the mouth of time. But I remember their voice, shrill and adult, not like I was pretending to be, but an actual grown-up. The adult called out the price I owed, $2.50, and I beamed at them, prideful and rich, my pocket full of plenty. I reached in my blue jeans and handed over the quadruple-folded $100 bill my mother had given me less than an hour earlier. Incredulously, they unfolded the flat green face of Benjamin Franklin, and held it up to the light. Again, I do not recall the person's face, but the voice is permanently etched. A bark, a demand, an accusation: "Where did you get this?"

The secrets that filled our house had followed me to the ice cream shop. They were plain to see; I was wearing them. I wasn't supposed to have that money. I was not supposed to be buying the Christmas gifts that barely two years earlier I still believed Santa delivered with Rudolph. When my mother handed me all the world's wealth—all our family's plenty—I knew it was wrong. That by having that money I was telling the world our secret.

I knew that my mother was supposed to be Christmas shopping, that she was supposed to be the adult I could only pretend to be. But she could not be that person, because whatever she did in the locked bedroom with her friends while my brother and I ate fast food on the floor in front of the television, that thing made her stop filling the fridge with food, stop doing the laundry, stop sending us to school, stop making me and my brother dinner each night. Whatever she did in the bedroom stole everything: television sets, bill money, and school clothes. Whatever she did in the bedroom took it all, except the single piece of plenty she had given me that I had just given to the nameless, faceless, shrill adult voice who knew I should not have it. That my having it meant something was not as it should be.

"Where is your mother?" the voice from behind the ice cream counter followed up immediately.

Without hesitation, and with great earnestness, I lied. "She's outside."

The adult's suspicion filled the shop, their glare seemed to multiply. Their one set of eyes became fifty sets of eyes all peering down on me from a single face—each eye aware that I should not have had the plenty that was in my pocket. The adult passed me $97.50 in change and a double scoop of cookies and cream on a sugar cone. On the way out, the voice said, "Next time, tell your mother to come in here with you."

I wore the stain of my ice cream shop encounter into the toy store that day—and into check cashing joints and finance companies twenty years later. But on that day in December, I hurriedly snatched up the slime pit for my brother in Toys"R"Us, paying for it with a twenty and a ten—bills small enough to escape scrutiny—and exited the store before any additional adults could detect my recently inherited shame. The skateboard I wanted, the one like Rizalynn's boyfriend, Jason, had, was sold out. I made the executive decision to forgo a Christmas gift that year. Who was I to have even a portion of plenty, when our refrigerator could offer up nothing more than condiments—when my mother could offer up nothing more than locked bedrooms, a shrinking frame, and the nondescript smell of tiny rocks burning in glass pipes? Who was I to have anything that resembled plenty when we were obviously in such lack? My mother had not given me riches at all. She had given me the fear of getting caught with "too much."

That Christmas, I became a martyr. If I denied myself, then maybe, just maybe, my mother would unlock the bedroom and take care of us.

When I got home, I gave my mother the change from the $100 bill. I was old enough to know it was unlikely to be spent on groceries or more presents. I was young enough to still hope that it would be. But my father would not return from overseas for three more months, and whether the ice cream shop keeper knew it or not, there was only one grown-up left in our house—and it was me.

Christmas morning came, and my brother radiated with joy at the sight of his slime pit. My mother saved enough of Daddy's check and the week's change to take us to Fisherman's Wharf for a fancy Chinese food Christmas dinner. I held on to a tiny prayer that I might awake that morning to a skull-and-bones skateboard beneath the tree we bought on Christmas Eve. That my mother might have stepped in, cleaned up enough to let me be a child on Christmas morning. No such holiday miracle occurred.

Many calendar pages later, my mother got sober for a while. And for that time, we were a family of plenty once again. Although my brother and I were adults, we had Christmas trees packed with presents underneath them—my mother's attempts to make up for the holidays her addiction stole from us. But she could not reverse time or the lessons her disease threaded into every fiber of my world. She could not reverse my expectation of lack.

That nameless, faceless, shrill adult voice from the ice cream shop followed me for the next thirty years, blaring out indictments from the bottom of wallets, bank accounts, contracts, and tax filings. Behind every dollar—whether twenty or one hundred—was a voice prosecuting me with "Where did you get this?" That same voice was there every time I dared to live above the poverty line. An adult who likely never thought of me after our one chance encounter on a December afternoon in 1986 altered what I understood about money, about myself, about what it meant to have "plenty." About who should have it, and who should not.

I am forty-two today, and it has taken eight years of therapy, a few twelve-step programs, and a lot of overdraft fees, repossessions, and abysmal credit scores to pull up what took root that day in 1986. I spent thirty years certain I had no business having plenty of anything: not love, intimacy, home, stability, and most assuredly not money. Remarkably, I always made this anticipation of lack work in my favor. I took my lack of stable housing and chose to become a touring performance poet. I transformed my fear of intimacy in partnership into a career built on sharing the most intimate stories from my life on stages in front of thousands of people around the world. My beliefs about lack became a vehicle. But it would only get me so far.

In 2011, I started a Facebook page called The Body Is Not an Apology, named after a poem I had written espousing the infallible beauty and power of our bodies, no matter their shape, size, race, gender, age, or ability. I called this foundational belief in our inherent "enoughness" radical self-love.

As I explored the idea of radical self-love for myself, I began to see how my story about money was also limiting the possibilities of this project. My money story was shrinking my vision. People were reaching out to me, asking if they could contribute content and write essays about radical self-love and social justice, but I had no way to compensate them. Others wanted to help the idea grow and expand. I refused their offers or sabotaged plans with missed deadlines and a lack of follow-up; fearful that if I let myself believe in a grander, revenue-generating version of The Body Is Not an Apology, I would be alerting the world to my act of fraud. I would be telling everyone that I had no business running a company. Everyone would know I was only pretending to be a grown-up.

Stepping into the work of radical self-love demanded I reckon with the three decades I spent in a prison of lack. In order to transform The Body Is Not an Apology from the Facebook page I launched in 2011 into a global media platform focused on the intersection of radical self-love, bodies, and social justice in 2015, I needed to raise $80,000 from our community. To grow beyond my fear, I had to ask my community to give me eight hundred of the very same bills my mother handed ten-year-old Sonya all those years earlier. Every time a donation came into our crowdfunding account, a shrill disembodied voice from a cell inside me would say, "Where did you get this? You are not supposed to have this money, Sonya!"

But one of the most powerful tools to come out of my work with The Body Is Not an Apology has been the ability to see my personal transformation as part of the transformation of the world. I know it is incumbent upon me to take up the task of healing. One of the most important realizations that came through doing radical self-love work was how my commitment to caring for myself and tending to my wounds was directly proportional to the creation of a just, equitable, and compassionate planet. It just so happens that my healing was also directly proportional to the money in my bank account.

Fortunately, one of the first projects I developed through The Body Is Not an Apology was the Radically Unapologetic Healing Challenge 4 Us, or RUHCUS. This thirty-day transformational healing journey is designed to put us into intentional relationship with our greatest pain, shame, trauma, and fear—challenging the beliefs underpinning these traumas and consequently dissolving what adheres them in our conscious and subconscious minds.

The fear I developed as a child with an addict parent was that I would never be taken care of, that I would always be in lack. Surely, if I were deserving/good enough/lovable enough, my mother would have gotten sober and cared for us. Surely, if I were worthy, my brother and I would have had plenty.

One of the most salient elements of the Healing Challenge is a self-designed ceremony created to launch the thirty-day process of exhuming a big ugly belief. The ceremony is the container that will hold you during the labor of birthing a new story, one with fresh roots in fresh soil. *Terror* is the only appropriate word to describe what it is to stare directly at those dug-up beliefs, to see their roots writhing and begging for water, and to intentionally let them dry up and die in front of you. I enlisted my community and friends to support me in the journey. Without them, it would have been an impossible feat. For my ceremony, I needed to be swaddled in the possibility of care. I needed to create the belief that it was not only possible but actually evident and obvious that the world wanted to take care of me—wanted me to have plenty.

Through my thirty-day transformational healing project, I learned that there was an entire planet of humans who wanted nothing more than to care for me. I developed the skill to ask for what I need without fear and shame. Most important, I began to see that my mother's disease of addiction was not a reflection of my failings. She was not an addict because I was not enough. And she would have cared for us if she could have. Her illness made it difficult for her to do so, but it did not change the fact that I deserved care. And no amount of my depriving myself could have made my mother sober.

Taking up healing work—from therapy to twelve-step programs like Debtors Anonymous, to practical money management strategies like actually opening up my bills, paying them on time, and keeping tabs on my credit—I created new money beliefs that manifest in how I live my life today. My life is plentiful, abundant. My refrigerator is brimming with my favorite delights, and my bank account is not in overdraft, but overflowing with resources to financially support activism, art, friends, and family. The crowdfunding campaign I did in 2014 did not raise the full $80,000, but we raised over half—enough to launch our media platform. Money was no longer evidence of my unlovability, my not-enoughness. Instead, it became a tool I could use to build the world I want to see.

Debtors Anonymous taught me to practice experiencing money as a neutral entity, like a spatula or an axe. It has no inherent meaning; what we do with money, what we believe about money, how we wield money is the weighted thing worth exploring.

And so, for my ceremony, I focused on allowing myself to be cared for. Friends made me dinner, tucked me into bed, and held me while I cried. And when it was all over, three women who love and care for me in exceptional ways walked with me into an ice cream parlor in California. As I approached the case, a beautiful young Black man's face smiled at me and asked me what I'd like. "Stracciatella, please," I replied, ordering the most grown-up, bougie version of my beloved cookies and cream. He pressed two heaping scoops of yummy goodness on top of a sugar cone and passed it across the counter.

I reached into my pocket to pay, because I could. Because I had earned money, not by pretending to be an adult but from hard work and using my talents to be a contribution in the world. I was learning that it was possible to have my own plenty without shame. But before I could get to my debit card, my best friend grabbed my arm and handed a card to the cashier. "We got this," she said, gesturing to my two other friends. "We got you."

I took a breath, turned around, and walked out of the shop and into the sun, licking my cone, trusting that they did. Yes, I could both care for myself and allow myself to be cared for. Finally, these two gifts were not mutually exclusive.

ARIA

SAM REGAL

SOMETIMES I'M shopping online, which is something I love to do, shop online, as every store is a new puzzle to solve, like, which clothes would I buy if I shopped here, and sometimes I end up buying the clothes, so I guess you could say it's very meta and works on a few levels, and I stumble across something that I didn't know I needed, like, say, a black Bardot crop top, and it's like suddenly I'm meeting the lord Jesus Christ or found the path to Enlightenment because I feel, out of nowhere, absolutely convinced that this is the one clothing item I have always been missing, like since infancy or conception, and that having this thing, wearing it but really just the owning it, the possessing it, will finally Change My Life in the ways I've been waiting for it to change, and it's like I enter a fugue, I short circuit, I hit Purchase and there I am, sort of shocked, addled, kind of postcoital, like exhausted but satisfied but not totally satisfied, and if I've ordered, say, a pair of bright pink palazzo pants that I know will need tailoring and I know I will never tend to, I feel itchy, and blue, and a little dumb, maybe, or sexless and vast like the last woman on Earth, and I start wondering after creepy stuff, like regarding my personality and whether I am worthy of love despite all the raisins in my bed, and I open another website and hope I don't get struck by a thunderbolt of object fancy but sometimes I do, sometimes it happens, I hit Purchase and the cycle repeats itself, and has been, really, repeating itself for some years, you should see my dresser, the drawers don't close, they're all overstuffed with shit, with pink and sateen fabrics that I don't wear or know what to do with, that I drape around my hips like a hand, like a gift, and I know, at least at home in the mirror, alone among my things, objects too precious for this city with its leers and grime and violence and dripping virulent ugly, that I am beautiful, a Chaos void spotlit in pink, singing my body's sweeping arias.

composting capitalism

adrienne maree brown

in 2013, i was in a grocery store, about to binge after a period of extreme dieting. i had a cart full of oreos, chips, ice cream, and frozen pizza. but when i went to check out, none of my cards worked. i called my bank, the institution where i'd opened my first account when i started a magazine store job back at age thirteen.

on the other end of the line, a polite, emotionless voice informed me, with no loyalty at all, that the federal government was responsible for freezing my accounts. even in my shock, some part of me had been waiting for this day: i'd been a war tax resister for the past thirteen years. i was ready to take my stand but surprised by how terrifying the loss of control felt.

i stood by the wilted flower arrangement at the grocery store door and called the number my bank gave me. this time, i reached a curmudgeonly new yorker.

"i am a war tax resister," i told him.

"ya gotta pay your taxes, honey." he was gruff but kind.

"but i don't want to support the wars in iraq and afghanistan!"

"there's a lotta things in life i don't wanna support. but ya gotta pay your taxes."

feeling the tension between my righteous activist stance and the social shame he was sending my way, i still somehow sweet-talked my way back into accessing my funds that day, and reluctantly entered a payment plan with the irs.

once a month, i had to pay them more money than i had in the bank. i borrowed from family and friends, called back in loans i'd made to others, and learned how to strategically delay paying bills until right before the moment of shutoff or eviction. at this rate, there was no end in sight.

in the years that followed, i paid my taxes until the 2016 election. but i couldn't bring myself to pay taxes into 45's administration.

i want to tell you the story of why i became a tax resister—twice—and what i learned.

my parents grew up in the deep south, at opposite ends of the class spectrum: my black father in persistent, every-thing/space/bite-is-shared poverty, my white mother in ambitious, upwardly mobile, pony-and-pearls wealth. when they eloped, my mother was disowned. she chose my father over financial security, and growing up inside that story made me a young believer in love as the most important resource to accrue in a life.

i still believe it. i was born into abundant, unconditional love, and i often say it's my greatest privilege—i have parents who believe in me, support me when i falter, cover me when i'm foolish and idealistic, and tell me often that they are proud of me. their love and pride came far before i began to be successful in ways that translate to mainstream america: today, i am a bestselling author with a successful self-started facilitating business and critical acclaim of my work. but they also told me they loved me when i failed my french oral exam and didn't complete the college degree they'd sacrificed to pay for. said they loved me when i couldn't make the rent after getting fired from my first job and needed a $2,000 loan. said they were proud of me as i took one movement or nonprofit job after another, where the pay and benefits were paltry and the righteousness high.

this emphasis on love over money had an impact: my parents unintentionally raised a postcapitalist—someone who values people and planet over profit. even though my father was in the military, and growing up on bases outside the u.s. allowed me to see how capitalism impacts power and quality of life around the world, on a base, there was a near uniformity to the living conditions and my parents were very focused on being loving, and on teaching me that everyone had a right to think for themselves. they encouraged me to question things (while still being obedient), and those questions eventually pulled out the rug on capitalism for me. but it took a political education for me to understand how to bring the cooperative loving spirit of my childhood to bear on my economic stance.

by the time i finished college, i understood that an economy based on severe inequalities, which gives a few people the profits of the earth while masses toil to generate that profit, and which exhausts this abundant home of ours with no sense of obligation to protect or regenerate nature's wealth, was incompatible with the future of our species. that capitalism leads to hoarding and competition where we need humanitarian, earth-centered decisions.

initially, i was convinced I was an anticapitalist, that the primary work i wanted to do was to dismantle the current economy. but as i learned more about nature's complex, interdependent operating systems, i became more interested in how we become postcapitalist: how do we recognize capitalism as an outdated model for human life?

how do we compost capitalism?

it began in 2001. i was facilitating at the harm reduction coalition at 27th street and sixth avenue in manhattan. one morning, i got off the train and heard an odd, loud sound. i stepped to the corner of sixth avenue and looked down the grid of the city. one of the twin towers was on fire.

i ran to my office to call my dad, who, at that point, worked at the pentagon. there was no answer, and shortly after that call, i learned the pentagon had also been targeted and damaged. i spent that morning watching footage of the u.s. bombing of afghanistan and emailed everyone i knew the link to the footage. i made a sign demanding to stop the bombing and walked out, by myself, to stop traffic with it.

that day cemented a change in me: i'd been antiwar in theory, which was already a great leap from my military upbringing. but i'd never been covered in ashes made of people before, i'd never felt anything like the terror of being unable to reach my father, whose office was destroyed. hours later, when i heard from him that he was alive and had been away from the office, i felt clearly that i would never be able to support this kind of violence. i knew that my father, and my country, were hungry for war. but i was starving for calm, safety, peace.

when the american government chose to retaliate in rage—to put the same fear i felt that day into strangers and children in iraq and afghanistan, humans as innocent as i was that morning on the train—i knew i had to increase my radical efforts to shape the future. as i realized my tax dollars would mostly be spent on this national rage, i felt the depth of radical pacifism: as marvin gaye sang, "war is not the answer, for only love can conquer hate." in many ways, this was when i really began to think for myself, to compost what had been given to me into a worldview of my own.

i wanted everything, everything in the world, to stop. the bombing, the bullshit, the systems of colonization that fueled our capitalism-entranced world. i searched for a way to have the biggest impact in my war resistance, and i thought, at the time, that not paying my taxes was the answer. i thought, if i got arrested, it would be politically important that a child of a military household was making such a radical choice. i also thought everyone i knew was going to stop paying taxes alongside me. i underestimated how ready people would be to defy the system.

i thought the same thing when we let 45—the very embodiment of every oppression i was fighting against—be elected. and so, when it was time to pay my 2016 taxes, i couldn't. once again, i didn't think anyone would. once again, i was wrong.

this time i knew the risk. they had emptied my accounts before. i knew the irs was watching me, that i was no longer floating under the radar. i considered that i could spend four or eight devastating years behind bars. but i still couldn't bring myself to pay taxes to the current administration.

i was politicized to know the importance of political prisoners, i'd read mumia abu-jamal, angela davis—i thought this was as important as the fights they'd served time for.

once again, i didn't pay. and once again, everyone else i knew did. i was disappointed and confused: if this wasn't a moment for divestment, then when was? it was a moment of personal crisis. and when the hammer came down for the second time, in january of 2018, it was all encompassing.

the irs is a sentient, angry being. this time, there was no sweet-talking. they froze and emptied my accounts, garnished my wages, and demanded exorbitant payments. i have never known financial desperation like i did that year: i was working but unable to earn an income, my wages were garnished down to nothing, and the irs still expected me to pay them. i don't know how people without safety nets would survive. my guess is that most would not.

during these years, i learned what it meant to have to ask for help, to beg, to skip meals, to stagger unpaid bills, to say no to social outings that required money. but more important, i learned what it is to be functionally poor in the united states—to rub elbows and lead meetings with those who were financially stable, knowing i needed to eat whatever they provided at the meeting. knowing i would have to fumble around the fact that i couldn't front business expenses and get reimbursed. i lived from an empty bank account for the eight months before i turned forty.

at forty, i once again began to consider my value behind bars (the final stage of punishment for those who don't pay their taxes and don't have funds for the fines) versus out in the world doing my work as a movement facilitator and writer. as i sat with these questions, three different black liberation groups that i love asked me, with some desperation, for help. i took it as a sign from the universe to surrender the money to the irs and move forward with the work i knew was my distinct gift to share. the resistance was not worth the prison time.

this led me into rituals of abundance and release. i did a burning ritual to release my attachment to the money i was going to have to give the irs. i recognized that the money in and of itself was not mine. all resources come from human labor, or the abundance of the earth. the trick of capitalism is to make us value printed paper and digital numbers over water, joy, soil, kale, time with family. money, even excessive amounts of money, wasn't real wealth. it was simply the cost of living in a capitalist system.

i also expanded my practice of radical honesty, telling people explicitly what i was facing, and opening myself to help. at the same time, i began a daily gratitude practice to bring my attention to how much i had in my life, and how many people wanted to help me.

as these practices became a part of my daily life, i experienced a direct correlation between my detachment from money and my ability to experience authentic postcapitalist abundance. i had heard similar realizations from those who had lost everything to fire or foreclosure. the projection of financial security is common practice in the u.s., where most people are living on dreams and credit, two checks from broke. losing the ability to project wealth forced me to get into a real relationship with what was enough for me, and with the abundance of enough.

i also experienced, again and in new ways, the abundance of community. i survived because people loved me—some even with small loans. my parents, with whom i'd left a small nest egg (about five months' rent) after the first bout with the irs, paid some of my bills directly. friends sent money to paypal that i could use to buy things online. people fed me, and covered meals and trips. my community loved me enough not to make me beg, and the biggest generosity wasn't from those who had the most, but from others who were also making ends meet. i found this liberating: we could move from capitalism to cooperation, generating abundance where we thought only scarcity existed

i also survived because of detroit—a city that makes a way out of no way. i'd made a home there since 2006 and knew that drought year would likely have broken my life if i had been in new york city, los angeles, or oakland. but in detroit i was able to stay in the home i'd been in since i moved. i could get affordable local produce from the farmers' market, or ramen noodles packets from the party store.

maybe most important, no one locally shamed me for my war tax resistance. in fact, many of the organizers i knew gave me props for being brave enough to try and resist.

i believe we should all be tax resisters at appropriate political moments. i am appalled by how easily we pay for the punishment of a racist, sexist, cruel, and unqualified administration. but after more than a decade of trying to opt out, i learned that it is impossible to wage a solitary economic resistance against an empire.

i won't try that strategy alone again, but in its aftermath i committed my whole self to increasing the effectiveness of collective strategies for living into justice and liberation work. i am living in my purpose by putting my superpower behind the work of organizers i believe in. it is not my place to galvanize, or to organize. instead, i have been given a different gift: to increase the impact of those called to lead, to facilitate their growth, their connectedness, their power.

love, still more valuable than money, directs and gives meaning to my life. it is a measure of postcapitalism. and money, which for years only flowed away from me, is beginning again to flow toward that love, and toward me.

now, my work is to pay down my debt, stay generous and connected, and be part of generating a truly abundant ecosystem that sustains each person through this violent economic time where we can have nothing, but look good.

CALCULATING MY NET WORTH

JAMIE WONG

"We hate suffering, but love its causes."

—Shantideva

I STARED at the giant golden statue of the Buddha before me and bent down, clutching a white envelope containing two ten-dollar bills in my right hand. I knelt to the floor to prostrate three times and deposited the cash at the altar.

The Tibetan lamas say this practice is a way to "accumulate merit," and according to my lama, merit was something I urgently needed. I had arrived in Kathmandu one day earlier with my teacher and a dozen Buddhist practitioners from Spain and Bolivia to embark on a monthlong pilgrimage to Nepal and India.

In Kathmandu, I set off each day, leaving traces of my past life behind in the form of $10, $20, and $50 bills tucked into white envelopes at the feet of awe-inducing Buddha statues I found in the dozens of temples, schools, and monasteries that circumscribe the famous Boudhanath Stupa in Kathmandu, Nepal. I had given away everything I owned a few months earlier, and the one suitcase of belongings I still possessed had been lost in transit between Delhi and Kathmandu. The lama's mother had given me a pair of disposable paper underwear that I wore beneath pants I had borrowed—along with a shirt, socks, and deodorant—from other members of our group. All I had left were small wads of US dollars that I was stuffing into gilded shrines in a race against myself to accumulate the ethereal merit that I didn't quite understand, yet had enough faith to believe I needed.

When I wasn't making these offerings, I was doing *koras*—the Tibetan word for "circumambulation" or "revolution"—around the large *stupa* (sacred dome) in the center of the ancient city. The Tibetans consider *koras* another great merit-accumulating activity designed to help us meditate on the cyclic nature of a mundane existence. If not an expert, then I certainly considered myself an advanced practitioner in mundane existence. I found myself at age thirty-six chanting mantras around a holy site alone, wearing underwear that didn't belong to me with no home, no belongings, no job, and no plan. All I possessed in that moment was the deep, overriding certainty that for the first time in my life, I was exactly where I should be.

How I got here was not obvious or easy and it would be disingenuous to suggest that I had much of a hand—at least consciously—in any of it. In this moment, I could only understand my transformation from a venture-funded Silicon Valley CEO to a woman on her knees with her hands clasped in prayer as a consequence of a series of great misfortunes.

WORLDLY EXISTENCE

It all started innocently enough. My goal was to start my first company before I was thirty. It's easy now to see how many errors riddle that premise, but to a half-Chinese, half-Jewish Ivy League graduate in San Francisco in 2009, it felt like a divine mandate on the path to the pursuit of happiness.

I had invested years in working hard at my dream jobs (as a paralegal at the country's largest civil rights law firm, a researcher for Michael Moore, a producer for *The Daily Show with Jon Stewart*, a writer at a fancy ad agency) and found genuine satisfaction in none of them. I was aware enough of my privilege to hate myself for being unhappy but not aware of it enough to see that my sense of entitlement to happiness itself was making me miserable. By my late twenties I had to face the fact that the common denominator in my job dissatisfaction was *me*.

My first attempt at fulfilling my own human potential came in the form of a start-up. I felt that devoting my life to executing other people's visions was stifling and that manifesting my own vision would yield a much higher return—both financially and existentially. I had also developed an insatiable thirst for travel and adventuring into the daily lives of locals in more than thirty-five countries; there, I discovered how malleable my own identity could be, and in that, I experienced a sense of freedom so vast I needed to share it. So, I started a travel start-up. We wanted to create transformative experiences for travelers and transform the travel industry by helping local experts and aficionados of food, art, and culture create and sell their own activities and tours in their cities.

In some ways, I don't think I was wrong to seek fulfillment and personal growth by building my own business. I felt more job satisfaction, I felt more attuned to my natural abilities, I was able to exercise my strengths, and I satiated my curious nature. But what I failed to understand is that my existential angst and material longing were in fact disguised, deep spiritual yearnings that no form of entrepreneurship, business, or creative project was ever going to satisfy. Yet, I was too green and ambitious to understand this: I only experienced it as fuel that propelled me toward achievements. I could not have found a better echo chamber to validate and encourage this worldview than Silicon Valley circa 2010, and I took to the start-up race like a millionaire to a Tesla.

Unlike some of my Silicon Valley peers, I never had fantasies of wearing black turtlenecks, ringing the opening bell at Nasdaq, inventing software that would transform computer programming, or of historians committing my success story to history books. I scoffed at that kind of hubris and instead wanted something far more modest: to change the world. The logic seemed obvious: if I could change something outside of me that made the lives of lots and lots of people better, then those people would in turn impact other lives for the better, and on and on until reaching a certain critical mass, when the whole world would be better. But I never really asked: And then what? Redemption? Freedom? Happiness? I just figured I'd find out when I got there.

For a year, I took meetings with other entrepreneurs, experts, and investors. I built a customer base, then wireframes, a website, and, within a few months, launched into a business that had small but growing sales. Artists offered street-art walks, street-food bloggers offered exotic food tastings, a homeless man offered homeless tours. A year into running the business, I found myself at the world's top start-up accelerator, Y Combinator, pitching my start-up in front of an audience of five hundred investors packed into the auditorium of the Computer History Museum in Mountain View, California.

"And it turns out, when you build something people want, they tell their friends about it!" I boasted, flashing up a growth curve on the PowerPoint presentation behind me that investors lovingly refer to as the "hockey stick." "We are profitable and growing fifteen percent week over week," I lauded.

The audience erupted in applause and giddy laughter. We had shown them what they wanted to see: early signs of a company that could grow up to be a unicorn, a company worth a billion dollars or more. The next few days became a flurry of meetings, term sheets, and wire instructions. Within a couple of weeks we had $2 million in the bank, were renting office space, hiring engineers, and making runs to Ikea.

The team grew to eleven people. We ate catered organic lunches and drank coffee prepared with one of five different technologies available in the kitchen of a converted Victorian duplex and neighbor to other start-ups, several of which are now public companies. Each night, I worked well into the early-morning hours and found company in other founders on social media with our shared 2:00 a.m. battle cry: #TeamNoSleep.

I lived within a one-block radius of several bars and hordes of single, male founders, and I let off steam by drinking too much and dating the wrong people. I then tried to offset the toxicity with exercise. I took up Muay Thai and ran a half-marathon. As I raced against the clock to sufficiently grow the value of our company to qualify for a new round of funding before we ran out of money, my life began to run away from me and turn into a lifeless series of business opportunities: on Halloween, I dressed as the company logo, and didn't show up to Thanksgiving with my family because I couldn't stand leaving work unfinished. What's worse, I thought I was choosing this. I thought I was happy. Little did I know at the time, I was in a race against myself: would I awaken to the causes of my own deep suffering before I destroyed myself? I had no idea I had fallen into a trap I had created: my entire sense of self-worth was dependent on the worth of my company.

External conquests powered my internal sense of well-being. We were hitting our monthly revenue milestones and were on track to a million-dollar run rate. Customers loved our product and so did the media. *Glamour* magazine came to my apartment for a photoshoot of me. The *New York Times* covered my company several times, along with the *Wall Street Journal*, *Forbes*, the *Guardian*, *USA Today*, *Travel + Leisure*, and dozens of other widely circulated national and international publications. I appeared on *CBS Morning News*, Bloomberg, CNN. We became big in Taiwan.

But by the following fall there were signs that the business wasn't growing at the rate that investors required to give us another round of funding, and we weren't yet making enough revenue to support our operations. My inner world began to collapse.

Just eighteen months after successfully pitching a room full of some of the world's best tech investors and being named one of Silicon Valley's top ten start-ups, our future was not looking so bright. We had arrived at what start-up investors and entrepreneurs often refer to as "the valley of death," where start-ups who can't get another round of funding go to die. Unable to apprehend or accept this, I personally began to deteriorate. My living room began to look like a scene from *A Beautiful Mind*, my walls smothered with multicolored Post-its, each with business ideas scribbled in Sharpies. I became easily agitated. I wasn't able to sleep. I developed an ulcer, then shingles, and eventually a second-degree sunburn (I had been on my first vacation in years but only had seventy-two hours, so I used tanning oil in the hopes of speeding things up). Then one day at Muay Thai practice, I was jumping rope to warm up and heard a loud *snap*. My gastrocnemius muscle had ripped, and I was forced to put my right leg in a cast for a month. My physical state painted a generous picture of my mental state, which had become so distressed, I could no longer recognize it as my own.

Due to my newfound immobility, I turned to the pile of books I had accumulated over the months and had planned to read—a joke for someone who barely had time to read the name on an incoming call. *Crucial Conversations*, *Man's Search for Meaning*, *Who: The Method for Hiring*, *Loving What Is*, and three identical copies of *When Things Fall Apart* by the Tibetan Buddhist nun Pema Chödrön—each one purchased by me, apparently (according to my Order History, not my memory), within weeks of one another. All unread.

Amazon knew I was having a nervous breakdown before I did.

This would have been a good point in the story for me to go on a meditation retreat and have a spiritual awakening, but I didn't. In fact, it would take me several more years for the idea to even cross my mind.

It's funny and also kind of creepy how many times we allow ourselves to step in the same pothole before we learn a lesson, thinking the minor adjustments we make to our daily lives are sufficient to bring about the inner transformation we actually yearn to experience. So, instead of going inward, I adjusted everything outside of myself. I spent the next few years running a small and lean team to rebuild our product enough to generate the income we needed to support the business. I looked for a "soft landing," a start-up term that describes a kind of sale of a company that saves face by partially or fully repaying investors and gives the product or the team a home in a bigger company, but without the big payday or glory. It was my last-ditch effort at preserving any sense of dignity after what I had internalized as a personal failure—not performing the elusive alchemy of turning $2 million into $2 billion.

Despite all my attempts to fight against the karmic winds of my start-up, I once again found it, and myself, in a similar state I had been in years earlier: diminished, disenchanted, and unmoored. I began moonlighting as a consultant to bring in more cash flow as I looked for an exit. I bought and read more books. I began meditating again. I joined a writer's group. I went on weekend retreats alone in the woods. I finally had enough money to discover how spiritually impoverished I was.

What I didn't realize was that without my knowing, a slow process was already taking place inside me. The bright and shiny objects of power, fame, and money were all losing their luster. One of my best friends sent me a link to a five-week meditation retreat she was going on in Spain and suggested I apply for admission. A few months later I boarded a flight to Valencia.

RENUNCIATION

As the white taxi snaked up the paved roads of Mount Sella, I was both thrilled and terrified to be on another new adventure—the kind, I thought, that had inspired me to build a travel business in the first place. To quell my mounting doubts about meditating for six hours a day with a group of strangers and teachers I did not know, I told myself that even if I didn't enjoy the experience or find much value in it, there would be an opportunity for growth, somehow. There always was.

Within a few days, my life had transformed in a manner that I had no way of knowing at the time. Rather than staring into the glare of a laptop screen, I began to turn my focus to my five senses, then to my mind, then to cultivating love, compassion, and joy. I actually enjoyed not talking and not listening to anything other than the sounds of the trees rustling in the wind on my afternoon runs. Less pleasing, however, was the incessant chatter of the thoughts that I had finally stilled my mind and body enough to hear. For five weeks, my only job was to gently quiet the storyteller inside of me and observe. I experienced a type of satisfaction I never had before.

I began to feel very at home in my life, but it wasn't clear to me yet whether it was Spain (where I happened to have lived for a year during college), the sea breeze, the silent company of others, or my mind turning toward something much more sublime and enduring than products, metrics, and press releases.

"Are you going to the teaching?" Marcos, one of the center's volunteers, asked me after dinner. "The lama gives a teaching every Wednesday night. Tonight, it's on attachment."

He had me at attachment.

I found my way to a room on the third floor of the five-story monastery. The walls were lined with books on one end and a wall-to-wall window that overlooked the sea on the other. Large, cloth-wrapped paintings of Buddhist deities adorned the walls, and several bowls—filled with saffron, water, candles, rice, and flowers—sat beneath them. Under a large painting of Shakyamuni Buddha was a monk draped in maroon robes. He sat cross-legged reading prayers out loud in Spanish.

"I take refuge in the Buddha, the Dharma, and the excellent assembly, until I reach enlightenment," he read in a monotone, hands clasped in prayer. Several dozen Spaniards who looked to be in their fifties and sixties spoke with him.

The scene was both terrifyingly foreign and reassuringly familiar at the same time. I did not grow up religious, but I did grow up going to our neighborhood temple for Bat Mitzvah training and High Holiday services. We chanted prayers in Hebrew, and my limited vocabulary granted me the freedom to recite prayers from my heart and not my head. Meanwhile, my Buddhist and Daoist father bookended our days by lighting incense and making his own prayers and prostrations to Guan Yin, the Chinese name for the Buddha of Compassion, whose statue my father housed in a custom altar he built in our home.

After a few short prayers, the monk opened a book titled *A Guide to the Bodhisattva's Way of Life*, written by the celebrated seventh-century erudite and yogi Shantideva, and began to read from it:

Perhaps we'll claim that by our wealth we live,
And living, gather merit, dissipating evil.
But if we are aggressive for the sake of profit,
Won't our gains be evil, all our merits lost?

The room fell silent—surely from confusion more than awe—and the monk filled the space with a soft-spoken, slow, meandering commentary that eventually would become as familiar to me as my own voice in my head. He spoke slow enough and with simple enough vocabulary that I understood his words and even more, they hit me like a meteor.

It would be misguided for me to go into detail as to what I experienced in that moment. It was part intellectual, part emotional, part physical, and fully spiritual. However, I can tell you that from that point forward, I have not seen the world the same. I do not experience myself the same. In that moment, for the first time in my life, I began to believe that there could be no greater achievement in life than to gain command over my mind and to cultivate a heart of love and joy.

A new north star had come into view, and its light was bright enough to pull me away from all the distractions in my life that had left me depleted.

THE CAVE

What started as a five-week meditation retreat evolved almost effortlessly into a two-year spiritual journey.

I returned home from the retreat and got rid of my apartment, my car, my company, and my life as I knew it, and returned to the monastery a few weeks later. To live.

At the Buddhist monastery, I lived in what they call a *selda* or "cell"— a solitary-confinement-sized room with a small bathroom and single bed. I had some clothes hanging in a closet, a meditation cushion, an altar, and a small stack of books.

My daily life was programmed along with those of the other dozen or so volunteers at the Buddhist center. The day began with 7:30 a.m. prayers, meditation, and the recitation of the Heart Sutra, followed by breakfast, and then the workday began at 10:00 a.m. There was a three-hour break in the middle of the day for lunch and siesta, a few more hours of work, then an evening meditation session, sometimes followed by philosophy class in which we explored the teachings of great Buddhist scholars and yogis such as Shantideva, Nagarjuna, Atiśa, and Dharmarakshita.

I observed my thoughts. I also observed the balance in my bank account going down each month. I worked long hours, seven days a week in the center's administrative office as an unpaid volunteer in exchange for room and board. I canceled all my subscriptions—cell phone, Netflix, Amazon Prime, and Dropbox. Owning things began to feel like a nuisance. I tried to buy as little as possible—not on principle but because I had genuinely lost interest. I would imagine having to pack everything I bought and lug it on an airplane. I valued my peace of mind over having more things. Some of the best beaches in the world were five kilometers away, but I rarely went, both because I had no means of getting there without a car and because I knew that while reading a novel beneath the Mediterranean sun would bring me pleasure, it would also distract me from unearthing a more sustainable source of joy within me. I prepared my own meals rather than eating out. I turned down invitations to meet with new friends because I preferred to stay home and read the autobiographies of Tibetan yogis and about how karma works. Until this point, I had spent my entire life trying to string together moments of pleasure hoping the sum of their parts would create happiness. Because it never worked, I assumed the problem must be inherent to me.

For the first time in my life, I was dedicated to conquering something far more influential and valuable in my life than run rates and revenue: my own mind. Through my studies and practice I grew more optimistic that perhaps *I* was not fundamentally flawed, but that my ideas, thoughts, and emotional responses were.

I had every reason to believe I would find freedom in the monastery, away from the stress of Silicon Valley and in the Mediterranean where life was slow, siestas were long, and the only person I had to answer was a monk. But in the desolation of living without context, references, and material benchmarks, I instead retreated to my old, familiar internal world.

I looked to escape my discomfort and insecurity by throwing myself into work. I hid from the awkward silences I didn't have the vocabulary yet to fill by eating meals at my desk. I stayed in the office at night to distance myself from the sounds of the other residents living their lives on the other side of the paper-thin walls. And I took on more projects at the center to turn down the volume of the critical voice in my head shaming me for anything and everything. I worked to feel progress. I worked to feel worthy. I worked to avoid discovering that my optimism was ungrounded: that my deepest nature was flawed.

Within a few months I was building a global platform for online meditation courses and running the operations of the center. I trained the team—composed mostly of openhearted, computer-illiterate Spaniards from the countryside with an affinity for the Buddha's teachings—in how to use Gmail, then we graduated to productivity tools, CMSs, and online payment systems.

While the center's projects benefited in many ways, my work ethic was making me no friends. People quickly dubbed me *la chica Americana de informática* ("the American girl who does IT")—along with a slew of other less-than-warm nicknames: *pija* (snob), *princessa* (princess), *ambiciosa* (ambitious, which the Spanish consider a highly derogatory term), *la perfeccionista* (perfectionist). The names soon escalated to rumors: I had come from a wealthy family that provided me with everything I wanted. I had moved to Spain to have an affair with the resident lama. And finally, I had joined the team of volunteers to turn an altruistic Dharma project into *una multinacional*—another derogatory term in Spain—a multinational corporation.

Thinking that a Dharma center would be full of people practicing Dharma was like thinking the government was full of people following the law. I hadn't given up everything in my life to move halfway across the world to let petty, small-town gossip and a few Dharma bullies obstruct my path of awakening, I told myself. So, rather than fighting back, I retreated further into my meditation practice and studies. I increased my meditation practice to several times a day and consumed the Dharma as if I were in a race to conquer something ephemeral: "It's now or never" became my mantra. I would embark on several days of silent, solo retreats and begin to hear my own voice pushing me to meditate better, harder, faster. I felt like I was behind. I had to make up for all the lost time I'd spent in misguided, worldly pursuits!

When I arrived at the Buddhist center the year before, I imagined that the warm Spanish winds atop the monastery on Mount Sella would somehow herald magic into my life the way I imagined it would in an Almodóvar film. Instead, I had developed a full-fledged case of spiritual materialism. I can only imagine that you can't get further from enlightenment than entrepreneurship. Yet I was chasing spiritual conquests as blindly and desperately as I had chased revenue in my startup. I was attempting to create hockey-stick growth out of my spiritual development.

By the time I discovered this, I had already spent more than a year living in the monastery. Any notion of the free-spiritedness, romance, and excitement I had sensed coming into the experience had faded away, and I felt defeated, with no path out other than withdrawing to the depths of my suffering in order to burn through all my negative karma and hopefully, someday, millions of lifetimes from now, awaken.

I was not going to be able to Eat Pray Love my way to enlightenment.

As I retreated further into my mind and meditated more, I developed what the Tibetans call *rlung*, a state of severe distress that results from pushing the mind too hard. Apparently, it's most common among Western practitioners who seek efficiency in their practice. My friends and family urged me to leave the center, but I wouldn't. I believed there was nothing left out there for me—my emancipation from suffering could only happen within my mind. Worldly pursuits were only going to harm me. In a few short years, my inner pendulum had swung from the extreme of existentialism to another extreme of nihilism. The only aspiration I had left was that of becoming a Buddhist nun, and even that fantasy was fueled not so much by optimism as it was by inertia: I was a mere shaved head and maroon skirt away, after all.

If my ego wouldn't hear the pleas of my loved ones and instead interpreted every yearning I had to seek a more balanced and wholesome way of living as a craving to be ignored, then my body was going to have to speak up again as it had years earlier on the other side of the world. I began to develop chronic neck pain. I lost my appetite. Fatigue stronger than any siesta could manage monopolized my days. I didn't feel sad, and I didn't feel happy. Blood tests showed I had heightened levels of cortisol, and doctors ordered me to go on vacation and relax. What I didn't realize until many months later, when I had regained my energy levels and healed my neck pain—which ended up being a result of chronic migraines I didn't know I was having—is that what the Tibetans call *rlung*, Western medicine calls depression and anxiety.

Life at the monastery felt like it was spiraling downward for me with my physical symptoms increasing in severity each week. The workload for our online projects was growing, and the center was increasingly dependent on my work, a dynamic that was so familiar in my life that I could no longer avoid taking responsibility for my role in creating it. My understanding of the teachings and my personal experiences of their power kept me from turning against the spiritual path, so instead I turned against myself. I was failing at my spiritual path.

Just as my physical and emotional pain began to escalate, I booked a flight to return home for a family reunion. I wrapped up my work at the center, packed a bag, and flew back to California.

THE VALLEY

I touched down at Oakland International Airport as I had every summer for twenty years and for the first time, rather than feeling overwhelmed by the stale air and hungry ghosts of my hometown, I felt joy.

I saw beauty in the rustling trees and felt the blue sky cast its glow of optimism on me. Traffic jams were a portal to compassion, and the stores that lined the city's main streets were expressions of ignorance and confusion. My new experience of these old things was not operating through my intellect—they were my heart's raw and spontaneous findings as I observed my surroundings. I felt light again. I felt free.

One morning soon after I returned, my mom and I were in the kitchen preparing coffee and oatmeal.

"I have never seen you look so bad," my mom said. "It's like your spirit is gone." Clearly, I hadn't actually transcended my suffering yet. It turned out that my newfound contentment was not enough to override the physical and emotional residue of months living in isolated depression at the monastery.

I decided then that I would stay in Berkeley for as long as it took to regain my physical strength and heal my chronic pain before returning to the monastery.

I spent the following weeks spending quality time with loved ones, going to doctor visits followed by physical therapy, taking up Tai Chi, receiving teachings from Tibetan lamas who came to town, continuing my daily meditation practices and studies, and working part-time. Slowly, my headaches and neck pain began to improve, I regained my appetite, my energy levels went back up, and I felt a sense of strength, autonomy, and peace I had never experienced before. It was as if I had finally grown a new layer of skin after a long bout without one. I wasn't getting "back to myself." I was becoming a new self.

THE CEMETERY

The Buddha taught that we suffer not because of the object, but because of our relationship to the object. I decided to give the Buddha a run for his money by seeing if my changed mindset could actually change the objects of what I experienced as the three greatest sources of adversity in my life: my childhood, romance, and work.

After a few months at home healing, I decided I would move back to the city where I grew up. I booked a round-trip flight to Spain to say good-bye and collect my belongings from the center. Upon returning to the States, I set up camp for the first time in two decades—since chanting as a teenager "Friends don't let friends go to Berkeley" (we were all from Berkeley and getting away was one of the greatest allures of college)— directly in the eye of my past emotional storms: my childhood home.

To my great surprise—and that of my friends and extended family—the storm had passed. The ghosts and demons were no longer where I had last left them. Emotions that my parents stirred that used to feel like a laceration now felt like nothing more than a prick on the finger, pain dissipating with a few long breaths. The gray filter that had saturated the streets of my North Berkeley childhood neighborhood had regained its transparency. I no longer felt like a child in a straitjacket when I frequented the local restaurants and bookstores that remained from my childhood. For the first time in twenty-one years of living away, the ghosts were gone. (I am guessing they moved to Spain.)

When the familiar demons I expected to find coiled in the Berkeley Hills were not there, it gave me the space to invite in new ones. A couple months into an unprecedented stretch of peaceful cohabitation with my mom, I met a man. This posed a conflict for me because I had discovered tremendous joy in disengaging from romantic relationships over the past few years: in my process of detachment, I had attached myself to staying single. And now here was this great man opening his heart to me, calling forth the ghosts of past relationships, losses, and fears. With my ego far more attached to maintaining discipline in my spiritual growth than to the success or failure of the relationship, our connection had a chance of blossoming into something meaningful—a form of spiritual practice for us both. The strengthening of our bond stirred up my vulnerabilities, anxiety, and unsettled inner debts. Then I did the unthinkable. I returned to work full-time with the travel company I had sold years prior—returning to the source of my existential crisis and breakdown that led me to nearly becoming a nun. What years earlier would have felt like a series of painful, involuntary regressions were now deliberate choices I was making to work with my new inner resources. I was resolving once and for all old karmic debts that had left me mindlessly circling the same problems for years.

The Vajrayāna tradition, or tantric Buddhism, follows three macro-stages of spiritual training based on the teachings of the ancient Mahasiddhas, or wandering yogis in India who brought the Buddhist tantra to Tibet. My teacher refers to these stages as the Cave, the Valley, and the

Cemetery as a way of guiding those of us who are not ancient Mahasiddhas. Before one can enter into any of these phases, she must undergo renunciation. Once a practitioner has renounced worldly pursuits and taken refuge in the spiritual path, she embarks on the first phase: entering the Cave, or a period of separation from the primary triggers of her afflictions. The cave artificially distances the yogi from the primary issues in daily life she is not able to overcome—triggers, temptations, distractions that arrest her—in order to grow and cultivate mental stability. For the yogi, the Cave stage is the time she spends in silent retreat.

Once she has mastered her practice in the cave, her teacher will instruct her to go into the second stage, the Valley, a natural, real-world environment that provides a gradual, spontaneous, and sporadic encountering of the practitioner's greatest personal challenges or adversity. In classical tantric Buddhist terms, this is the stage of the wandering yogi. In psychological terms, the Valley is the place where integration takes place. In worldly terms—for me at least—Silicon Valley was where my greatest disintegration had happened.

The third and final stage of spiritual practice is the Cemetery. Like the Cave, this is another artificial environment we create to induce a greater spiritual leap. If the Cave is designed to insulate the practitioner from the greatest sources of adversity so she can build a solid foundation without being constantly triggered and in distress, the Cemetery is designed to overwhelm the advanced practitioner with constant exposure to the same triggers and adversity, to help her once and for all scale the last stretch of the cliff of her own inner demons.

The Buddha found enlightenment sitting on a pile of weeds under a tree in an unremarkable forest. He awakened once he accepted that the extremes of both the decadence of his life as a prince and the deprivation of his life as an ascetic were blinding him to his own nature and human potential. It's quite obvious to me now—in a way it was not then—that I am never going to find freedom in the Himalayas, Silicon Valley, Spain, Berkeley, or on any of the adventures I had designed for myself to help escape the mundanities of my daily life.

The friends I have made who remain living at the Buddhist center in Spain ask me when I will return. My friends who are entrepreneurs ask me when I'm going to start my "next thing." My teacher asks me when I am going to become a nun. "Not right now" is the most certain response I can muster. I had built an identity, a business, and a life on the idea that one's destination is inherently valuable and that it actually exists. I'm not sure I believe this any longer. I'm exploring what it means when the destination is no longer the hero of the story.

EXPLAIN IT TO ME

AN INTERVIEW WITH RACHEL CARGLE

1. What were your thoughts about money while you were growing up, and how did they shape your childhood and teenage years?
Growing up I knew I was poor. But, interestingly, our housing project sat within a fairly wealthy neighborhood in Northeast Ohio. A small town called Green. This configuration I lived in—seeing the sharp contrast in social class yet having a lot of access and exposure to the opportunities money brought—really informed me.

I was hyperaware of what I didn't have and what others did—but it was never necessarily a sad contention. I just took it as "Hey, this is where we are." But I had a vision for the financial upward mobility that was possible. I don't think I connected money with "more money equals more goodness." I just saw it as a key, a tool to create even higher levels of convenience, options, and opportunity.

I remember being eight or nine, and my soccer team had an end-of-season party at the soccer coach's home. It was my first time there, and I remember pulling up and feeling awe that someone could have that much space and comfort in their home. To my little eyes it seemed like my entire home could fit in their basement alone.

While my teammates were outside playing yard games their mothers had organized to keep us entertained, I snuck inside to find the father, who was preparing our food inside their gorgeous kitchen. I sat down at the counter and asked, "Can you explain to me what you had to do in life to get a home like this? What is your job? Explain it to me." And he did.

I sat there with my pigtailed braids and legs swinging from the counter stool while he told me about his career in computer engineering. I could comprehend almost nothing of what he described, but I do remember thinking, *So, there* is *a formula. I don't know it, but there are things I* can *do to possibly have a home like this one day.*

That continued curiosity, plus access to people—like friends' parents, job managers and mentors, and people I looked up to online who could answer my questions—shaped the conversation I had with myself about money throughout my childhood and teenage years.

2. Has your view and experience of money changed over the years? In what ways? What changed your view of it?

It certainly has. I think I concretely decided early on that I wanted a different narrative around money than what I recognized in my family. I was determined to have more security and not to get thrown into the exhausting cycle of living paycheck to paycheck. I was also intrigued by the ways that people were indulging in creative and successful careers as opposed to routine-based jobs.

I pursued money with both necessity and a deep curiosity. I realized there was so much I didn't know, hadn't experienced, or hadn't learned, and I took any opportunity to really hear others' viewpoints as I tried to develop my own financial practices. Whether through playing Twenty Questions with the owner of the Hallmark where I worked, in skimming personal finance books I could barely understand, or by inquisitively observing the ways the rich families I nannied for would spend, save, and prioritize their money, I was constantly learning.

The biggest changes were in my perception of possibility—of what I was capable of as an earner, and of what money was capable of doing for me in life as I pursued my values and goals. The more I learned, the more both of those would rise. I always thought that I was capable of breaking a lot of financial cycles that seemed to exist in my family. I thought I could get creative in developing a financial life that left me feeling more free than frustrated.

What I learned was that I had a set of skills and a vigorous curiosity that, when combined, presented me with options for carving a path for myself that has led to a new and powerful space in my personal finances.

3. What do you believe about money now, and how do those beliefs inform your work and your daily life? How do they affect your professional and academic choices, including your decision to leave Columbia University in favor of becoming an independent scholar?

Today my belief is simple: money is a tool. It's a device that carries out a particular function, whether that be to keep me housed, to put quality food in my body, to save as a means of mental ease, or to pass on in an effort to give those same things to others.

I've been working on taking the emotions out of money and being really smart in how I'm both pursuing it and using it on a daily basis. I have come to a point in my career where I have a financial security that little me would be in awe of and for which adult me is deeply grateful. This security has also given me new levels of choice and flexibility in my professional and academic decision making.

My decision to leave Columbia, for instance, was a radical one, based on years of grappling with institutional racism, our country's capitalism, and my own pursuit of unlearning the whitewashing curriculum that was spoon-fed to me my whole life. It was, nonetheless, a decision situated around a level of financial security I had, as a successful writer and public lecturer, which allowed me the flexibility to explore other options.

That is a privilege. It's something I recognize and I make sure to convey when people tell me, "I'm disappointed in my institution, I want to leave as well." I try to guide them through the process of deciding if leaving is the absolute best way to fight the system for them. Because leaving a college or university often means that one is leaving access to health care, leaving work-study income, leaving a sense of community built with other students.

So, while finances are a big factor in one's ability to wipe their hands clean of an institution they feel so wronged by, there are many implications to consider. We all must do what makes the most sense for ourselves and our long-term goals.

For me, and many others like me, we felt we could engage in bigger and more meaningful scholarly work outside of the academy. For others, resistance to institutional racism and the whitewashing of curricula might look like leveraging the resources those institutions offer and using them for the good of our community. Both are completely valid.

I can now put my money into more intimate modes of learning, like taking classes at smaller community institutes, working one-on-one with scholars whose work I value and want to learn from, buying more books to explore topics myself, and applying to fellowships and residencies where I can continue to develop my craft and get meaningful critique.

4. The Loveland Foundation is a project that began in the wake of your successfully raising $250,000 for the Therapy for Black Women and Girls initiative. How did this fund-raising experience begin? Did it shift your beliefs about money? Do you think it shifted your community's beliefs about money, and what they should do with the money they have?

My Therapy fund began as a birthday project. I was turning thirty, and I decided that I wanted to turn the excitement around entering a new decade into an opportunity to support people in a really on-the-ground and meaningful way. At that time in my life, I was really finding value in my therapy sessions and the ways I was unraveling all the mess in my head and learning skills to help me navigate the world. I would often think, *I wish more Black women and girls could pursue their healing.* I decided to create a fund-raiser to help pay down the cost of therapy sessions for Black women and girls, to make mental health care more accessible. I remember sitting in a Starbucks uptown developing the

GoFundMe and thinking, *This will be really cool, I hope my followers show up*. And they did!

In the first twenty-four hours, we raised ten thousand dollars, and over the next several months, two hundred and fifty thousand dollars in donations had been gathered. That fund-raiser was such an unexpected and incredible moment for me and my community. At the time, I didn't have nearly the number of readers as I do now, yet they were a group that was moved not only to learn from me but also to take action on the knowledge they now possessed. That is always the goal of my work, and to see it in such a tangible way was just incredible.

For many of my white followers, the therapy fund-raiser was the first time they were intellectually engaged with a giving process. Suddenly, they had the opportunity to consider what they'd been learning from me—particularly in regard to the historical context of Black mental health and systemic injustice—and with an awareness of their privilege, in the words of Brittney Packnett, pay that privilege forward.

5. Friend Care Friday happens every week on your Instagram—you encourage friends to send small amounts of money to each other using Venmo or PayPal to fund quotidian acts of self-care, like a morning latte. How did Friend Care Friday start, and why is it an important part of your practice not just on a personal level, but as an educator to hundreds of thousands of readers on social media?
Friend Care Friday came out of a time when I sent five dollars via Venmo to a few of my girlfriends who I was really missing since we all moved to different parts of the country. I thought of it as a virtual coffee date to let them know how much I missed them and our time together. When you send money via apps, there is often a space where you can leave a comment on what the money is for. When I was considering what to tell them, I remember thinking, [it's] just because I want them to feel seen and loved regardless of what I knew or didn't know about what was going on in their lives. I saw the positive waves of connectedness it had brought my friendships, so I decided to share it as a suggestion to my readers.

I quickly got lots of comments and messages from people, telling me how valuable or exciting that little act of kindness on Fridays was. On a personal level, Friend Care Friday is important because as I move into my thirties, life is getting more and more complicated and full. Connectedness is one of my highest values, and something I'm committed to not letting slip away. Friend Care Friday is a good way to push a constant reminder to the people around me that even when we're apart I am invested in them as a person, and in us as friends.

I hope that my readers are able to make some sort of powerful connection between Friend Care Friday and their own values as well. At the very least, it's a weekly reminder to check in on your people and love on them a little—however you can.

6. As a writer and educator, you say your income comes from paid engagements as well as from your supporters on Patreon. You also encourage your social media followers to invest in the education they receive from you by sending money to your PayPal account. Are these digital platforms—PayPal and Patreon—a sustainable, lucrative way for you to support yourself as an educator, or more of a symbolic act?
My labor as a writer and lecturer is no more or less sustainable, lucrative, or secure than any other career path in a capitalist country like ours. Historically, we have lived with the idea that any work in the sector of public service—especially that of teaching, activism, and even writing—equated to a limited, low income and often burnout. As I moved into this work, I decided I wasn't going to subscribe to that.

I made this clear by giving my readers several opportunities to contemplate the exchange of knowledge I was offering and consider how they'd like to show up to compensate me for it. I believe this is the type of tangible support activists should have had all along; I just happen to live at a time where this is a true possibility. Imagine if we could have had the ease that we have now to donate monthly to Harriet Tubman, Florynce Kennedy, or Lorraine Hansberry. We could have collectively contributed to their financial security, allowing them to continue fighting for and creating major shifts in our country. It should have always been this way.

Asking for money is always complicated, and not always easy. But I had to make a commitment to my purpose in the world. If I was going to stay afloat, to remain unweathered, to practice self-care for the sake of staying alive in this tumultuous climate, I was going to have to ensure I was financially compensated for the work I was doing.

Once I established that expectation with my readers, it created a culture within my community such that I no longer had to say, "Hey, I offered you a lot of value—it would mean a lot to me if you would consider investing back so I can continue to do this work." It's now an understood and respected stance I take, and people are now showing up not just for me, but for other educators they are learning from online and in person.

Having the financial support from my community means that I have the financial security to continue pushing boundaries and making change in spaces that often don't give Black women a voice at all, let alone one that will shift culture.

7. As a Black woman devoting much of your time and energy to educating white women, could the flow of money from your students to you be seen, in part, as a mechanism of reparations? Or does the labor required on your part negate that for you?

The white women who pay me for the education they are receiving from me are paying for my work, not giving me any type of reparations. As with any service position, there is an exchange happening. It's important not to get those mixed up, because the learning is not the anti-racism work in and of itself. It's not enough to just read about and intellectualize the racial injustices in the world—you have to take intentional action based on what you know. Them investing in their education is not connected to a reparations-style atonement.

8. How do projects like Therapy for Black Women and Girls and Friend Care Friday engage the question of reparations?

When I first started the therapy fund, I was situating it around a conversation of reparations. I soon stopped as my peers and other activist-scholars expressed that using the concept of reparations in such micro ways could be pulling away from the prioritized conversation of governmentally mandated reparations programs.

While I do think that critical conversations around white America's responsibilities and the debts owed to the Black community can begin to be had in these small and meaningful ways, from that moment on, I committed to maintain my discussions around reparations in larger contexts. I don't intend to stop.

THIS ISN'T WHAT I CAME FOR: TESTIMONY OF AN EX-WHITEFLUENCER

LILY DIAMOND

The patriarchy is in the algorithms.

—Claire Fitzsimmons, founder of Salty

Large technology monopolies . . . need to be broken up and regulated, because their consolidated power and cultural influence make competition largely impossible. This monopoly . . . is a threat to democracy, as is currently coming to the fore as we make sense of information flows through digital media such as Google and Facebook in the wake of the 2016 United States presidential election.

—Safiya Umoja Noble, *Algorithms of Oppression*

Whitefluencer (n): A white, cisgender woman with a large social media following who profits off of product placement and endorsements and remains socially and politically neutral at all costs to maximize followers and profits.

—Jessica Lawmaster, founder of Kindred Leaders

THE INTERNET is a terrible place to make money.

In this era of fake news and deep fakes, anti-vax conspiracy theorists radicalize millions on Facebook, Instagram filters cause body dysmorphia,* Russian bots rig presidential elections, and cancel culture dictates who we must like or shun on any given day. Search engines and artificial intelligence algorithms reinforce racism.† A megalomaniacal white supremacist president engineered an attack on his nation's own capital from the safety of a Twitter account. And white liberals' overwhelming response to rediscovering racism in America in the summer of 2020 was to refine their Instagram meme activist skills to performative allyship perfection.

And yet, I am a full-time blogger. Or I was. I hate the word and its connotations: frivolity and ennui, self-absorption and privilege chief among them. I hate them because—aside from a hefty dose of birth-inherited middle-class white cis heteronormative privilege, I hardly fit the stereotype. I did not blog out of boredom or for fun, as most assume bloggers do. I don't have a trust fund, an Instagram husband,‡ or even a boyfriend, for that matter. I am rarely selfie-ready. My bloggerdom was not born of an Instagram-ready home filled with marble and unnaturally verdant potted plants. No. My blog was, quite simply, my full-time job.

In other words: I blogged to survive.

My business emerged from the need to pay rent in a city where people bleed thousands of dollars to live in apartments far too small and dilapidated for their price tag. The $28,000 I made my first year in LA—cobbling together paychecks for freelance copywriting and editing and groveling at the altar of any place that published my essays and poetry—placed me squarely below the city's "Very Low Income Level."§ My father began to

---

*Susruthi Rajanala et al., "Selfies—Living in the Era of Filtered Photographs," *JAMA Facial Plastic Surgery* 20, no. 6 (December 2018): 443–444, https://doi.org/10.1001/jamafacial.2018.0486.

†Safiya Umoja Noble, *Algorithms of Oppression: How Search Engines Reinforce Racism* (New York: New York University Press, 2018).

‡"An *Instagram husband* refers to a person who helps a partner manage their Instagram social media channel, especially by taking photos. You may have seen them patiently waiting to drink their oat-milk latte until their partner snaps that perfect pic first." Dictionary .com, 2021.

§The US Department of Housing and Urban Development's Very Low Income Level

subsidize my Obamacare health insurance. And each month, I forked over an out-of-budget check for a one-bedroom apartment with a photogenic yet termite-ridden vaulted ceiling, one noisy and tepid AC unit, and a kitchen only slightly larger than a bathtub. I woke up most mornings to the ruckus of trash hauls, fire trucks, and the onslaught of gentrification construction. At night, I plugged my ears to keep out the jittery thrum of LAPD helicopters seeking so-called criminal suspects.

I came to Los Angeles in 2013 because—for as many ways as it's corrupted—the city's lifeblood is still creativity and art. Writers there, working in "the industry," actually got paid. LA offered the promise of being remunerated for work I loved to do, of having others read my work, and of making a living at the same time.

I was born into a family of entrepreneurs and learned a dogged work ethic from my parents, who built a natural body care business from the ground up. Their parents, too, were self-made—Jews in Indiana and California who assimilated as department store owner, jeweler, first female president of the temple. If I wanted success, I knew it was up to me to go out and get it.

I began my own version of the LA hustle: Daily meetings with producers and showrunners. Grooming a new copywriting clientele. Reeling off spec scripts and pilots, true-to-life dark comedies about the New Age industry, and my angst as a motherless daughter and chronically single lady.

At the same time, a growing digital movement was shifting the terrain of media, social and otherwise. In 2012, I started a food and storytelling blog at the insistence of friends. Instagram had arrived, and with its growth, the readership of the blog expanded swiftly. Shortly after I learned how to use a hashtag, I started to receive offers for paid product promotion. And by 2014, I realized I could make as much of a living

---

threshold in Los Angeles in 2010 was $29,000. The 2020 Very Low Income Level threshold for Los Angeles is $39,450. And anyone who makes less than $63,100 a year in Los Angeles is officially deemed Low Income. From laalmanac.com and the US Department of Housing and Urban Development.

off my blog as I was from my freelance editing and writing. The internet moved toward me far faster than Hollywood ever did, with one crucial difference: my blog gave me a built-in readership.

Los Angeles whispered to me of celebrity, of the cult of personality, of the possibility that I could make money just for (gasp) being myself. The rising clout of social media as an advertising platform and personal soapbox made it feel like anyone could become the next Chrissy Teigen or Gwyneth Paltrow—not just a model or an actor, but a lifestyle brand. To be not just a person but a brand was an identity that everyone wanted; a selfhood that could be packaged and sold.

And thus, from my thoroughly aspirational existence, I began to make a living as a food and wellness blogger. I taught myself how to use a camera. I wrote stories about my mother's death, my single-lady woes, and the string of heartbreaks I weathered over the past decade. I developed recipes for green juices and honey face masks, and—equipped with a blog URL, an iPhone, and a steadily growing internet presence—I began to create #sponcon: sponsored content for brands, propagated by social media.

With the wind of a multibillion-dollar influencer marketing industry* beneath my millennial wings, I became that dreaded social media succubus dubbed an "influencer": one whose virtual presence sways the wants of an ever-hungrier audience.

Suddenly, my very presence was commodified. I was paid to attend branded PR events, to talk up products to my followers, and often, to play pretend at blogger friendships—a performance of social bonding engineered to ooze relatability even as it sold the goods. As I got to know the fellow Instagrammers of LA, I was drawn to an elite set who seemed to have it all: hundreds of thousands of followers, Instagram husbands at the ready, wildly successful businesses, and most often, staff flanking them at home, in office, and in public. I was in awe. The first blogger outing I attended, a new influencer friend picked me up in a $150,000 Mercedes

---

*Brands will spend up to $15 billion on influencer marketing by 2022 based on Mediakix data (*Business Insider*, January 5, 2021).

G 550 SUV her parents gifted her for her twenty-first birthday, which engulfed her like a metal aura of money.

I had no access to such trimmings of wealth, but riding through the streets of LA in that G 550, I began to take notes: only show the pretty parts of the day-to-day; never talk about politics, racism, or the patriarchy; never emote too deeply; never reveal the privileges you hold or the work you must do to make things palatable; laugh; smile; post constantly; accept money, but definitely do not talk about money.

Elements of this design seemed problematic from the start, but I needed money, and sins of omission—or "curation," as we called it— seemed a small price to pay for cash in the bank. I could not see I was building a life that was ultimately unsustainable and relationships that were transactional before all else.

The Instagram illusion comes in many forms, but in the wellness industry, it's mostly a mirage of health, spiritual bypassing, and financial privilege: *Look at me bask in the effortless glow of my wellness routine and total self-acceptance, which certainly has nothing to do with the prohibitively expensive serums-superfoods-supplements-vacations given to me for free because I project an appearance that conforms to white supremacist heteropatriarchal beauty standards, thereby stoking the flames of digital hypercapitalism.*

Yet no matter how much influencers appear to spend on workout clothes, groceries, vacations, and "self-care," there is rarely any discussion of how they've paid for it.* These women seem to exist in a world apart from the concerns of basic safety, health care, and paying bills—a world where "authenticity" has been twisted to mean the curated absence of socioeconomic and sociopolitical accountability.

---

*Dr. Ellen Hesper of the London School of Economics writes, "Being open about the amount of work [read: "labor" or "money"] that goes into maintaining a cohesive, true online persona [is] a no-go in a digital world where authenticity is key." From Barbara Speed, "The Lies of Instagram: How the Cult of Authenticity Spun Out of Control," *New Statesman*, November 13, 2015.

But what could be more authentic than the need to make rent? The incongruence stung, but I tried to accept that maintaining an illusion of plenty—even when I couldn't pay for my own health insurance—was as much a part of my new job as any other duty.

As offers of free luxury kitchenware, expensive skincare products, workout classes, and trendy probiotic beverages filled my inbox, I was initially thrilled. Boxes of gleaming stainless steel and elegant cast-iron replaced the heat-blemished pans and dull knives I'd bought on Craigslist. Before I even knew I could ask for money, I was given product for free, in exchange for "sharing my thoughts" with my audience.* Thus began the accumulation of wildly aspirational products that seem to appear out of thin air in the lives of influencers, signaling wealth, ease, and privilege.

As the initial exhilaration of free shit wore thin, I realized that accepting product was a swift path to never making money—and to continuously misleading my audience. If I worked for free, acting as a stylist, photographer, model, photo editor, copywriter, and advertiser for a brand that would otherwise have to spend thousands of dollars hiring people and media outlets to do each of those jobs individually, it would be hard to get paid for my work in the future. But because many blogs are created by women as so-called passion projects, companies often expect them to work for free—and to be grateful for the opportunity. Bound by the dual need to have my work taken seriously and my rent paid, I bristled against the grim reality of heterocapitalism's ongoing devaluation of women's labor.

Moreover, I was uncomfortable with the knowledge that I might be receiving—and plugging—products, supplements, and gadgets I'd never have the budget (or the desire) to buy in real life. I was the first line in a culture inured to being sold something we didn't know we needed from the comfort of our very own phones and ad-targeted social networks.

---

*Bound by Federal Trade Commission regulations, influencers are supposed to tell their audience when they share about gifted products—thereby rendering their opinion heavily biased—but many fail to do so.

My willingness to have my life on display now determined how much money I could make, from my ability to pretend to like a certain kind of toothpaste to my capacity for feigning daily contentment regardless of what was happening in the world. And my long-term fiscal livelihood—my ability to move out of my apartment, to pay for health insurance, to one day buy a house and have a child—would be guided by my willingness, or lack thereof, to participate in a charade of free will, ease, and beauty.

To lie.

Of course it wasn't all façade: There was a pure, solipsistic kind of fun to posting a picture of a sexy peach galette and watching thousands of likes roll in. A thrill to knowing I could always get the trendiest superfood for free. There was some delight in being paid to be creative, to share myself with a readership, just to be, yes, me.

But was it really me? On the internet, I posted two new articles and recipes a week, seemingly from a pristine wonderland of taste, scent, and thought. At the same time, I was writing my first book, which I'd sold in a six-figure deal predicated on exponential projected growth via social media—Instagram in particular.

IRL, manufacturing illusion was exhausting and isolating. I was deeply lonely, breaking out in stress hives, shooting a cookbook from a kitchen with six square feet of dingy linoleum counter space my audience never saw. As deadlines crept near, I often worked until midnight to keep every aspect of my business and social media accounts at a rigorous foment and the dishes clean. I repeated that old adage: I'd sleep when I had a hundred thousand followers.

Monday through Friday, my closest relationship was with my phone, where my attention was sublimely attuned to the constant refresh of Instagram likes and comments. In the evenings, I huddled on my couch gripping a cold metal device instead of cuddling a significant other.

Now that I'd trained a content-hungry following to expect a world filled with curated kale salads, DIY facemasks, and bon mots–laced sunsets, I was scared to deviate. I had a formula that worked, satisfying current readers and drawing in new ones by the thousands. An illusion that may have deadened my spirit and wreaked havoc on my body, but that definitely, if barely, paid the rent.

All that changed in March 2016, as the United States hurtled toward a cataclysmic presidential election and Instagram's parent company, Facebook, changed the photo-sharing app's functionality from an egalitarian visual playground to a pay-to-be-seen business model. Overnight, Instagram traded out the organic, chronological order of its photo feed for an order determined by a supposedly personalized algorithm. The company claimed this algorithm would show each user pictures based on its knowledge of "what you will care about the most." In practice, this seemed more like "what we (as a business) have decided you should care about (because it's good for our business)."

Suddenly, personal users couldn't find photos from their cousin Julie, while photos from Kylie Jenner perpetually hovered at the top of their feeds. Creators like me saw likes, comments, and follows—which translated into advertising potential and overall influence—dwindle. At first, this new and improved version of Instagram seemed to prioritize visibility solely for large accounts and for posts that paid to be boosted to the top of their followers' feeds. At the same time, the app also deprioritized visibility for many creators regardless of size, ostensibly to goad us into paying them to ensure our posts reached more of our existing followers.

Even more maddeningly, many accounts with far fewer followers might see engagement five to ten times my own. Yet no matter how much of my heart and mind I poured into creating content, Instagram's algorithm often only showed my images to 5 to 10 percent of the community I'd worked for years to create. As engagement dropped, so, too, did the amount I could potentially charge to work with a brand.

Worse than the diminished engagement, though, was the way the app locked you into an identity based on your previous posts. The algorithm now seemed to reward accounts and posts that adhered to a monoculture they'd built for themselves: if it was pretty food pictures my audience expected from me, then in a self-built prison of food the algorithm wanted me to remain. If I posted a photo of a fancy brunch or frothy green smoothie, I'd reach tens of thousands of people. But if I shared my thoughts about white supremacy, the post's reach would be cut by half or more. The only difference? The algorithm decided that my audience would rather see the delectable eats than the calls to stand with the Black Lives Matter movement. I was, as they say on the interwebs, shadowbanned.*

Ultimately, nobody—except for the robotic mechanism running the algorithm from the shelter of Silicon Valley—knew why certain accounts and posts were favored over others. Perhaps the best explanation is that, "The Instagram algorithm is designed for one thing: [to] convince more people to spend more time [on the app] so Instagram can show more ads and make more money."†

Every attempt I made to outsmart this system felt not just like a business failure, but a personal one: building an income stream dependent on the behavior of a privately owned app with its own fiscal aims was a swift path both to losing money and to betraying my own core values and interests. It meant I was allowing a supposedly omniscient and omnipotent— yet entirely unintelligible—entity determine who I was, and who I should be in the future.

Simultaneously, the world convulsed in the era of Trump, marked by horrific acts of racism, white supremacist violence, xenophobia, and misogyny. On my website (where I turned more and more often because it remained, for now, outside of Instagram's algorithmic grasp), I raged against the inequities of the political administration as a prelude to edible body scrubs and adaptogenic nut milks. But on Instagram, my luscious salad posts began to feel willfully ignorant, a feast of privilege with the

---

*According to Oxford Languages online, "shadowban, verb: to block (a user) from a social media site or online forum without their knowledge, typically by making their posts and comments no longer visible to other users."
†Posted by Aime Cox-Tennant, @studio.cotton, on Instagram, February 8, 2021.

occasional #BlackLivesMatter sprinkled in for virtue-signaling activism effect.

The day Alton Sterling, a thirty-seven-year-old Black man, was murdered by two white police officers in Louisiana, I begged a sponsor to delay a post about women's empowerment and activism spelled out in ice cream. I was mortified at the thought of turning a profit by tokenizing the murder in a display of performative Insta-activism. The brand acquiesced, but within days the media cycle had moved on, and I was back to making money from within the bubble of my Insta-illusion.

But something in me cracked. In case it wasn't already blatantly clear to me, none of this was anything like what I'd intended when I started my blog—or when I moved to Los Angeles seeking a writerly life of creativity, collaboration, and freedom.

I never meant for my blended green juice habit to become a business. And I never thought about the long-term implications of using food porn and curated lifestyle images as a lure to get people to read the writing I actually cared about. But that's exactly what had happened. Now, I spent hours each week trying to appease a tyrannical and literally nonhuman entity, deluding myself into thinking I could somehow make a difference by dressing up antihegemonic thoughts in the clothes of their capitalist oppressor.

Perhaps I was the only fool here: I was the one who presumed my audience actually wanted to read my writing, rather than just consume a steady stream of uncomplicated food and beautiful photos. I grew both obsessed with and repulsed by my work and by my inability to step away from a system I'd trapped myself in. I wanted nothing more than to please the algorithm—to make money, to eat, to house myself—yet I wanted to destroy it: to be free to work in accord with my own values without risking my livelihood.

Fighting anxious thoughts of cannibalizing my own business, I started to experiment with changing the content I posted—to show up more honestly as who I was becoming. A farmers' market report was replaced by a #BelieveWomen post about the Kavanaugh hearings; Sunday waffles supplanted by conversations about indigenous land sovereignty; and a Martin Luther King Jr. Day truism uprooted for dialogue around dismantling white supremacy. As expected, the algorithm deprioritized my visibility, and followers fled, their good-byes sometimes accompanied by the taunting suggestion I create a separate account for my "personal thoughts."

But in that sociopolitical moment, it wasn't just a question of whether or not my Instagram captions could fulfill my highest creative aspirations. I now had a digital following the size of my entire hometown county, and not using my platform—a business I built of nothing but my "personal thoughts"—to address the racist violence and institutionalized misogyny transpiring around me felt like collusion. After all, such transgressions occurred just as frequently in the digital sphere as they did in real life, where silencing and policing the voices and bodies of Black and indigenous women of color was commonplace, if not systemic.

If I did not use a digital space I spent years cultivating to address these crises on equal footing with discussions of how to live, eat, and care for ourselves as women, wouldn't I be complicit in caring solely for the well-being of a white, privileged few? Yes. I would be.

Of all the kinds of influence (or what in 2021 was finally coined as *whitefluence*) I might exert on an audience, I did not want to stand only for what could be bought with white privilege and the denial of the very real suffering of many. This was complicity in silence, a true crime of privilege—and I no longer wanted to offer an audience of predominantly white women a digital space for antipolitical escapism. Myself included.

I had been the first line not just in convincing other women they needed a product or way of living that was unattainable to most, but also in convincing myself I was happy to trade honest self-expression—and my lifelong dream of being a writer—for money and delusions of fame. With enough in the bank to provide a small buffer of perspective, I knew I could no longer play a role in suggesting that the life of a so-called influencer—replete with an avalanche of free, ostensibly covetable products—was the best kind of life, or one even remotely within reach.

After all, Instagram's capitalist-driven fantasy was just one more distraction from the daily ravages of heterocapitalism and white supremacy on women and communities of color—and one more space for largely male-owned companies to remind women of their inadequacies (as most advertising does).*

If I continued to play the game, to perpetuate the illusion, to be a bona fide "whitefluencer," then I was implicitly agreeing to the very terms of the illusion itself—that, despite the world on fire all around me, my whiteness, my privilege, my access, my influence might save me. Or at least distract me from the gnawing pit of personal and creative dissatisfaction growing inside.

But if I opted out, how would I pay the rent?

Desperate to reconnect with tangible values I believed in, I began to search for a place I could afford outside Los Angeles. Rent had climbed so astronomically that it took a year, but eventually I found a small apartment far below market value, nestled into a remote hillside in prime wildfire territory, a long drive from friends, meetings, and reliable cell service. Here, my mind relaxed enough to know I could not continue business as usual. I began to investigate how I might bridge the chasm between what I cared about most—writing, wellness, and a voice for all women, rather than a privileged few—and what I talked about on social media, where the bulk of my business took place. I didn't know what was on the other side of telling the algorithm to fuck off, but I was ready to find out.

In a flurry of frustration, I shared my current state on an Instagram Story (a feature that allows users to share content that disappears after twenty-four hours): disheveled and makeup-free, in bed with a headache at 4:00 p.m., still wearing pajamas from the night before after a full day's

---

*Advertising leverages a psychological precept called compensatory consumption, which "refers to the consumption behavior which aims at coping with psychological deficit or threat." Zheng Xiaoying and Peng Siqing, "Consumption as Psychological Compensation: A Review of Compensatory Consumption," *Advances in Psychological Science* 22, no. 9 (2014): 1513–1520.

work, crying over *Grey's Anatomy*, disillusioned and angry at all the ways I had to contort and silence myself to remain relevant. As an afterthought, I invited others to join me in sharing what they were going through behind the Instagram illusion, using the hashtag #honestinsta.

I was shocked by what followed: a cascade of truth. Hundreds of comments shared personal and professional vulnerabilities, echoing the feeling of being stifled by social media's limited range of acceptable self-representation. Bloggers with large followings shared rabid discontents, some later returning to delete their comments. Non-bloggers confessed their assumptions that the aspirational content they saw on Instagram was what life was really like for the influencers, actresses, and models they followed.

Mothers lamented being overworked and sleepless, exhausted at home and on the job. People divulged their anxieties and mental illnesses. Their financial instabilities. Chin hairs. Hormonal fluctuations. Helplessness in the face of political chaos.

And in everyone, a longing to be seen.

Over the following days, people began to refer to #honestinsta as a movement. Ironically, for the first time in months, my following on Instagram grew. I continued to shepherd the movement, devoting one day a week to a topic that required raw honesty from me, and encouraging the same in others. #honestinsta became a space to undo the many ways I manipulated myself to please the algorithm, a place to talk about the things that hurt, that make us human.

Almost instantaneously, though, I saw people using their honesty as a tool of the algorithm: employing vulnerability and "authenticity" as a pathway to likes; crying selfies that leveraged emotional shock value to gain followers. I was tempted to intervene, to burst yet another illusory bubble I'd created, one that seemed to suggest Instagram was an adequate space for confession, therapizing, and the development of the human spirit. But I demurred, certain that whatever I did, my entrapment would ultimately commodify the action—a snake eating its own tail.

•   •   •

As a knot in my stomach tied and untied itself each day, I realized that my only choice was to change the game I was playing. Instead of trying to please the algorithm and the people who were only there for the smoothies, I would focus on building the community of people who were interested in the bigger picture. I would share only content I truly believed in and do my best to speak honestly to my followers about the issues that mattered most to me.

Over the following months, I began to speak out against the systems in which I—and we all—are bound. Though I still worked with brands to make rent, I railed against the inequities of the beauty and wellness industrial complexes, and the peril of remaining complacent to the terms of a culture that prioritizes whiteness and wealth. Day in and day out, I reminded my audience and myself that true wellness—which wellness entrepreneur Sinikiwe Dhliwayo defines as agency—cannot be bought.

Instead of activated charcoal and ashwagandha, we talked about Audre Lorde, the male gaze, and the political roots of self-care. I began to share pathways to lasting mental and physical health that were free—a birthright, not a commodity. I shared stories of my own loneliness, guilt, grief, and the obsessive self-editing required to live a life that looks "perfect" from the outside. And I helped introduce the use of a brand partnership inclusion rider for white influencers who wanted to take meaningful action in their own businesses.*

What happened next was, of course, what I both wanted and feared: The more antihegemonic truth I spilled online, the more influencer

---

*Vix Meldrew modified the inclusion rider (an addendum to a business contract stipulating conditions that must be met by both parties, in this case specifically regarding diversity, equity, and inclusion measures) initially created for the film and television industry in 2014 by Stacy L. Smith of the University of Southern California's Annenberg Inclusion Initiative. I then published and marketed this inclusion rider to white influencers, asking them to insert language into brand partnership contracts to ensure that companies reach out to and partner with "people who identify themselves as females, people of color, disabled, Lesbian Gay Bisexual Transgender or Queer, or having a combination of these attributes," and report on the demographics.

connections and work relationships—which had been about selling a fantasy—fell away. Within nine months, the business agency that represented me called to let me go. They didn't give me an answer when I asked why. Whether it was the result of my outspokenness itself or that the outspokenness meant decreased engagement on Instagram, I'll never know.

All of this, of course, happened before the summer of 2020, when millions took to the streets for months of Black Lives Matter uprisings in the wake of George Floyd's brutal murder. Before the meme activism of #BlackOutTuesday and the tidal wave of white tears shed by influencers and businesses suddenly committed to being actively antiracist. It happened before it was cool to be political on social media, before the algorithm (and corporate responsibility) rewarded whiteness for taking accountability for its privilege. But I had effectively ruined my financial viability as an influencer by doing just that already.

And I—well, I no longer cared.

I now knew I'd rather make less money being honest and losing hundreds or thousands of followers a week than make bank suppressing the truth about the forces threatening the well-being, the agency, of millions. Wellness wasn't culturally appropriated and commodifiable crystal face rollers, yoga, and golden milk lattes. Wellness began with safety, with every human's basic right to breathe. And if I couldn't be truthful about that kind of intersectional well-being, if I couldn't name the white supremacist underpinnings of the wellness industry, I no longer wanted to play the game. No matter what social justice hashtags were trending for the week, I would find another way to pay the rent.

As journalist Diyora Shadijanova tweeted in the spring of 2021:

> at some point we have to recognise that the financial anxiety young people are living through is not normal. monetising all your hobbies is not normal. hustle culture is not normal. glorifying precarious work is not normal. self-optimisation is not normal.

Watching sponsorship inquiries trickle to nothing, I moved my money-making endeavors away from social media. And I moved my home from California to the land where I grew up, on Maui, to live in a two-hundred-square-foot studio. Here, I am confronted daily with questions of what it means to be a white settler living (and making money) on occupied Native Hawaiian land, particularly during a global pandemic and financial crisis. What does it mean for me to be a coconspirator in ensuring wellness for all in this place, in this community?

I haven't yet figured out how to dismantle capitalism or white supremacy, but I took on a consulting job for a nonprofit that allowed me to do nothing but be honest about the challenges our human and earth communities were facing. I published another book, the result of years of collaboration and relationship conducted entirely beyond the realm of social media. In this interactive journal, my coauthor (Rebecca Walker, editor of this book) and I offer sets of questions for people to rewrite the tired, dysfunctional stories of their past in order to move into a new narrative for a more honest future.

And in rewriting the ways I wanted to make a living, I began to examine how I could be accountable to the digital community I'd built over the past decade. Because of this community—and the many creators I met there who became lifelong friends IRL—I still love Instagram. It's now a tool I use to create content for educational purposes, and to build relationships based on truth and service, rather than delusion and extraction.

But most important, I also had to rewrite the ways in which I was accountable to myself. I had to be honest about the insecurities, obsessions, and social media addictions that threatened my own sanity and sovereignty, my ability to see myself and the world around me clearly, without the distortions of an app (and a society) that profited off my own lack of empowerment.

I don't want to monetize every part of my life. Nor do I want to broadcast it as a model to which anyone else should conform. My experience as a neurotypical, able-bodied, straight cisgender white woman from a landowning family of multigenerational entrepreneurs is just one tiny prism of the vast human experience. I don't have all the answers, and I make mistakes all the time. But I'd prefer that my presence, my work, my writing make space for a symphony of unique voices, realities, and truths rather than compound a silencing by the normative whiteness, exploitative capitalism, and patriarchy to which social media is largely enslaved.

I just want some version of normal that doesn't make my existence—with all its privileges, problems, and irreplicable, unfiltered delights—anyone's aspirational delusion. A normal that doesn't leave me aspiring to someone else's curated internet life. A normal that reinforces human connection, sanity, and honesty over technological supremacy. A normal my ancestors knew, by which they survived.

No algorithm has cracked that one yet. But humans have done it for millennia, and that's the technology I'm taking to the bank.

MONEY WOUNDS

LATHAM THOMAS

MOMMY WAS always dressed. "Dress for the dreams you have" was her mantra. Never leave the house in attire that you would regret being seen in.

On that day, my mom stood, six feet tall, wearing what I came to learn were called "pumps." A red patterned pencil skirt and a matching pussy-bow blouse hugged her slender frame. A pair of perfumed pantyhose clung to her arabesque thighs. Her hair—a perfect French twist—was held in place by geometrically arranged pins, which were hidden out of sight. Oscar de la Renta perfume scented her wrists. If you were close enough, you could detect the faintest trace of it—but few were allowed that close.

I know that scent by heart.

Mommy was an impeccably dressed Black woman in the late '80s and early '90s, working with a Black-owned real estate company in Oakland, California. Making that money. I remember thinking my mom was rich, because she was always first to have the latest technology—pagers, cell phones, laptops.

I learned from my mom how to spend money, but never how to save it. It always seemed better to spend money than to have it because having it could get you in trouble. I learned when I was eight years alive that if someone who looks like me or my mom, someone brown and female, is in possession of money, we are criminalized; seen as incapable of earning or having our own money legally, on our own terms, in our own right.

That there are systems in place to keep money out of our hands.

"Wait here, I will be right back," Mommy said. She pulled down the sun visor to open the mirror, applied a fresh coat of antique-red lipstick, and blotted her lips. She slowly opened the car door and stood up, shimmying her hips to adjust her skirt and tilting her head back to give her bow a refresh. She leaned in to grab her purse and locked me in the car.

I was used to Mommy taking quick trips into the grocery store and bank, leaving me in the car to wait. I climbed into the front seat, rolled up all the windows, and closed my eyes to feel the warmth of the sun coming through the windshield. I waited, and waited some more. At a certain point, I remember feeling like she was gone for a long time. I'd sat for longer periods and felt safe, but my spirit nudged me: something was not okay.

Mommy enters the vestibule of a bank that looked like a holy place, complete with high vaulted ceilings and masonic imagery. Her steps echo as she glides across the marble floors. She looks like money. The eyes of everyone in the bank fall on her: at first in awe of her beauty and poise, quickly dissolving into a dangerous, biased curiosity. Every white person in the bank is already thinking she can't possibly have any money.

Approaching the teller, Mommy presents a cashier's check for $21,562—the amount of her latest commission. Cashier's checks are like a wad of cash bulging out of your pocket. The teller looks at the check, takes a good look at my mother, and she asks for ID.

My mom passes her driver's license to the teller, who then holds the check up to the light, expecting it to be fraudulent. When she realizes it's not, her face unknowingly distorts with disappointment. Without saying a word, she excuses herself and walks into a private area. But she doesn't return with the cash or the check. Instead she calls the police.

When the Oakland PD arrive, they come in force, striding to where Mommy stands. They grab her by the arm and ask her how she got ahold of that amount of money. Before she can speak, she is thrown to the ground. They pin her arms behind her, place a knee into her back, press her chest against the cold marble floor, and handcuff her in front of everyone.

My mom has done nothing wrong, is not told why the police were called or why she is being handled with force. She curses them as they remove her from the bank. And that's when I see her: exiting the bank escorted by policemen. In custody. Like a criminal. When it's over, she tells me how it happened, every moment playing vividly in my mind.

They were forced to release her thirty minutes later, but for days, she was physically sore, her ego bruised. I remember the bluish-purple marks on her wrists. She was humiliated in front of the entire bank, assaulted in broad daylight by at least two officers, while three others watched. "Why don't you sue?" I asked her.

"Sue who?" she replied. "They will do nothing."

Race and money are inextricably tied. I intuited that day that, like my mother, I would never be seen as someone worthy of having access to money. That I would have to jump through fire to adapt to a system designed to siphon my economic value while giving me back very little respect, or even basic decency.

My mother's trauma took root in my marrow, my cells. I was okay depositing checks at my bank because I knew the teller. But my emotional motor system would signal when I was in an unfamiliar bank or a place where I was othered and outnumbered. It was an imperfect intelligence that, while keen, might also forecast a perceived threat when there was none.

I once read that when a woman is under-resourced and feels the threat of economic pressure, the brain perceives the event as life threatening. A life-threatening event initiates a stress response in the body, sending cortisol through the bloodstream and preparing the body to flee the danger. But what if the threat is your rent, your tuition, your electricity bill?

As a young woman, and then a single mother, I lived on Strivers' Row—one of the most treasured historic blocks in Harlem, with the projects just a few blocks north. I was keenly aware that I was living in an economically depressed region of New York City, of anxious people, all trying to get by. Yet nothing in our sociopolitical, educational, or health care systems was designed to help us address rampant economic stress.

I became accustomed to this tension and the accompanying stress cycle—I witnessed it as I was growing up and seem to have inherited it. I was raised by a single mother and remember the pressure she felt raising two girls and providing a life for us with little to no child support. But once I gave birth to my son—and after three years, became a single mother—I found myself repeating a pattern. I did not want to carry the cycle forward. I wanted my son to know economic freedom, mobility.

It was time to uproot my limiting beliefs, some that I'd held since that long-ago day in Oakland.

I started an entrepreneurial venture in women's health, and it took a few years, but it soon began to stand on its own. As an independent entrepreneur, I began to see it all as an ebb and flow. There were times when I made huge lump sums of money, but I couldn't keep it because I never learned to save. And there were times when I had little.

We often design our lives around narratives of doubt, sabotaging ourselves consciously and unconsciously because we believe there is a fixed amount of abundance or success we can actually achieve. Every day, I swam upstream, working against the beliefs I held about money: I knew that I could make it, but I still wasn't sure if I could keep it.

I needed to learn that even if I was under financial stress, I could control my thoughts and start a new thought pattern, a new belief system.

I had to expand my capacity to receive.

As I built my business, Mama Glow, I began to invest in a different type of capital: social currency. Social currency broadly refers to the value of effectively functioning social groups, including interpersonal relationships, a shared sense of identity and values, and most important, a commitment to reciprocity.

I believe in cultivating relationships like tending a garden: building powerful relationships with collaborators and other folks who serve as supporters of my work. In this space, there is trust, beauty, and love. As these relationships have grown, I've uncovered a currency of abundance, which begets money, and which holds value far beyond my pocketbook. It is the currency of human relationship, the human spirit's longing to connect, to share, to honor, to do the right thing.

Now I realize this isn't necessarily new: wealth has been deeply embedded in social relationships for generations. This is why my mother wanted me to attend Fountain Valley boarding school and Columbia University; she wanted me to build social capital like the white men who were beneficiaries of the "old boys' club"; in other words, a community that helps its own. This was a club she didn't have access to but saw as critical for my advancement, relationships, and opportunity. She was right, of course. But I'm blessed to be able to build on what she knew; to do it with my own sense of integrity and well-being at the center. And to do this work at a time when a whole new generation seems to want to do the same.

Today, I invest in social circles and surround myself with people who support each other, from women's groups to our Mama Glow doula community. Because while I now understand that social capital is a currency I can both nurture *and* keep, it's also a wealth circumscribed by the same systems of whiteness that seek to limit the power of people like my mother, like me. We work together as a community to counteract the stress of what it means not to have money or power. We leverage our circle and invite those with privilege to do their part and contribute currency. We redistribute money through networks, from folks who have more of it to communities that do not.

As I do this work, I often think about my ancestors, enslaved people who were forced to come to this country and then brutally and opportunistically used to build its economic foundation. The wealth held today by white men in power was made off the backs of our ancestors, and they've had it for so long, they believe it's theirs and theirs alone. But facts are facts: conservative estimates claim that upwards of $14 trillion in reparations is due to the descendants of slaves. That money belongs to us.

Money is a structural tool of whiteness, and this is the fundamental relationship that must change. Whether we make these changes legislatively or through a shift in our approach to all types of currency, we must acknowledge that there has never been an effort to restore and make right the wrongs of the past, or the present.

This must change.

We live, and earn our livings, in the wake of slavery, of a trauma that the US government wants us all to forget. We are under constant attack, but the government refuses to acknowledge the generational inequity that keeps Black folk well behind the starting line while white people move to the homestretch of the race, powered by privilege, access, and advantage. This system is steeped in supremacy and domination.

The teller that called the police on my mother that day was not an anomaly. She was an operative of a racist system that criminalizes Black women for earning money. A system that saw Black women as economically valuable—as chattel. A system that refuses to accept us, even when we have money. And so, in a system that will never recognize our value, we have to reclaim it for ourselves.

Money is currency. Currency is a current. Money is supposed to move, and when it isn't moving, or when it is only moving in one direction, something is wrong. Every day we participate in an economic system that centers on greed and exalts whiteness. My work today, as a Black businesswoman and a mother, is to keep money moving toward everyone, to make sure money—and social capital—is not only a tool for whiteness but for all of us.   .

CRACKING OPEN YOUR HEART WITHOUT BREAKING THE BANK:
Financial Tips for Single Mothers

NANCY McCABE

YOU'D SPENT most of your twenties in school, and when you reached your thirties, it felt like time was running out. So, you chose to adopt a baby from China by yourself for whatever insensate reasons anyone wants to raise a child.

So what if you made poverty-level wages the year before you initiated the adoption? Even though you were a graduate student, you were still far more privileged than the many single parents who live in poverty. You had underemployed, underpaid friends who were parents and somehow managed to make things work. And then you accepted a tenure-track university job, and despite a single income, no partner to offer emotional support when money is tight, and no child support, you still had a comparatively flexible schedule and decent health insurance. You felt that you were ready.

The adoption turns out to be the best decision you ever made. The first time you met your baby, your heart cracked wide open. And now you're sure that with a little organization, determination, and discipline, establishing and maintaining lifelong financial health as a single parent ought to be a breeze!

All you have to do is follow a few simple tips:

REMAIN DEBT-FREE.

Your own parents grew up poor during the Depression, and when you envied your classmates' nice clothes and beach vacations, your dad would say, "I'll bet their families are in debt," the worst possible insult. You put yourself through three degrees by working part-time and competing for scholarships, fellowships, and assistantships. You financed your China adoption—which, with some economy on your part, cost about $13,000—through loans paid back by adoption tax credits and a couple of extra courses, adjunct classes at other universities, and teaching jobs at summer camps and conferences that kept you on the road four or five hours at a time during breaks. Be proud, in the midst of your exhaustion: you managed to transition from graduate student to parent with a minimum of financial stress. You can do this!

ESTABLISH A SAVINGS ACCOUNT WITH THREE MONTHS OF LIVING EXPENSES.

Except that you teach at a private college and can barely scrape together day-care fees. Toward the end of each month, you often don't have the twelve dollars it costs (twelve dollars!) to fill your gas tank. Your daughter wears hand-me-downs generously passed on by other families. You feel fortunate since you teach heavy loads and aren't sure when you'd find the time to scour thrift stores or clip coupons. As for the savings account, your only option is to cultivate denial that anything bad could ever happen, because you don't have a penny extra.

Then you're denied tenure because, according to the appeals committee, you are rumored to be a "feminist." You are aghast because you were hired, with specialties in women's literature and feminist criticism, to teach critical theory. At your appeal, a board of male professors clears their throats and say, "We've heard that you don't like men." One male professor overheard a male student say this in a restroom. Another male professor was approached by a male student unhappy about his grade.

And by the way, why would you adopt a child with the intention of raising her without a father?

You're pretty sure that all of this is illegal, but after contacting lawyers and the American Association of University Professors, who are sympathetic but not optimistic about your prospects, you realize that you don't have the time, energy, or resources to seek recourse.

Anyway, says your chair, who voted against you, isn't it great that you've been booted from this conservative college? Now you can have more time to write! You stare at him blankly through the fog of panic. You have a child to support. Like all of your male colleagues, he has a stay-at-home wife who raised his children and freed him to focus on his career. Who does he think will subsidize you?

For weeks you eat soup and oatmeal for dinner, whatever's in the cupboard, and wander around the house with your blinds closed, caring for your two-year-old daughter, terrified for your future. How will you ever be able to summon the energy or money to find a new job and make a major move, alone, with a toddler, find her a good day care, start all over again? How will you even begin to find employment in a job market so tight that when you received your PhD, there were a thousand graduates in your field and only fifty tenure-track positions? Not only does the academic job market remain practically nonexistent, but you were denied tenure late in the fall, at the end of the annual job cycle. At this point, you can only find two jobs to apply for.

But you're grateful that as you fret, your daughter plows cheerfully, obliviously, through each day, arranging her stuffed animals around the coffee table and throwing teddy bear picnics, breaking eggs all over the kitchen floor while squealing with delight at the satisfying cracks of fragile shells, the gloppy mess of yolk and whites, cracking through your own haze of worry as you rush to stop her. The wonderful thing about having a toddler is that it's hard to stew very long. She forces you to be in the moment. Her presence in your life reminds you how lucky you are, no matter what.

Miraculously, because of a couple of eleventh-hour national awards for your writing, you get interviews for both of the jobs you apply for, and a surprisingly quick offer, with a substantial raise. Your self-esteem reappears, but you don't have time to celebrate. You start packing for a move a few states away; unbelievably, you're able to buy a whole house in your new town for $59,000. Even though your daughter's potty training stalls as you set off from South Carolina to Pennsylvania, as she patiently sits in the backseat, paging through books and watching videos on a tiny portable TV wobbling atop pillows, periodically calling, "It's going to fall on me!" you are buoyed by a sense of hope. You remind yourself of why you're doing all of this as you pull over to rearrange the backseat.

When you arrive in your new town in rural Pennsylvania, the air smells like the oil refinery that dominates the town, and your new house is dim. You replace all the bulbs with one-hundred watts and soldier on in this small town where the white neighborhood kids gather around your daughter and say, "She looks like an Indian." A town where there are no other single parents by choice or adopted Chinese children, where you stop by the Y to ask about the single-parent-family memberships advertised in their brochure. "There's no discount," the college student at the desk tells you with a broad smile. "That just means that we'll allow you to join even if you don't have a husband!" Your daughter will long after remember the Y as the place where she was rapidly yanked out the door by her mother.

It's a relatively safe town, and people generally approve of you. In fact, you find it unnerving how they seem to regard you as saintly for "rescuing" a child from an orphanage. They smile blankly when you try to explain that, no, it is she who has rescued you. You focus on establishing stability for your daughter, refusing to dwell on the dearth of relationship prospects in this place where it's winter seven months of the year and you often feel lonely and confined and panicked about making sure that you get tenure this time. The good news, though, is that you should be able to make ends meet, at least for now, even if saving three months of living expenses seems like a pipe dream.

PROTECT YOUR CHILD'S FUTURE WITH A LIFE INSURANCE POLICY.

Your insurance agent tells you that you need more life insurance. "Enough to cover your daughter's college," she says.

"Already covered," you say, because your job carries with it a tuition benefit for your dependents.

"And your mortgage," she adds.

"Why?"

She raises her eyebrows as if the answer to this question should be obvious. "So your house can be paid off."

"Can't the bank just take it back? I mean, I'm dead," you say.

"I don't know about you, but I just don't live that way." She peers at you over her glasses. "I take care of my debts."

"Well, yeah, me, too," you say. "But I'm dead."

"You still owe the money," she says.

"Even though I'm dead," you repeat incredulously, and when she purses her lips, you feel shockingly, wildly irresponsible, positively criminal.

But you realize when you perform an annual review of your employee benefits that another of them is a life insurance policy. Your credit rating will be safe beyond the grave. You're briefly relieved; now you can think about other things. You can't bring yourself to think about your death, or the possibility of leaving your child parentless, any more than you can bear to think about the day when she'll grow up and leave you.

REMEMBER THAT PSYCHOLOGICAL NEEDS AND MATERIAL NEEDS MAY BE ALTOGETHER DIFFERENT THINGS.

Unfortunately, even as young as five, your daughter feels different, out of place, in this town where she is one of a handful of minority students. You apply for some other jobs in more diverse places, leaving her with friends to travel to interviews. She cries at school, can't concentrate, throws up, clings to you when you come home. Your child, who spent her first year in an orphanage, is so traumatized by your absence that you withdraw from the job market and settle in, conflicted all the time about raising her in a place where she endures daily racial slurs that school administration mostly refuses to address.

You tell her that someday she'll go to college, where things will be different, and you hope that you're right.

START SAVING FOR COLLEGE WHEN YOUR CHILD IS YOUNG.

Better yet, since your new university offers free tuition to dependents, all you have to do is amass enough for four years of room and board, if you can convince your daughter that she wants to attend one of the university's campuses. So, even though your child is very young, you launch a long process of persuasion. As she grows up, you sing the praises of your university's main campus in Pittsburgh, which is a city, you point out, far more diverse. She'll be at a highly ranked research university where people will be more enlightened. You're undaunted that your college's main campus is a top-ranked public university; after all, your child is smart and precocious and proving to be an excellent student.

TAKE ADVANTAGE OF DISCOUNTS, DRIVE A USED CAR, GET RID OF CABLE TV, PACK SACK LUNCHES.

Except that every second of every day is tightly scheduled, and by evening you're often too tired to cook, much less produce frugal, nutritious meals. When the car breaks down, a ceiling collapses, the roof leaks, you try to disguise your descent into panic mode with big smiles and chipper tones. Your daughter absorbs your anxiety anyway. When you rock frantically back and forth in the La-Z-Boy chair you bought years ago to gently lull her to sleep, she crawls in your lap and pats you on the head. At six, she assumes the task of clipping coupons. You quickly discover that the majority are geared to large families. Buy three boxes of granola bars and get the fourth free. Get forty cents off two enormous bags of laundry detergent.

You don't want to crush your daughter's helpful spirit, but you just can't eat that many granola bars, and the detergent pods turn yellow long before you've worked your way through them.

You can't cancel your cable because you've never had it, and you resist obtaining a cell phone until your daughter's school can't track you down in an emergency. You rarely travel home to the Midwest. You drive a small used car in an area with six months of daily snowfall. Your daughter joins a YMCA gymnastics team—a fraction of the cost of a private club—at the Y that you once resolved never to return to. There, her teammates' parents, who complain about the expense of the team but have state-of-the-art smart phones and drive expensive SUVs, make fun of your car. You shrug and channel your dad: "I'll bet they're in a lot of debt," you tell your embarrassed daughter, "and probably aren't saving much for college." Nor do those other families, you point out, get to travel as much as the two of you do.

WELCOME WINDFALLS, EVEN IF THEY COME AT A COST.

You are always applying for grants, devising writing projects, and putting aside money that will allow you to travel, particularly because as your daughter gets older, it becomes increasingly apparent how vital it is to her identity to maintain connection to her Chinese heritage. You drive long distances to culture camps, New Year and Moon Festival celebrations, and Asian festivals. Fortunately, when your daughter is eight, you find a great babysitter who she loves to stay at your house when you accept a second part-time teaching job in a low-residency MFA program that requires you to travel to Kentucky for twenty days a year. This enables you to afford your first China trip, but what makes the second one possible is your mother's death one month before the crash of 2008. You've only been able to afford one visit with your mother every year, since she lives in Kansas, but you talk to her on the phone every week even though you know that she is too deaf to hear most of what you and your daughter tell her. After she dies, your brother says that if it hadn't happened when it did, the stress of the crash would have killed her. But even after the resulting financial losses and even after the money she left behind is divided between you and your brothers, you have a small college account for your daughter, the beginning of your own retirement account, and enough to cover the extra travel.

Much as you wish your mother hadn't fretted so much about leaving you money, much as you wish she'd enjoyed her last few years more, you are relieved to have this cushion. And then you become your own mother, nervous about every penny that you spend, fearing that there won't be anything to leave to your own daughter someday.

REMEMBER THAT YOUR CHILD DOESN'T HAVE TO GO TO AN ELITE SCHOOL TO GET A GOOD EDUCATION.

Though for years you've tried to convince your daughter that she should use your educational benefit to go to college in Pittsburgh, by the time she's thirteen, she looks at you skeptically and instead pores over college guides, circling the schools with the largest Asian populations. You're haunted by a persistent low-grade grief, knowing that to live the life she wants, your daughter may have to go far, far away, that your heart is going to shatter, that you will miss her terribly, and that you may not be able to afford to help her. But every day you are astonished that you get to be her mom, and you try not to think about any of this stuff because it makes you too sad to imagine all the ways that your relationship will shift as she inevitably separates from you.

But you take her on campus and city tours in Pittsburgh, hoping she'll fall in love with it, and gradually, to your relief, she does. "When I go to college in Pittsburgh . . . ," she'll begin sentences.

ENCOURAGE YOUR TEEN TO GET A SUMMER JOB AND OPEN A SAVINGS ACCOUNT.

By the time your daughter hits her sixteenth birthday, she has volunteered for a couple of years as a gymnastics coach, but now, thankfully, she wants a paycheck. You help her obtain a work permit and open a savings account. You're proud of her industry. She's a hard worker, an A student, a gymnast, a hurdler at her school, a yearbook photographer. She wants to play the violin. And with your own extra job, you can much more easily afford lessons and team fees.

Your daughter works a few months as a waitress. But she frequently suffers from fierce headaches and nausea and long bouts of fatigue. She begins to throw up daily and develops hives and swellings and ear infections. She misses weeks of school. Takes a leave of absence from work. The money that used to go to gymnastics goes to doctor copays. You wonder: *Do people without your resources just give up altogether? Or is this just what it means to be a parent? That you can't figure out how to give up?*

Your daughter often can't get out of bed. You'll visit twenty-seven doctors over the course of the next few years and get nowhere. No one seems to think that it's a problem that a teenage girl has lost her ability to function. She's diagnosed with migraines, depression, and then chronic Lyme, which is not recognized by the CDC or covered by insurance. You come to doubt all of these diagnoses, but only after you have spent thousands of dollars making exhausting twelve-hour round-trip drives to New York City to see a Lyme specialist. You eventually trace her issues, including severe allergies and tachycardia, to hyper-aroused stress reactions, a result of infant brain development in circumstances of neglect. You embark on another exhausting search for a specialist who can help her. Good thing college will be free.

That is, if she ever goes to college. Because she's essentially a high school dropout by the middle of her junior year.

This is not what you planned.

But you fight to obtain homebound tutoring, which with a doctor's order is financed by the state, and she squeaks through high school, mustering the energy to complete requirements but struggling with college application deadlines. You wonder if it matters. You wonder who's going to accept a student with a terrible attendance record who has barely completed the minimum requirements to graduate.

And then the letter arrives. After your campaign, all of these years, to readjust her aspirations, to plant in her the dream of going to the main campus of your university in Pittsburgh, with her once-stellar academic record so ravaged the last couple of years, she doesn't get in.

All day, you feel like you can't quite catch your breath. You have to go teach a class; you leave her sitting on the couch, staring off into the distance. You come home two hours later, and she is still sitting on the couch, staring off into the distance.

You offer hollow words. It's not her fault; she was always an excellent, conscientious student. Maybe it's too ambitious to try to move that far away just yet anyway. She stares into space and doesn't answer.

Soon after, she's admitted to Sarah Lawrence, a school with the same selectivity rating as the Pittsburgh campus that turned her down. Her spirits rise. On one of your trips to her specialist in New York City, you take her on a campus tour. Her hope and your despair swell in equal proportions. Here, she sees her chance to go away after all. But all you can think is that there's no way you can afford it.

On the way home, you hand her a paper listing figures: the cost of four years there ($280,000), the amount of her scholarship ($144,000), the amount you've saved ($40,000), the additional amount you anticipate contributing ($40,000), and that's if you both completely give up new clothes, restaurant meals, and summer trips. She'd have to come up with another $14,000 a year. You hold your breath, thinking about how Sarah Lawrence is six hours from home, way too impractical for a chronically ill young person.

She stares at the paper for a long silence. In it, you imagine a hysterical high-pitched sound of desperation only dogs can hear, the sound of dreams shattering like eggs cracking all over the floor.

Then your daughter announces that she'll be starting college at the regional campus where you teach.

Not her dream. Not even close. You are sad for her, but secretly also relieved by the savings, by knowing she'll be close by for a little longer, by your renewed hope that her health will improve and her dreams will soar again. After all, she feels well enough to attend the last two weeks of high school and the mandatory scholarship ceremony. You watch the same group of twenty students congratulated again and again for their achievements and you wonder about all of the other kids forced to be their audience. How many of them have fought illness or had to take care of younger siblings or work to contribute to their families or dealt with a million disadvantages and yet are still here, preparing to graduate from high school, their own achievements invisible? You consider the correlation between accomplishment, health, ethnicity, gender, and economics. You think about the prices paid by non-nuclear, non-white families.

You never expected to feel so relieved, watching your daughter walk across the stage at graduation. So proud just to see her reach a milestone you used to take for granted.

But she's not going to be able to afford a car, and there's no public transportation where you live. Finally, you give her your old car and buy your first new one ever, an SUV that will get your daughter to doctors' visits even in the winter.

PLAN TO PAY FOR COLLEGE THROUGH A COMBINATION OF LOANS, SCHOLARSHIPS, SAVINGS, AND PART-TIME JOBS.

These financial tips begin to seem less absurd when your daughter moves to the dorm five minutes from your house, which, because of scholarships and tuition benefits, is practically free. She still struggles with fatigue, but by the end of her first year, she has the grades and credit hours to be accepted to Pittsburgh, and she thinks that by force of will, she'll be well enough to succeed.

You push away your misgivings and help her move. Tuition is still free, but living expenses rise exponentially. She's sick all the time. She totals her car, can't get home from work because the buses stop running at 11:00 p.m., can't come home for visits. She drops down to a part-time schedule and can barely complete those classes. You worry and worry. You know she loves Pittsburgh, and her friends, and her sense of independence, but she'll be in college for ten years at this rate. The tuition benefit, which allows for twelve semesters, will run out before her education is complete. And you dread the idea of having to take out loans if she has no guarantee of health or the ability to pay them back.

ACCEPT THAT SOME FINANCIAL STRESS IS INEVITABLE. COPE WITH IT BY TAKING CARE OF YOURSELF: EXERCISE, DEVELOP NEW INTERESTS, MAINTAIN A SOCIAL LIFE.

Whenever you think you're going to crack open with stress, you write, you ride your bike, you focus on your classes. You make budgets, getting carried away, projecting costs for the next ten years if your daughter is only able to attend school part-time, and for the next twenty years if your daughter can't support herself. You have enough money for now, but you still panic, afraid that these scenarios will send you into massive debt.

You date for the first time in years. You get involved with a man who retired when, widowed at forty-five, he was faced with raising his children alone. At first, this endears him to you. Gradually you learn that he's a multimillionaire as the result of settlements related to his wife's untimely death, though he sees his financial status as an accomplishment. You come to find him controlling, critical, mercurial. He denigrates your accomplishments. Finally, you trade him in for a poor but emotionally supportive boyfriend who fixes things around your house. Money is not, after all, everything.

WHEN FINANCIAL WORRIES THREATEN TO OVERTAKE YOU, MAKE A LIST OF THEM. CHECK BACK THREE MONTHS LATER: MOST OF THEM WILL HAVE RESOLVED THEMSELVES.

Being constantly sick, your daughter is struggling to get through a science class. Her off-campus roommate has an alcohol problem, with phases of being mean and violent, but the landlord won't address the situation or let you out of the lease and you anticipate a huge drain of time and energy to find a new place and get her moved mid-semester. She's not making any progress on finding a new apartment for next year. You worry about the financial and psychological costs of repeating classes, and of leaving her in her current housing situation vs. moving her.

You look back at this list three months later. Nothing has resolved itself. The roommate's violent behavior has continued to escalate. Your daughter's stress and illness have left her incapacitated. She's not going to pass the science class. The landlord still won't address issues with the roommate or with mold and sewer gas. Your daughter has located a new apartment for next year, but her new roommates are taking forever to sign on to the lease. And you still have a stomachache trying to figure out how to deal with all of this long distance.

LOOSEN THOSE APRON STRINGS LITTLE BY LITTLE: TEACH YOUR CHILD TO BUDGET AND ENCOURAGE HER TO TAKE ON INCREASING RESPONSIBILITY FOR HER OWN FINANCES.

But how do you do that under the circumstances? Money and health are the subtext if not the text of every conversation. You miss discussions of books, politics, fashion, TV shows, friends. Texts ping in: she needs more contacts, another pair of glasses, needs to pay for allergy shots, her rent is due. Meanwhile, you worry that she'll someday have to come home and live with you in a town where she grew up socially isolated. You're terrified that she'll relapse and be unable to finish college. You work extra hours and then feel angry if she doesn't appear to appreciate your sacrifices. "I'm stressed," she'll say. "I have so much to do. You have no idea how much I have to do, Mom. Can't you call the doctor for me/pay the rent/mail me my favorite shampoo?" And you find yourself sending constant schizophrenic messages, like, don't go to the ER unless it's a real emergency. Call an ambulance regardless of the cost if it's a real emergency.

She comes home between semesters. The furnace isn't working right, the dishwasher is making a loud noise, her car is in the shop, you never have a break from work. "Will you cut me an apple?" she asks, as if you don't have a ton to do. Already, you're on each other's nerves. What is becoming of your intense, close relationship? She announces she wants to move to New York City.

"You don't really want to live there," you tell her at the pizza place with the large pans and small tables, so that when you get your pizza, there's no place to eat.

"Why would you say that?" she asks. "Why are you killing my dreams? You always do that. Like when you told me that I was a failure and would have to come back here to finish school."

"I never said that," you protest. "I said I couldn't afford to keep you in Pittsburgh indefinitely. I said I couldn't keep you there if you were only completing six credits a semester."

She glares at you. She refuses to hear what you're really saying, or maybe you just said it badly.

"I can take out loans," she says. "Everyone else has tons of loans."

"But what if you're sick again? You have to consider your future earning power." You think about parenting articles that say that sometimes, in trying to help your child, you instead impede them. You instead deny them the chance to solve their own problems.

But does that rule apply when your child has a chronic illness? Should you let her take on debt she might not be able to pay back? If you someday leave her money, will it all go toward debts?

As you face off at the pizza restaurant, as you worry about these cracks in your relationship with your daughter, you know, deep down, that this is just another recasting of the age-old collision between generations, the struggle of a daughter for independence, of a mother for respect and appreciation. You see your daughter's optimism as denial. She sees your worry as catastrophizing. And you're both a little bit right and a little bit wrong, but it doesn't matter because separation is necessary and no one ever has any control anyway, and you can only hope that someday she'll be well again, and that someday you'll be able to retire, and that if she ever has to move back home, you can avoid killing each other. That these fissures are only temporary.

You remind yourself that dreams shift, and that people adapt, and that you are lucky, better off than so many people, and that you've survived lots of things, and so will she. Including, if necessary, debt, right? But it still terrifies you.

Your daughter glares at you fiercely. You breathe a sigh of relief. A fierce glare means she hasn't given in to despair.

WE ALREADY PAID

The Frasier-Joneses

From: Student Financial Services (MFS) <mfs@███.edu>
Date: Thu, Jul 18, 2015 at 8:47 PM
Subject: ███ College Financial Aid
To: Sarah Frasier-Jones <Frasier-Jones@███.edu>

July 18, 2015

Dear Sarah,

Your financial aid has been determined and is available to view through your student portal.

Student Financial Services

On Thu, Jul 18, 2015 at 6:11 PM Sarah Frasier-Jones <Frasier-Jones@███.edu> wrote:

To whom it may concern at MFS,

I have received my financial aid award and my first bill statement, but it is extremely unclear how much my family is expected to pay. The first bill is over $14,000 (which is more than twice as much as my family was expected to contribute for the entire 2014–2015 academic year).

Is this number just one installment? Is it the bill for the entire fall semester? Or is it the balance we are expected to pay for the whole year? Regardless of which it is, may I appeal to have my financial situation reviewed and aid reconsidered?

I appreciate your help clarifying this for my family and me. It is vital that we know as soon as possible because my family is financially unstable right now and the amount we are asked to contribute is the factor which decides whether I will be able to continue my education at ▉▉▉ or not.

Thank you sincerely,
Sarah Frasier-Jones

On Thu, Jul 25, 2015 at 3:35 PM Helena Frasier-Jones <▉▉▉@gmail.com wrote:

July 25, 2015
To: Director of ▉▉▉ Student Financial Services
CC: ▉▉▉ President, ▉▉▉ College
▉▉▉, Dean of Admission
Re: Financial Aid Award for Sarah Frasier-Jones

Dear Gretchen Djokovic,

Our daughter Sarah is due to continue on with her education at ▉▉▉ in the fall of this year. She will be a sophomore. This year, as in the preceding years, we applied for financial aid from ▉▉▉ on the understanding that ▉▉▉ will meet the "full documented need" of the applicant. We have accepted the former awards granted with gratitude and we have made the necessary sacrifices, juggled our finances and increased our debt load in order to meet our end (as determined by ▉▉▉) of Sarah's college costs. It has not been easy and we have never felt that ▮▮▮ has in fact met our financial aid needs. This year the amount of aid granted to Sarah has been reduced drastically for reasons we cannot understand. We simply cannot afford to pay the bill with which we have been presented. The numbers we have provided to the college via income tax forms and so on prove that. We don't own our own home. We rent our home but don't have a lease to protect us. The nature of our work means that our income fluctuates. We have no tangible assets except a 2009 Toyota Highlander, our family car. We have no savings, stocks, shares, pensions or other hidden income. We have massive debt.

It has taken me (Helena, Sarah's mother) a good moment to sit here and compose myself enough to write to you and to ▮▮▮ College at large. I have really been thinking about the diligent and optimistic efforts that as a family we made for our daughter to take up her place at ▮▮▮. ▮▮▮ is meant to be a transformative experience. It is meant to open the doors to an exceptional education, to encourage leadership, to integrate a global perspective into the lives of students. That Sarah is at ▮▮▮ is a great achievement for her. She stands at many intersections of race, class, politics, culture and economy both within her mixed culture and mixed-race family identity and within ▮▮▮ historical occupation as an elite institution of higher learning. I know that she is not unique in this at ▮▮▮, that she forms part of a fabulous minority grouping at ▮▮▮. I have come to believe however that ▮▮▮ is not fully grasping, appreciating nor celebrating the radical and courageous presence of these students on campus. Their challenges are often not merely intellectual—in fact they are at ▮▮▮ because they crave intellectual challenge!—but also financial, social and cultural. The mental grit and resilience that Sarah at least has been forced into stringently developing just in order to meaningfully occupy space and to feel worthy enough to be in the room has been staggering. There is access to these spaces and then there is survival in these spaces. There is a massive gap between the two and students too often fall by the wayside. That is a great shame. It's a wrong that needs to be corrected.

These financial aid decisions taken by Student Financial Services have real impact on destinies; they change fortunes. In this second year of filling out the various forms and adding up and taking away, I have been thinking that it really feels inappropriate and an exercise in humiliation to continue to "demonstrate need" and to be forced into finding different and compelling ways to perform poverty year in and year out for the four-year arc of Sarah's college attendance. We did not create the brutal structures and systems that caused the staggering inequalities in our society and we are actively forced into negotiating it in order to survive, to find a way for our children to thrive. It is absolutely degrading. I cannot find a way to think about it without feeling an erosion of my dignity and self-respect and self-worth. Most people who are at our income level and below, with zero assets to speak of, are not going to suddenly come into great wealth over the course of our child's college career. And if we do, we are the least likely to lie about it. We are the most likely to invest with alacrity and pride in our child's education, which we have, which we do.

It feels as if all we do is knock on the door. The door opens a crack, just enough to slide into the room, but then it begins to close before we are able to enter that room fully. And so we knock and knock and knock some more. How are students who come from different backgrounds to the wealthy, white, dominant occupiers of privilege meant to embrace their unique strengths and intelligences and creativities if they are asked to demonstrate the opposite at every turn? If they are constantly asked to ask for permission and for access? How are they/we to break the real and punishing cycles of need and debt? How are they/we to demonstrate justice and equality? How are they/we to evolve and move forward into self-awareness, self-determination and freedom?

This is an urgent matter of equality, true inclusion, and recognition of value—of our daughter's value. And without a doubt, the value of other students, primarily BIPOC, who are struggling with and utterly exhausted by financial difficulties, who are striving to keep up appearances and critically, to keep up with their education and ambitions, who are trying to embrace their unique strengths and let their passions flourish. Instead of joyful integration, punishing processes like these require painful assimilation and the burden of it is shouldered by students like Sarah and families like ours, and like us. It is absolutely grinding. How are these decisions made holistically? It feels as if Sarah and our family are barely recognized let alone valued as an integral part of the ████ community. What are the goals for your financial aid programs? How do you open the door and hold it open?

How do you stop punishing bright minds and bright hearts for not being quite wealthy enough? It seems to me as if ███ as an institution has an opportunity for leadership guided by integrity in thinking about how to really invest in students who truly need and deserve proper investment, support, encouragement, celebration and mentorship.

When we tell people that our daughter goes to ███ College, the response is always one of admiration, awe and congratulations. We don't tell them that we don't really feel as if we belong there. We don't tell them of the extra-huge financial struggle it is for Sarah to remain there. We don't tell them of our caution in communicating with the college because we are afraid that she will lose her position there because we don't have enough money or that we might strike the wrong note. We don't tell them of some of the difficult issues she has faced there that are entirely to do with race, culture and financial power.

We do tell Sarah that she has choice and agency in her life and that she must keep moving forward with curiosity, intelligence and integrity; that she must trust what is happening in the moment and what is to come. We truly would like ███ to be a powerful and positive part of her journey. Please engage with us wholeheartedly in a way that demonstrates kindness and respect, empathy and understanding as reflects our entire interaction with the college and all the hopes that we had, and still have, for our daughter as she matriculates there.

We ask that the college review our application with a greater understanding of our situation and make an ethical financial aid offer that accurately reflects our ability to contribute and that does not drive us further into debt. This has certainly not been the case this year. It has been unbearably stressful.

Yours sincerely,
Helena Frasier-Jones
Samuel Frasier-Jones

From: Student Financial Services (MFS) <mfs@███.edu>
Date: Fri, Jul 26, 2015 at 3:27 PM
Subject: Re: Financial Aid & First Bill
To: Sarah Frasier-Jones <Frasier-Jones@███.edu>
Sarah Frasier-Jones
ID #█████

Hi Sarah,

Thank you for your email. Your award letter included a message that the
parental contribution for this year has increased from the prior year due to
an increase in income. If there is additional information that may not have
been considered initially in your file review, you are welcome to submit a
Review Request Form (attached). We will begin the review process after
August 15. Your mother recently sent an email with a request for review, so
we will add her letter to your file for committee review.

After review of your file and billing notification, you will need to complete
the loan acceptance/decline process (for the loans you were offered) on-line
through the portal for your loans to be reflected on your bill. This process is
completed by logging into the ███ portal with your ███ email address
and password, click on the SFS link, and access the drop-down menu in
the upper right corner to select "Aid Awards." At that point you are able to
complete the process. Additionally, you would be eligible for another $3,000
in federal unsubsidized loan for the year. If you would like to add the
additional loan, please send an email request to our office.

If you need further assistance or would like to set up an appointment
with a director to discuss your concerns and options for moving forward
financially, please give our office a call. Any of our advisors would be happy
to assist you.

All the best,
Grace Miller

From: "Student Financial Services (MFS)" <mfs@█████.edu>
Date: Fri, July 26, 2015, 5:02 AM
Subject: Re: Sarah Frasier-Jones, ████ ID #█████████, Review of Aid
Award
To: Helena Frasier-Jones <athena.lands@gmail.com>

Dear Mrs. Frasier-Jones & Mr. Frasier-Jones,

My name is Leonard Barrington and I am the Director of Student Financial
Services here at █████. The President has asked that I respond to the
concerns about financial assistance. Let me first say that our primary goal
is to be fair and equitable in the financial aid process. As it is true that
we say we are committed to meeting the full demonstrated need, we do so
by measuring the family's ability with the standard methods used for all
students. The increased family contribution for this year was concerning
on our part because it seemed to be a large jump from the prior year. We
can certainly work with the family to make sure we have all the facts. My
office will be sending Sarah the "Review Request" form so that we can get
a complete picture of all that is going on in your household. The two primary
issues that I can see for this year's change in aid is the substantial increase
in income from 2013 to 2014 (357% increase) and the reduced private
school costs reported on the CSS Profile application for this year. We ask
that you take a look at the Review Request form and submit it with a letter
explaining your situation so that we can determine if any adjustments are
possible. It might even make sense to send along your 2014 Federal income
tax return if it is substantially different than 2013.

Please know that I am scheduled to be out of the office for the next two
weeks and will not be able to respond to any follow up questions or concerns
during that time. I am happy to discuss upon my return if you feel that
would be helpful. Our Front Desk staff is able to set an appointment with me
after that time if you feel it would be beneficial.

Sincerely,
Leonard Barrington
Director
MFS

On Tue, Aug 6, 2015 at 12:06 AM Samuel Frasier-Jones <███@gmail.com> wrote:

Re: Sarah Frasier-Jones, ID #███████, Review of Financial Aid Award

To Whom It May Concern at ██████ Financial Services

As per Leonard Barrington's request in his email dated July 26, please find attached three documents regarding our daughter Sarah Frasier-Jones's financial aid award. The Review Request form, a letter explaining our particular circumstances, and a chart giving an overview of our household expenses.

We filed for an extension on our 2014 taxes until October of this year, so at this point we only have estimated numbers for our personal gross adjusted income. I have been in touch with my accountant and these numbers are close, however they will probably be slightly lower once a few remaining business expenses have been subtracted.

Thank you for your consideration.

Respectfully,
Samuel Frasier-Jones

On Tue, Aug 20, 2015 at 05:40, Student Financial Services (MFS) <mfs@██████.edu> wrote:

Dear Samuel,

We have begun to review your financial aid appeal but need some additional information. Can you please provide us with the following:

- 2014 taxes, including any W-2s and business taxes. If taxes have not been prepared yet, can you please clarify your estimated income for 2014? (The

Review Form reported different amounts in comparison to your letter dated 7/26/15.)

- The amount of one-time income in 2014
- 2015–2016 educational costs for your oldest child. How much will be paid by your parents?
- Amount of financial support of family in ▒▒▒▒ in 2012, 2013, 2014. Please list amounts separately.

Please let us know if you have any questions. I thank you in advance.

Best regards,
Gretchen Djokovic
—

▓▓▓▓ College
Student Financial Services

———————————

On Tue, Aug 20, 2015 at 5:23 PM Samuel Frasier-Jones <▓▓@gmail.com> wrote:

Dear Gretchen Djokovic,

— As stated in our letter our 2014 taxes have not yet been finalized. Attached here is a tax estimate as prepared by my bookkeeper.
— The 2014 income in the letter was minus tax. In the Review Form the figure represented gross income.
— There were three backdated one-time payments in 2014 amounting to $11,222. This amount may have to be adjusted to reflect payments that I in turn may owe collaborators per contract. Please note that our income in 2014 is the highest that our annual earnings have reached since 2000.
— Tuition for our oldest son for 2015–2016 is $22,460 (including a deferred payment fee of $500 and insurance in the form of a Tuition Refund Plan of $200). The full tuition is paid for by Samuel's parents. We pay for books, mandatory enrollment fees, athletic fees, extra tutoring, and any other educational costs approximately $1,500.

— Regrettably we have not been able to offer financial support to family in
██████ in the past 4 or 5 years due to our own difficult financial constraints.
The reference made to helping family in the past was to illustrate past extra
financial responsibilities. These are responsibilities that will inevitably have to
be shouldered again in the future.

We are concerned about the timing of the review process. We have already
incurred late-payment fees while we wait for a decision to be made as we
simply cannot afford to make the first installment fee of over $3,000. We
don't have that amount of money. However, we understand that Sarah will
not be able to register for classes until our payments are made. Is this true?
Is it possible that a good faith waiver be applied so that she can register
for classes when the time comes while we (you and us both) figure out how
to finance this college year? If we make a good faith part payment in an
amount that we can currently come up with would that help?

We have no further questions beyond comments and concerns made in
our previous communications (both written and verbally) and an ongoing
confusion as to how to continue to prove that we truly do need the need-
based aid ██████ promises its students. The process demanded by ██████
feels to be an inimical one inclined toward opacity and seriously tricky to
navigate.

We have answered all questions truthfully, transparently, and to the very best
of our ability even when it has felt invasive and unnecessary. However, we
trust it is to be for the very best for our daughter.

Please let us know if there is anything further required from us. We hope
that what we have thus far provided will result in a favorable outcome for
our daughter so that she can continue on with confidence in her tenure at
██████.

Best regards,
Samuel Frasier-Jones
Helena Frasier-Jones

———————

From: Samuel Frasier-Jones <█@gmail.com>
Date: Tue, August 20, 2015 at 7:22 PM
Subject: Re: Subject: Re: Sarah Frasier-Jones, █████ ID #████████,
  Review of Financial Aid Award
To: "Student Financial Services (MFS)" <mfs@█████.edu>
CC: Helena Frasier-Jones <athena.lands@gmail.com>

p.s. Just to reiterate that the income reported in 2014 was an exception—
because it was mostly from back payments—and even then we did not
make ends meet at year end because of historical debt and present, normal
ongoing necessities. Our income in 2015 looks like it will drop again to a
figure below that of 2014.

From Allison Warner, █████ alumna and member of Board of Trustees:

On Thu, 22 Aug 2015 at 11:31, Allison Warner wrote:

Hi Helena,

Thank you for talking with me yesterday. I understand your concern for your
daughter and was so sorry to hear about your frustration with █████.

I was able to connect with Abigail Hunt, VP for Enrollment, this morning.
Abigail is responsible for all aspects of admissions and financial aid. Abigail
was troubled to hear about your experience in dealing with Student Financial
Services and would welcome an opportunity to hear directly from you about
how █████ can improve interactions with students' families.

Abigail might also help by hearing more specifically about Sarah's life at
█████. President █████ and the College has made inclusion an important
priority, so hearing back from students and families about their lived
experiences on campus is an important way for us to learn as a community.
Abigail would know who on campus could take your and Sarah's important
feedback and improve our practices.

Please let me know if I can connect you directly to Abigail by email.

As for Sarah's financial aid, I understand that an appeal has been filed and that your case is in process. Of course, Abigail couldn't share any details but she did say that you should be hearing from ███ very soon about the outcome.

I hope I get a chance to meet Sarah on campus soon. I'm at ███ 3–4 times each year and have connected with several students from ███. It would be wonderful to meet her!

Best,
Allison

———

From: "Student Financial Services (MFS)" <mfs@███.edu>
Date: Thu, Aug 22, 2015 at 5:33 AM
Subject: Request for Review
To: Samuel Frasier-Jones <███@gmail.com>
CC: Sarah Frasier-Jones <Frasier-Jones@███.edu>

Dear Samuel,

The Review Committee has carefully considered your request for a review of Sarah's financial aid eligibility. I am pleased to report that the Committee did agree to adjust our calculations, and as a result have increased Sarah's ███ Grant amount by $10,247 for a new total ███ Grant amount of $55,406. To accommodate this additional grant, a portion of Sarah's spring federal work study has been switched to campus work. The rest of her award remains unchanged. We do hope this additional aid helps.

Best regards,
Gretchen Djokovic
—
███ College
Student Financial Services

From: Helena Frasier-Jones <athena.lands@gmail.com>
Date: Thu, Aug 22, 2015 at 12:37 PM
Subject: Re: Follow up to our talk yesterday
To: Allison Warner

Dear Allison,

I so appreciate your time and your patient attention and willingness to hear our story.

Yes, it would be great if you could connect me with Abigail via email. I would happily speak with her. In my communications with MFS re Sarah's financial aid, I had cc'd President ████ and ████ ████, Dean of Admissions. I didn't hear from either of them directly but my email was passed by the President to the Director of MFS, Leonard Barrington, who wrote me back and invited me to fill in a Review Request Form, which we did. It just went in circles basically back to the first person that I spoke to—Gretchen Djokovic.

We heard from Gretchen Djokovic this morning. Our financial aid has been increased by 10k which is a cause for celebration but it is by no means a sigh of relief for us! We are taking a breath to try and figure out a way to proceed forward. More personal debt, if that's even possible? Or keep knocking? It is truly exhausting.

I will forward to you the initial letter that I addressed to MFS and ████ ████. Please read, if interested, so that you can have a deeper sense of our process.

I've already told Sarah about you! She is very much looking forward to meeting you on campus! She loves Holland and is already inclined to think that you're her kind of people if you also love spending time there!

With appreciation,
Helena

From: Helena Frasier-Jones <athena.lands@gmail.com>
Date: Thu, Sep 5, 2015 at 09:44
Subject: ▮▮▮ Financial Aid Program
To: Abigail Hunt <ahunt@▮▮▮.edu>
Cc: Allison Warner

Dear Abigail,

Forgive me for emailing you again. As my mind is not at ease and I have
been continually thinking about college and the costs I wanted to reach out
to you one more time with some thoughts. I have cc'd Allison here because
I think it's important for a member of the Board to hear concerns from its
constituents as it were—or the parents thereof!

I want to state that I believe that it is exceedingly important for ▮▮▮
College to become clear, transparent and progressive in its Financial Aid
Program. As my younger child (senior in high school) is preparing to go to
college, we have been receiving all the usual brochures and information. A
cross-section of those colleges that interest him—Williams, Swarthmore,
Colgate, Brown to name a few—have exceedingly clear Financial Aid
programs and guidelines, whether they are need-blind or need aware. It is
clear whether there is an expectation that families take out loans or not.

Increasingly and by a majority (for the colleges that we are looking at) the
colleges have no-loan initiatives built in. There is *zero* loan requirement
and needs are met. Very specific figures of incomes and family size are
given as examples. There has been across the board an *increase* in loans for
families in need. The minimum family income where aid is automatically
and substantially awarded has also *increased* in keeping up with the cost
of living. Across the board our family falls well within that income bracket.
There is *more* aid awarded to students who continue on at the college
rather than *less*—this demonstrates commitment to and relationship with
their students on the part of the college. I have spoken to students and
admissions and financial aid officers at some of these colleges and the
feedback is overwhelmingly positive.

In comparison, the ███████ Financial Aid program is not clear. It is not progressive or responding dynamically to the needs of some of its students. It is static and opaque. Beyond that, there is a refusal to look at or acknowledge blind spots in its governance. Please, there is an opportunity here for ██████ to render compassionate, practical and just, equal assistance to ambitious young students. Let's really positively look at that!

Sarah is having a meeting with MFS today to see how much more in loans she can take out so that she/we can pay for her college costs this year. We are actively hoping that by the time she graduates, student loan debt cancellation will be a priority for the next administration. Beyond that, we are still in arrears with ███████ and do not know where we will find the money to pay the bills. Believe me, we are working toward it.

All the very best,
With appreciation,
Helena Frasier-Jones

From: Abigail Hunt <ahunt@███████.edu>
Date: Thu, Sep 12, 2015 at 3:45 AM
Subject: Re: ███████ Financial Aid Program
To: Helena Frasier-Jones <athena.lands@gmail.com>

Dear Helena,

I apologize for taking so long to respond; I have been traveling for ███████ the past week. We are well aware of the relatively small number of institutions that have reduced or eliminated loans or provided a guarantee of aid for families at certain income levels. Each institution is in a very different position; ███████ has a larger share of students receiving aid than the institutions you name as well as in almost all cases fewer resources per student. That said, raising funds for financial aid is one of our president's highest priorities, and we hope to be able to do more in the future.

We regularly review our communications in print and on-line, as well as our individual communications in an effort to provide a clear and accurate picture to students and families. We will include your feedback in our next review.

I do hope that Sarah's meeting with MFS was a productive one and that her semester is off to a good start.

Best,
Abigail
Abigail Hunt
Vice President for Enrollment
███████ College

From: Student Financial Services (MFS) <mfs@████████.edu>
Date: Thu, Sep 12, 2015 at 9:54 AM
Subject: Review Follow Up
To: Sarah Frasier-Jones <Frasier-Jones@████████.edu>

Sarah,

I met with the Review Committee to see if there was anything additional that could be done to increase your ███████ grant eligibility. Unfortunately, the committee determined that there is nothing further that can be done. The director Leonard Barrington has offered to meet with you to discuss the aid policy at ███████ and to talk about the different loans available to you. I would be happy to meet with you again to discuss loan options as well.

If you have any questions, please let me know.

Take care,
Rachel Exeter
—
███████ College
Student Financial Services

ABACUS

NEELA VASWANI

I

The waiting room. In the time-before-seeing-the-doctor, we pause like blanched cauliflower. We will pass through here again, transformed. Terminal or cured or better or worse. For now, there are surgical masks for the immunocompromised. A water cooler. Other waiting people, thirty, forty years our senior. The TV bolted to the wall blares game shows, court shows—never cooking shows. Food on TV, as nauseating as the real thing.

The waiting room is one of my work spaces. My work is caring for the patient, my husband. My work week is 168 hours, unpaid.

I am a snake swallowing its own tail: in a hospital, waiting to see a doctor for my husband while on hold with an insurance company waiting to speak to someone about having been to a hospital to see a doctor for my husband. Sometimes I practice deep breathing for forty-five minutes before speaking with a representative. Sometimes it helps. Sometimes we are called in to see the doctor and I have to hang up on the hold music, a piece I find myself humming in the shower on the days I am able to shower.

Administering his subcutaneous chemo injections and catching his vomit in a pink plastic basin don't rattle me as much as the financial weight of illness.

In a cloth satchel, I have a freezer-size Ziploc that holds our hospital bills. Each day we receive ten to twenty. When there are more than fifteen, our mailman, who serves our block and five others in New York City, has to twist the envelopes to fit into our 6-x-5-x-14-inch box. If I happen to see him, he places the bills directly in my hands. He is gentle as if he, too, understands their mass in a visceral way.

We have a lifetime limit of $1 million on our insurance. In health, this seemed opulent. In sickness: ruinous. The insurance company lists our balance toward $1 million on the bottom right corner of each bill. In the waiting room, before I call the company to review or argue charges, I take the sheaf of bills from my Ziploc and fan the bottom right corner. I have organized the bills by date so the increasing balance jumps like a cartoon as the papers flip against the tension of my thumb. The bottom right corner of the bill at the top of the stack reads $937,000.67.

We are both on my husband's insurance, a union plan. We are fortunate. The plan covers most of our bills. But my husband must make a minimum of $30,000 a year or we lose coverage. It is difficult to make $30,000 a year when you have spent four of the last five months in the hospital. My husband is an actor, a voice-over artist, a narrator. He must audition to land a job. He is a snake swallowing its own tail: a sick actor playing a well actor in order to get a job to keep his health insurance so he can continue being an actor who is sick but alive. Most of his work is now voiced, not on-camera. It is easier to sound than to look healthy. At least with acute leukemia.

One night with leukemia in this hospital costs $60,000. The day before we were released after a ten-day emergency stay. All the blood in my husband's body had turned to fat, a rare allergic reaction to a chemotherapy. His triglycerides went over 5,000, a number so high residents from other departments came by to take pictures. He nearly died. Again. It was Labor Day weekend, a skeleton crew, but our room was crowded with onlookers.

Now we are $62,999.33 away from hitting our lifetime cap. If we are admitted to the hospital one more time, we will lose coverage. The options then become bankruptcy, death, or both.

A nurse stands in the doorway between the waiting room and clinic. She is calling our surname. In health, it is not my last name, only his, but in sickness, it is ours. In health, people addressed us as a unit; in sickness, there is just one question: "How is he?"

I would like to be asked how I am, followed by a silence that invites me to answer. Though, in truth, I am too distanced from myself for an accurate response. There is not enough time to know. I am always thinking in numbers. How much time do we have? How much money? Dollars, cents, minutes, hours.

II

The first year of sickness. My husband and I have been together for sixteen years, since I was nineteen and he was twenty-two. We married twelve years after we started dating because I wanted to wait until everyone I loved could legally marry.

My husband was always the lifter, the carrier. Suitcases, garbage, laundry, the dog. A vigorous person in constant motion in many directions at once. He was a child actor with his own earnings that he learned to invest at the age of fourteen. In college, where we met, he paid for two abortions for friends whom he had not impregnated, bailed one friend out of jail, bought everyone breakfast on weekends, handed out packs of cigarettes. Taking money from him felt less complicated than taking money from parents.

His money made me nervous. I didn't want anything to do with it. Never a borrower nor a lender be, my mother had raised me. On my twenty-first birthday, he said, "No arguments, we're going on a trip." It was fall. He liked orchestrating surprises and implied we were headed upstate. But we boarded a plane for Bermuda and stayed at a shimmering resort. I could not get comfortable, tallying costs—including a bikini I had to buy in order to swim. I remember snorkeling for the first time, the blueness and joy. Riding a moped, hot in a sweater, feeling like I owed something I could never repay. Like I had been made small, lesser. I asked him to promise not to do anything like that again. He was so shocked and saddened by my reaction that he has kept the promise ever since.

For sixteen years, I considered money his and mine—or his and not-mine. I confused separate with independent. I thought if I didn't owe, I wasn't owned. I thought autonomy kept me whole. I valued time over money. Time to write, to wander. I took flexible jobs that didn't pay well. No credit cards. Haircuts twice a year. I followed self-imposed rules that made me feel self-sufficient. When we married, I let him cover housing, though I continued to split food and utilities for some years. The truth is, I could never have afforded to live in New York City on my own. I still can't.

But illness has turned me into the carrier, the lifter. He used to write the gym off his taxes, saying that as an actor, his body was his office; now his office is closed for remodeling with a high probability of demolition. And illness hasn't inverted who makes the money. When his agency calls, I dress him, tie his sneakers, haul him out of the building, down two avenue blocks to the subway, down and up the subway stairs. I leave him at the door to his gig or audition so it appears as if he has gotten there on his own. I weigh ninety-two pounds to his one hundred and fifty. Now, to keep us in money, my body is required. My time allows for money to be made. Just not by me.

I am on leave from two jobs as an adjunct professor and have canceled the tour for my second book that was six years in the making and hit the shelves four months after his diagnosis. None of that provided health care. I am worth more at home.

For richer, for poorer, in sickness and in health. We did not speak these words in any language in either of our weddings to each other (one in India with my family, one in Montana with his). I was so angered by the word *obey* that I rejected the traditional vows in their entirety.

It wasn't until diagnosis that we had a joint bank account. In sickness, I stopped attaching money to my pride and sovereignty. I stopped feeling diminished by his generosity.

I think now of his diagnosis as the start of our true union. Our equality.

We used money to purchase time with each other. To extend our present. Sickness declared us husband and wife. As long as we both shall live.

III

Another waiting room. The second year of sickness. I have not watched or read the news in weeks. In each corner of the room, elderly white men slump next to brown or Black female caretakers. At first glance, I could be one of the caretakers, except the white man next to me is my age and my husband. Someone has left a *New York Times* on the seat beside us and I read the headline: "Health Care Law Prohibits Lifetime Caps." The first words of the article: "Starting Thursday . . ." It is Monday. I lift the article up for my husband to read but do not let him touch the newspaper, as his white count is a decimal. I hold an image of President Obama in my mind and shower him with marigolds.

When my husband was first diagnosed, we went to our local hospital, St. Vincent's in Greenwich Village. In the hematology waiting room, I looked around and became frantic. Where were the rich people? The doctor had stains on his white coat. There was a mobile AC unit with a tube sticking out a window, and a leak in the ceiling dripped into a garbage can.

In sickness, follow the rich people. We switched hospitals. The new hospital had a courtyard and traffic circle. Valet parking. Gilt-framed portraits of benefactors. A café in an atrium with a banner proclaiming: Voted Best Hospital in NYC Fourteen Years Running! The elderly volunteer at the information desk wore a sable hat to fend off the wind coursing down the marble hallway whenever the automatic revolving doors welcomed another person.

There were clean coats on well-paid doctors.

We can enumerate the value of my husband's life in procedures and hospital bills. There is something demeaning about this. There is something clarifying about this.

IV

While living in the hospital the first few weeks of his treatment, I felt soft and ineffective: just a writer-academic. I watched the nurses and aides and PAs with envy—how their hands made useful things happen. One night, 3:00 a.m., about two weeks into our stay, I was awake on my cot next to his bed, watching his chemo and blood transfusion setup. I noticed that the nurse had, after checking his name and wristband, hung the wrong blood on his IV pole: type A when he was type O. She had come in with blood for both my husband and our roommate and mixed up the bags. I pointed this out; she apologized and disappeared for the rest of the night. Another nurse took her place.

After that, I saw my PhD training as transferable. My value bloomed. I relied on my skills as a writer, teacher, anthropologist. I viewed the hospital as a culture, and its staff as a people sharing a common system and language. I became fluent in Medicalese and kept a daily log of my husband's medications, blood counts, mood, weight, changes in skin color, amount of exercise, food consumed, etc. Doctors would ask me what his hemoglobin was on a particular day or year or when he had received IVIG or when he had A-fib or aphasia or which lobe of which lung had collapsed. I would go to my memory and then confirm with my notebooks. They trusted my eye and recordkeeping. This earned me nothing except my husband's continued existence.

Some of it came naturally to me. I did not have to learn how to stand immobile so he could sob into my hip for a few hours. I did not have to learn how to witness, in stillness and kindness, seventy-eight spinal taps, twenty-five bone marrow aspirations, radiation, chemo, countless MRIs, CT scans, X-rays, PET scans, EEGs, EKGs, bone densities, blood draws, transfusions. How to hide my fear and sorrow? How to browbeat him into eating hospital food, taking a shower, walking a mile from nurses' station to nurses' station? He never spent a day or night without me in the hospital and we were in there for nearly four of eight years.

But there were things I did have to learn—well and fast. How to accept that he might die. How to keep going when he didn't. How to flush, clean, and heparinize a MediPort and PICC line, how to tap an Ommaya, how to do sterile bandage changes for the immunosuppressed, how to set up and run IV antibiotics, magnesium, fluids, how to handle a neutropenic fever, how to stay awake and functioning for seventy-two hours in crisis.

Sometimes my husband would say, "Our hemoglobin is down." Or, "We're getting Vincristine in an hour." We resisted the divide of "sick" and "not sick" between us. Every night in the hospital, he wheeled my fold-up cot out of the corner where it lived beneath the wall-dispensed Purell. He used what was sometimes his last bit of strength to push down the two sides of my cot. He stretched the fitted sheet, folded and tucked the corners of the flat sheet, unrolled the sleeping bag, plumped and stacked the pillows, shuffled back to his mechanical bed that whirred like a vending machine and, once under his sheet, smiled at me and said, "I take care of you, too."

I'd help our roommates—mostly elderly, stoic, "I'm good, doc," kind of men. They never minded me because I kept myself small and quiet. We were separated by a thin curtain with one of three sad patterns. I heard their gas and vomit and weeping and diarrhea and snoring and prayers, and I pretended to be asleep or listening to headphones. I didn't use the patient bathroom; I cleared their meal trays three times a day so they wouldn't have to sit with the smell until the kitchen staff came full circle. I followed doctors into the hall when the roommate lied and said he had a good night. I told the doctors, "No, he didn't. He never stopped coughing and he told his wife he has an itchy rash on his legs. Pull back his blankets and look."

Is there a point at which the caretaker also becomes a patient? When we were not in the hospital, I had multiple appointments per week: acupuncture, physical therapy, psychotherapy. Sleeping on a hospital cot and becoming the carrier and lifter did not agree with my frame or psyche. In the third year of sickness, I gave my money to women to help my body. To keep me going so I could keep my husband going. Whenever I caught sight of myself in a mirror, I was surprised by the youth of my face.

V

In our fourth year of sickness, we became receivers. My mother- and father-in-law, who was sick with myeloma at the time, received monthly non-insurance compensation through an Aflac plan they'd bought years earlier. They gave that money to us. I spent it on food and cabs to get to and from the hospital.

For the five months we lived in Houston for my husband's bone marrow transplant, my father paid our rent in Texas while we paid our mortgage in NYC.

Because we accepted other people's money, I rarely asked for the kind of help I needed, day to day. His condition was so dire and specific. He wouldn't listen to anyone else. The few times I asked for help, I ended up comforting the person who visited. It was just more for me to do.

Maybe I didn't have people in my life I could count on. Maybe I was steeped in the gendered idea of managing everything myself. Whatever it was, not asking for help caused my body to break down further and cost us more time and money.

I am a chronic caretaker. It's a reflex from childhood. The only way I know how to take care of myself is by taking care of the people around me so that everything doesn't explode. My response to my husband's illness feels historical.

He did not have the choice to leave the hospital. I could have. I chose to stay there, with him. I chose to keep our home, our beds, our lives together. I chose to spend whatever time was left, with him, no matter the cost to myself.

"In sickness and in health" defines every couple. It just came for us sooner than most.

VI

The fifth year of sickness. We are home. He sleeps and I sit up in bed holding my knees and a small flashlight. I click it on every half hour and swipe the narrow beam across his nose to make sure he is not bleeding because he has only three platelets and it is Saturday and we do not go to the clinic for transfusion till Monday and I want to keep us out of the emergency room. Sometimes, in these hours of vigilance—wretched with loneliness, tender with peace—I think about what it would mean to be paid for my work. What am I worth, monetarily, in this situation? Night pay, weekend pay, double overtime?

Once, in health, I went with him to a voice-over job for a TV spot he'd already recorded; the ad had been running for months, but the item changed price so he was needed for adjustments. I watched him in the booth. He said the number "One" into the microphone. Just: "One." With three different inflections. "One, One, One." He made $500 in two minutes. That month, I made $1,000 teaching and put another $1,000 toward paying off my grad school loans by cocktail waitressing at a fondue bar four nights a week, 4:00 p.m. to 4:00 a.m. For a year, I smelled of caramel and cheese—a rank combination.

How much does a doctor get paid? A nurse? A janitor? A cook? A social worker? A therapist? Should a caretaker's salary be all of those salaries together? Who would or should pay? What is the value of a patient's life versus a caretaker's? Of a husband's versus a wife's? A man's versus a woman's? What I do doesn't make money but would cost us money if I weren't there to do it. What I do is life-saving and volunteer. I resent that the world works this way, but he cannot take care of himself and I cannot make us enough money.

I think about headstones in old cemeteries marked: WIFE. And nothing else. Not even a date. A timeless state. WIFE. Is caretaker implied in the word WIFE? Is it in HUSBAND? Is breadwinner? Those headstones used to enrage me. But maybe WIFE on a headstone is a radical reclaiming of the word. A simple show of appreciation and respect. There is no way to list it all. What a wife does. Just say WIFE. People who know will get it.

VII

Put the word *care* in front of the antonyms *giver* and *taker* and they mean the same thing in North America.

My husband spent my time. From age thirty-five to forty-three, he used my time, laid claim to it. We were advised not to do anything reproductive (we'd started trying two weeks before he was diagnosed) until he had been in remission for three years. Two weeks after his three-year date, he relapsed. Time is money, and, in time, eggs die. And when the doctors said it seemed reasonable to take the chance on reproduction, only money allowed us to have a baby.

We had banked his sperm the day before he started chemo, which enabled him to dodge infertility. Nobody suggested I freeze eggs. Nobody said years would pass. Because I was not the patient, insurance would not cover any of the IVF, necessary because I was then forty years old. They would not cover the yearly fees of his stored sperm, or the yearly fees for our eventual stored embryos. I still think of all the women for whom it hasn't happened or for whom it's unaffordable; I was one of them for so long. I think about women of the past, across cultures and continents, when none of this science and technology was an option. Childlessness is not a place you fully leave. Even if you end up with a child.

What I wanted to be taking care of was a baby. A real baby, not an adult one.

When friends complained about their tiredness as new moms, I wanted to scream. I was as exhausted as a new mother but without the joy. There was no guarantee we would ever grow out of this phase of life. And growing out of it might have meant only one of us was alive. And childless.

Our daughter was born in the eighth year of sickness. Now that I have a child, I can say with certainty that caring for a sick husband is more difficult than caring for a child. One is supposed to care for a child. As a young woman, one is not supposed to care for a husband.

Using money to have a much longed-for baby felt a bit like a con. At whose expense, I am not sure. What the disease took from us, money bought back. Another life with a price tag. It is an uncomfortable privilege I won't relinquish or regret.

VIII

The math of sacrifice. What I gave up (time, momentum, security, health, ability to earn, have sex, have a child) in order to keep him alive. The state of a woman is to wrestle with the math of her sacrifices. I saw and felt my mother do this: "Don't have children; they ruin your life." I would like to be free of this gendered math, open and full of x's and y's like algebra; it would be easier if it were a closed shape like geometry. Even now that my husband is more than five years past his relapse and considered cured. Even now that our daughter is eleven months old. Calculations of time and money, what's lost and gained, click through me like beads on an abacus.

What does a woman give? (Everything?) What does she take? (Not enough?)

My husband's bone marrow transplant cost $1.2 million, retail. Faced with that big a price tag, I think I would have said, forget it. I would have let myself die so other people didn't keep spending money on me and wearing themselves out. A practical ruthlessness. I am still not sure how I feel about having felt this. Somewhere between proud and frightened. Now that I have a child, I feel differently. A practical ruthlessness.

The day we heard that stunning price, my husband had the same low-grade fever he'd had since relapsing. We sat in a waiting room and he leaned into me, sweating, groaning. We had a quiet conversation about the expenditures of him staying alive—or, rather, having a chance to maybe stay alive. About how it costs a fortune to be fortunate. How the system has never been fair. In those moments, when he was closer to dead than alive, it was clear. He wanted to live. At all costs. If insurance wouldn't cover the entirety or most of the transplant, he wanted to borrow, sell, find a way.

My husband has always had a strong sense of his own worth. Maybe it is entitlement. Maybe fear, or a strong will to live. Maybe it's that he earns good money. Maybe it's bluster. Caretaking taught me my worth. It made me trust myself, my instincts. The ability to keep someone, something alive, out of love, is incalculable.

That first year of illness, I brought a pink vomit basin home from the hospital. Nine years later, our ten-month-old daughter dumped out the breast pump parts stored in that basin and put it on her head. She laughed. Said, "Hat, hat, hat," her skin and eyes gleaming with well-being.

I stay home with her; we don't pay for child care. My body again in service to another. This time, joyfully. My husband again lifting and carrying. In sickness and health, we are lucky. It is exactly what we want to be doing. Being with each other. Being with our daughter, instead of hoping for her to exist. To have and to hold. We look at her and see across time. The time before. Sickness and health. The time ahead.

ROYALTIES

TERESE MARIE MAILHOT

BEFORE THE book, I was poor. The other side of a welfare worker's desk kind of poor. In order to receive assistance, you have to be small and needy. I would make my case and yet not speak up for myself. The seat on the other side of that desk feels like silence. In order to break away from that place and such silence, I wrote a book.

The book did well enough that I see staged photos of its cover on influencers' Instagram accounts, next to cold brews or succulents, and I receive royalties twice a year that are enough to buy a vehicle with, or pay off debt, or support my family for a year. With my first royalties, I thought I could restore myself, or reconstitute all the things that had been stripped from me, after years of being without. I thought I could bring people back or keep them here.

I remember when the first wire came; it was $50,000. My husband and I just stared at our bank account.

"We're going to see Rhonda. We'll head out tomorrow," I said.

"Sure," he said, without reluctance. He knew how important my best friend was, and how sick she had become. She had been in the hospital for months by then and constantly messaged me to say she was feeling better, not to worry, and that she'd be out any day now. I was used to her being sick.

She had Crohn's disease and was always in and out of hospitals, taking treatments, sometimes steroids. The year before, she had reconciled with the fact she wouldn't be able to have kids because of the disease. But it wasn't a fatal disease, from what I could research. There was always the idea, in my mind, that she couldn't die from this illness, that its complications are rarely fatal. There was also the idea that something as good as $50,000 would rub off on my entire surroundings, and that things might be better for the people around me, for good.

We went to see her—my two boys, myself, and my husband—we all got in the car and drove fifteen hours to see her, from Indiana to San Antonio. During the ride, I looked up florists and planned how I would fill up her hospital room with flowers. The kids were excited to see her and were kind of glowing with a playful, joking joy between each other. My eldest was happy we'd be staying at Rhonda's house, because he loved her pool, and her husband, Robert, and her brother in-law Mike and niece Mia, who all lived there. Every year, my son and I would visit in May so the whole family could hang out for Rhonda's birthday. I was mostly excited about the idea of bringing flowers to Rhonda. I had been sending them monthly via online order, but they never looked as impressive as they appeared in the pictures advertised. I would finally have a chance to pick the flowers out myself.

Somewhere between Indiana and Texas, in the midst of the excitement, there came a small revelation, that I could do more with my money to help someone: Shawnee Inyallie, a Native woman who went missing close to the Indian Band I grew up on. I had seen her "missing" poster for a few weeks. The faces of missing women are always on my social media timeline. For Native women, we go missing at alarming rates, and experience sexual violence at a rate, in some communities, ten times higher than the national average, so our timelines are full of "missing" posters and news reports of violence against people we know.

Shawnee was twenty-nine and looked like a cousin of mine. Her cousins were my best friends growing up. That's how I came to see her poster. My friend Kristie asked everyone to share the poster, so I reached out that day to see if I could put up a reward to find her. Her family thanked me for the offer and directed me to the RCMP, the Canadian police in Hope, British Columbia, where she went missing.

When I called, the police were mostly unhelpful, telling me that I could make a poster myself to advertise the award, and that if they received a tip, they'd pass along my information to receive the money. During my drive, I made several calls, and my brother was able to make the poster, and within an hour we were up and sharing the news of the reward. It was liked and shared more than a thousand times, and it gave me a lot of hope along that drive that maybe money could solve problems like these.

Maybe money, and placing a monetary value on a woman's life, could help find that woman, and things could be different with the more money I made.

We stopped at a hotel, and I watched as the shares grew. I slept easy that night, imagining tomorrow would be good for the kids, that a woman might be found, and I let myself be a little naïve. I didn't think about the danger in naïveté, when my whole life I had been aware of it. Something about having money made me less sharp—duller and simpler.

"Do you ever get survivor's guilt?" a Native woman asked me in Duluth recently, at a book event. I had just read for the Indian college there, and she was part of a group of women, the Kwe Pack, who are runners and all successful women in their own rights. The women had become artists and worked in politics, and they all told me similar stories about how guilty they feel for having things in life. Even having an iPhone brought them guilt. I understood, because we see so many people who don't survive. It's hard to enjoy anything when you think about the people who won't get to know a life away from pain or struggle.

My answer was complicated. Their answers were complicated. We all want better for ourselves, for our children. But we leave people behind. We can't take care of everyone. Our mortality rates, the statistics over our heads, and the burden of a history of colonization weighs on us.

Rhonda experienced a different life from me. She was white. It always made us laugh that we got along. I am hypervigilant and scared of white women. They usually hurt me, or hurt my money, or put me in vulnerable positions at work. I've learned to avoid them, and sometimes resent them. It's hard to say that to you, because you don't know me well enough to like me, or see beyond the worst of me. I can tell you, though, that Rhonda changed people for me—all people.

When I met her, I was an editor for the student paper at a community college. It was a slow crawl to a life in academia. I had received my GED a couple years before. I had to work hard to understand the function of grammar, or how to construct a sentence, and I didn't spell well. It took all of me to learn it and become an editor. She came into my tiny office at the college with her husband, Robert. He didn't speak. She did.

She was blond, blindingly white, pearl white, with something illuminated inside of her. Blue-eyed. The things I am not. I resented the lightness of her. She smiled when she spoke. Asked perceptive questions, on behalf of Robert. She was barely nineteen. She wanted Robert to write for the paper, for college credits. He stood silently, smiling in a pleasant way, pretending to listen to me while Rhonda took notes.

His first assignment was a baseball game. He was supposed to cover the opening game. When Rhonda sent me the story, I knew she wrote it. I line-edited it, harshly, and sent it back. She came to the editing room for real-time feedback. Back and forth, we fucked with each other. Until we saw the ambition in one another. We saw the desire to be better. She was living on her own because her home life was difficult, her relationship with her father was nonexistent, like mine—her father was part-Indian, like mine. He was a drunk, abusive, like mine.

I didn't find this out until later, but I sensed her hard life. At the time, I was confounded by her bubbly nature. I didn't think it was possible to be so positive and strong. And she spent a lot of her time trying to show me that things could be better, and that a positive attitude wasn't unnatural. It was a solution in her mind, I think.

But the part of me that had been a foster kid, who didn't like to make eye contact, who was on welfare, who had to fight for things, like bus tickets home, or food, or a bed—that person was afraid of her. The part of me who was radical, like my mother had been, didn't believe a white woman could understand me. The person who was a child, who invited a white girl to my house once, and the girl called home immediately—that child was scared, inside of me. But I relented.

I had to let Rhonda love me. She moved to San Antonio as I was finishing up at community college. She sent for me. She visited me. She called. She messaged me. She was like me, in that she took care of multiple people. During this time, she encouraged her husband to become a nurse practitioner, to go to school, and she moved her niece and brother-in-law in while her sister was in rehab, recovering. Rhonda wanted to take care of everyone.

During this time, I was taking care of my eldest son, being a single mom, helping out family back home when I could, sometimes receiving help myself. It was hard, but necessary, to live away from my community, and Rhonda was always there. We struggled together, me talking about moving away from my rez to make something of myself, and her talking about how difficult it was to be something like married, when she had never seen a good marriage in her life. She sent birthday gifts for me, and my son.

With this love, she changed me. I believed in her, and she told everyone I was a writer. Even when I wasn't.

My husband and kids brought her flowers and candy arrangements when we reached San Antonio. When we got to her room, she looked worn down but happy, forty pounds lighter than I had seen her before. She had lost hair, but her skin was still bright, shining from the inside out. She told me she would get out of the hospital tomorrow morning, and I think she had convinced or begged or demanded the doctors let her out so I wouldn't have to be with her in the hospital for longer than a day. Her husband thought that, too. She never liked me seeing her sick.

The next day she was wheeled into her home. She saw her house filled with flowers and a banner that said, "YOU ARE MAGICAL" in her living room. She didn't want to stay home, so I took her to get her nails done. She insisted on going to the aquarium next. So, I took her and we even had something called "a sloth encounter." I watched her stand up from her wheelchair and walk slowly toward the sloth, then feed it. She insisted I do it, and I was completely repulsed.

"You have to," she said. "Imagine if you missed this opportunity."

We stayed a few days, and she ate less each day. I brought her food from places she liked, but all I saw her eat was a pizza crust. That was all I saw her eat in three days. I look back and can't understand how I thought she would recover, or that things would be okay.

And still, there was no word about Shawnee. I slowly started to sink into myself and then we packed to go back home. We left in the afternoon and told Rhonda we'd be back soon. Thirty days later she passed away from an infection.

Money doesn't bring people back, but I thought it could keep some people here.

When I offered a reward to anyone who brought information about Shawnee's disappearance, I felt good. I imagined someone would want the money. I imagined that the problem with Indian women going missing was that people think we have no value, but even when you put value on us—they don't care. We may not be invisible anymore, but they still want us to disappear.

Shawnee was a mother. She was without a home. People might say homeless, but the word feels too definitive for her as a person, too limiting. She was a woman living in Hope, British Columbia, without a home. She was poor, like I used to be, before the book. She was a lot of girls I know. Her leaving the world felt definitive, and final. It felt like a horror story actualized—breathing next to you at night.

When she was found in the Delta River, her brother said she would have had to walk two hundred kilometers in the wilderness to end up in that river. He couldn't understand how the police didn't find it suspicious. But that's how the police labeled her death: not suspicious.

It hurts to tell this story to you.

I've been on highways, on busses, in strangers' homes, and I've begged for help before. That felt final, too, but for me there was always one small act, or one internal voice that saved me. I kept running away, into myself—into success.

I tell my students, people I read to, Native women, "This world and these rooms might not have been designed for you, but you have to walk into the room and take the knowledge you need. Walk out with it. Don't take anything else home."

I knew I could take what I wanted from the world. I knew I couldn't be stopped.

But nobody told me how much it would hurt. You can save yourself and your babies, but beyond that—everything feels uncertain. Like a shoe about to drop. All I can do is remember what I received in life beyond the money.

Things like my mother standing by the river, telling me I had power. She put down tobacco for me, she prayed things would be better for me than things were for her. Those prayers might be what saved me.

But money can't bring her back, my mother who ran her hand through her hair like she was pulling it out. She died ill. She died tired. She worked to the point she neglected herself, and me—and still, we didn't have much food in the house.

When I got the call that Rhonda died, I was at my mother-in-law's house. We drove home. I couldn't stop crying. When we got to my door, I checked the mail. Letters from my mother to my mother's best friend, Geri, were in the box. Geri had sent them, apropos of nothing. The letters were dated 1995, and later. They talked about sisterhood and love, and fighting for better things; about the need for money, but the resentment of it.

I don't look for reasons in the bad. Mom said colonization was like an abuser in denial. I started to think about how a lot of things in my past and future are not in my hands. Mom told Geri that she was worried about rent, and in the next letter, a relative put some cash in her hand and fixed the issue. This, she said, was life and community. I think about her teachings.

Some people's lots are bad, because of colonization, injustice, bureaucracy, because of hatred—because there's nothing more dangerous to the colonizers than us with cash in our hands, with food, with rent money, with education, with knowledge. It's why, when the royalties came, I gave my brother money for rent, before I left for San Antonio. With the second royalty check, I got my friend out of eviction. I told her she could do anything.

I don't look for reasons in the bad; I look for the good shoe, that comes every time, after every death, after every bad shoe, every sadness and hunger. That's what I have now, that—and royalties.

THERE COMES THE TALK OF MONEY

MARNIE MASUDA

I BECAME a widow suddenly, twice, so I suppose it gives me the dubious authority to tell people things they hope they'll never need to know, but chances are, they will absolutely need to know. Things like this: not long after the horror of the news, the phone calls, the awful preparations, the questions, the overwhelming wave of people and food, there comes the talk of money.

If there is life insurance, there is a moment of relief. At least we will be able to keep the house, and eat, go to the doctor, and hold our heads up when we run into concerned acquaintances in the grocery store. But I remember, in the very early days, before I knew anything about my late husband's insurance and retirement situation, a well-meaning friend offered to help me organize and get a grip on my new financial reality.

She sat on the floor of what was now my office, brows furrowed, poring over our bank and credit card statements, mortgage papers, utility bills, health and car insurance policies, and my paycheck stubs from my job at the local college. She sat for a long time, asking clarifying questions and sighing ominously. When she'd finished, she came and sat next to me on the couch. She held my hand and stared at me for several seconds, her eyes glassing over with tears. Finally, she sighed and said, "Well, there's always the food bank."

After the memory of standing in my driveway, listening to a stranger sitting behind the wheel of an unmarked cop car tell me that my husband had died, and the visceral memory of the sound of my children's pain when I told them their father was gone, the "Food Bank Moment" still holds serious sway in my imagination. Even now, five years later, when I recall my friend's words, my heart freezes and there I am again, sitting on the blue couch my husband and I chose together just before our daughter was born. The wind whips through mango trees outside, the late afternoon glow slants through the jalousie windows. I am suddenly a single parent of two, and poverty is a clear and present danger.

Widows with young children to raise—mine were eleven and twelve years old when their father died in a car accident—identify money as their second greatest concern, after their children's emotional well-being. A half century after Betty Friedan's *The Feminine Mystique* unmasked the postwar myth of the happy housewife, a heck of a lot of us are still living an insidious version of that myth: women as the secondary breadwinners and primary parents. We have, intentionally or not, internalized the paradigm of "staying home at least for the first few years" as an (often unrealistic) ideal, even though the data to support the long-term benefits of a multiyear work caesura are ambiguous at best. What's more, careers in which the occupational demands far outweigh and outpace the size of the paycheck (i.e., nursing, teaching, social work) are still mostly dominated by women, and I was one of those women.

I was also one of those women who thought I'd always have this other person by my side, so I didn't pay much attention to the piles of files under the desk: cable bills, homeowner's insurance, 401(k) statements. If I learned one thing early on, it's this: you need to know all the things—all the user names and passwords, which bills are due when, what's up with all those credit cards in the junk drawer in the office, how to access all the "Tax Stuff" behind the "Christmas Stuff" in the basement—because if you don't arm yourself with all this mundane, quotidian knowledge, you'll likely find yourself in a heap on the basement floor, amidst scattered love letters, baby shoes, and leftover wedding invitations, sobbing uncontrollably, smelling the inside of his favorite ski cap you've pulled out of the "Winter Stuff" box. If the unthinkable happens, which it will sooner or later, you'll need to take charge of your financial life as gracefully and stoically as possible.

You will need to know that you are not responsible for any credit cards issued to your spouse, even if you have a card with your own name on it. They might send you scary-sounding letters, but you can cross this one thing off your worry list. How did I learn this? A woman from the credit card company told me. "Now listen here, honey," she drawled, "you're gonna get letters that sound like you need to pay these bills, but you don't pay them any mind, okay? You have other things to worry about."

Countless women I will never meet, from financial institutions I can't even remember, stayed on the line with me until seemingly insurmountable issues were put to rest.

I learned this, too: when it comes to banks and creditors and insurance companies, and the IRS, call back and call back and call back until you get a woman on the line. A few good men out there were patient enough to stay on the line until I answered all the security questions correctly or figured out the four-digit code to close an account, but mostly they waved me off.

"I'm sorry, ma'am, we can't refund you for the flight until we get the death certificate. That's just our policy."

"First, let me say I am very sorry for your loss, but I am sorry to say, this death certificate is in French. We can't accept a death certificate in a foreign language."

"But my husband died in France."

"I'm sorry to hear that, ma'am, but there's nothing I can do."

These bureaucratic vortexes made me want to give up and hide under the covers forever, but I didn't. Listen: there is always, always something they—and you—can do.

My second husband died in France when he fell off the Dutch barge we were in the process of buying. He was sitting outside, working late. All we heard down below was a loud crash on the deck. I climbed up the

ladder immediately, expecting to find him sprawled on the slippery surface. He was gone. Silence. Nothing. I will live with the pain of his absence
forever, and the almost unbearable fact that we will never know how he fell
into the cold, swiftly moving river.

The shock set in again, but this time it sunk in even deeper. I felt
utterly numb, frozen in complete disbelief that this could happen twice.
I had serious business to attend to, however, and all I could do or see
was the task immediately in front of me: get the kids home quickly and
safely.

We made it home on the day we'd planned to, but without him. That
was the most surreal part of it. With my kids and his seven-year-old
daughter huddled by my side, I explained to the agent at the check-in desk
the reason our party had diminished. He had to check with his supervisor,
who asked me for proof. I pointed at my face.

Shortly thereafter, once again, came the talk of money.

My husband had not anticipated his tragic, early death. It was impossible, of course, completely unthinkable. He had recently taken on a new
job and let his life insurance lapse. I had invested my entire retirement
fund toward the down payment on the boat. We intended to rent it out
in the winter months, spend holidays on it, and share it with friends and
family. We'd drawn up a business plan and calculated to the penny how
our two incomes could cover the expense of owning and maintaining
this historic vessel. It was a new, fabulous adventure for us, but when he
died, there was absolutely no way I could buy that boat. I never wanted
to set foot on it, of course, but there was also this frigid fact: I could not
afford such a venture on my own. The investment was based on the two
of us—on our incomes and the deeply held belief that we had many years
ahead of us.

These types of hopeful presumptions are beautiful, but they are risky.

The woman from whom we were buying the barge did not return a
dime of my substantive deposit. I had lost my husband, and this woman
had made off with my entire savings. Two years later, I am still waiting for
the French court to settle the dispute. The ongoing struggle to recover at

least a portion of the deposit keeps the wound fresh. It entails trips back to Paris, spending money to get money, but I know I can't give up.

I tell this story not to make you feel sad, although it is very sad, and not to make you afraid to dream big, because big dreams get us up in the morning, give us hope, and bind us to one another. I tell the story with the hope that you will read it and consider how strong you are. I am still here. My children are still here. We are a bit worse for wear, yes, but we are okay. And you would be, too.

One afternoon, amidst countless calls to recover passwords, close bank accounts, and prove my identity again and again (when I barely even knew who I was anymore), I found myself on the line with a customer service agent in Delhi. She took the time to dig in deeply and help me recover the password to my business email account, when my entire livelihood depended on it.

"May I put you on hold while I look into this further?" she asked.

I worried and waited. The "on-hold" music made me feel sadder and more alone. Finally, she came back, and in a calm, lilting voice, told me exactly what to do.

"Okay, now I want you to refresh that page."

I refreshed.

Miraculously, after a full week of log-in fails and frustrating, fruitless calls, I finally saw my name appear as Account Administrator. A tsunami of relief washed over and through me, and I began to cry.

"I'm sorry," I quavered.

"You don't need to be sorry," she said. "I understand."

"Thank [sob] you [sob]."

"Remember this," she said, "we are not just survivors, Mrs. Masuda, we are warriors. You are a warrior. You are going to make it through this."

When she said "we" I knew she meant "women."

I think of her words, and of her, every time I start to wallow in fear and doubt. I imagine her in that big city in India—sometimes she is in a crowded, brightly lit room filled with endless rows of half-cubicles, sometimes she is in a modern apartment, sitting at her dining room table, helping her children do their homework. Sometimes she is in a makeshift dwelling, lying on a dirt floor next to her baby, having made just enough to feed them for a day. There are infinite possibilities of where and how this woman lives, but it doesn't matter. I will never forget her, and I repeat her words back to her.

"You are a warrior. You are going to make it through this."

After the memorial service and the scattering of ashes, after the parade of people and casseroles and plates of sashimi, after the sickly, sad smell of incense and drooping funeral flowers, after the wails of my sweet children, after the numbness and the vomiting, I looked in the mirror and there I was—still me, still Marnie. Yet something had shifted. The difference materialized in the area around my mouth, and just behind my eyes. This Marnie, the after Marnie, had exactly zero time for any brand of bullshit. I needed to be okay, and I needed my kids to be okay, and I needed it to start right now.

I was now the only adult in the room, and I had to learn about revocable living trusts.

Many people think wills and trusts are for rich people, or old people, or austere, gloom-and-doom types. That's what I'd always thought. It costs a bit to have a will or trust drawn up by an attorney. It's a disquieting task. Who the hell wants to walk into an office and spend an hour or more facing mortality head on, right after work, in the middle of a normal week?

Maybe later. Maybe, like, twenty years later, okay?

I certainly would never have hauled myself in had fortune continued to smile on our family, never imagining the bell might toll for any of us any time soon.

My friends made an appointment and escorted me to the small, tidy office of a local trust attorney. She walked me through the process of sorting out my personal and financial affairs. The point was to make sure I had a clear idea of what I had and what would be locked in trust for my children. The trust also contained specific instructions in the event of my death. What was now mine? What would happen to my children? Did I have enough to provide for them?

Did I hyperventilate when I considered the behemoth reality that I was now their only parent?

Indeed.

Was the whole process almost too much to bear?

Sure.

Did I feel way safer and more secure when, a few weeks later, her assistant handed me a hefty pleather binder, which somehow reminds me of Mr. Darcy in *Pride and Prejudice*—its surface stately and standoffish, its contents imbued with love and courage and, yes, trust?

Absolutely.

When we enter widowhood, we mourn the lost best-hugger, the lost spooner-in-bed, the lost keeper of our deepest secrets, the lost inside-joke-getter, the lost school band concert date, the lost mutual knowing-glancer across a crowded room when it's time to leave. When we wake up sobbing, we cry out for the person we called from the market to see if we should pick up a bottle of wine. If there are children, we cry for their sudden fatherlessness, for the family they knew as permanent suddenly vanishing into the night sky, a fire lantern extinguishing. We cry for the other death: the death of the third entity we created with our spouse, an unseen but omnipresent golem lovingly molded from the intimate clay of coupledom.

We yearn, too, for the economic partner who helped keep the whole business chugging along, the one we asked to transfer money, or reminded to get the taxes done, the one who told us to slow down the spending for a while if we wanted to take that summer vacation. Suddenly we find ourselves left alone. We can't help but feel disoriented, rudderless. If ample provisions and preparations have been made, there is a foreboding sense of responsibility, the fear of losing everything. The avalanche of unsolicited advice. The invasion of privacy. The impolite questions.

Stories of suitors who prey on "wealthy" widows run across your radar.

I discovered throngs of peripheral acquaintances waiting in the wings and the rafters. In they swooped, masking their judgment and gossip as sympathy and concern. These wing-waiters shake their heads in dismay disguised as pity, particularly if a widow dares to move through her grief and allow herself some happiness. A widow may stop to chat with a colleague, for instance, and notice the woman's eyes wandering up and down—assessing the widow's earrings, bracelet, handbag, and shoes. The colleague may offer a compliment steeped in toxic innuendo: "Well, don't you look stylish?" Gone are the days when a widow was expected to exclude herself from society, hide under a black mantilla, weep often (but not in public, please), worry a simple set of pearls, weak, undone, vulnerable; but the traces of such protocols and tropes linger, nonetheless. Widows are supposed to suffer endlessly, not move on. And sometimes we believe this ourselves.

Genuine compassion and empathy, on the other hand, are welcome salves, granted at random from the likeliest and unlikeliest of benefactors. One day I make a day trip to Oahu for work. The woman behind the desk happens to be the person who handed my husband his rental car keys several mornings a week for many years, a hearty local woman with a stoic, intimidating air about her. She looks at my driver's license, recognizes the name, asks how my husband is. "We were just saying we haven't seen him for a while," she says. When I tell her he died, she dissolves into sobs and embraces me. "No! No!" she wails. "We love him! We love him!" We hold each other tightly, for a long time, and allow ourselves to cry, in the gray Daniel K. Inouye International Airport parking garage at 6:30 a.m. on a Wednesday, while a line of tightly wound businessmen forms in front and behind us, but we don't care.

Moments like these help me move through seemingly endless money issues, mounting heaps of bills and tax forms and insurance notifications, always worried there won't be enough for college tuition and retirement, terrified I'll mess everything up.

I hopscotch along the path, from tolerable to serene, sometimes all the way to nearly joyful. Somewhere along the way, I've come to think of my widowhood as a mysterious, unsolicited gift, wrapped in thorns, bound with agitated cobras.

I'm afraid of it, but I unwrap it nonetheless, slowly and gingerly. Over weeks and months, a new resourcefulness emerges from the place in my chest that hurts the most. I bewitch the writhing cobras of my grief. I hold them, and they entwine me in a tight embrace that sometimes feels like love. I untangle the brambles, branch by branch, every day a little closer to discovering who I have become.

COME FUND ME

POROCHISTA KHAKPOUR

ON AND off since 2012, I have been asking strangers for money. Some friends, too, but mostly strangers. It feels like begging, this particularly modern and somewhat acceptable form of panhandling, but it's online and it gets a fancy name: "crowdfunding." Both stints were long and at the urging of others. Both times it was incredibly hard for me—I was a kid who never wanted to ask my parents for money, much less people I didn't know. But both times, I would have died without it, so when life and death are on the table, you do what you gotta do.

The first experiment in crowdfunding happened in 2012, at the urging of a friend, and former students, and another chronically ill internet friend. Over months they had watched me deteriorate from a mystery illness—the root of which seemed to be a black mold infestation in an apartment I was given in Germany while on a fellowship stint—and so here and there, over and over, they'd mention that I really should turn to the internet for help. I'd been active on the internet almost all my life, and it's been no secret to any-one who has ever known me that I never have had any money. I don't come from it (my Iranian American family lost everything on the way over), and I've never acquired it (I graduated from college just before a major stock market crash in 2000, and then 9/11 happened—plus: I'm a writer).

I kept waving off the suggestion, mostly because I could not imagine anyone would do this. I had donated to others the few times I felt I had money, but somehow, especially as I was without diagnosis, I could not do it. Once I received a diagnosis—Lyme disease—I still felt like an impostor asking for money. But eventually, one sweltering summer day in a café in Los Angeles, when my body felt like it really could not hold on, a friend told me we could not leave until it was completed. Friends and students had already started it: it was simply waiting for me to put aside my pride.

With shaking hands, I entered my banking info on a site I did not know well, called GoFundMe, and hit Send. I avoided my email for a good day. The text, partially composed by others, read:

Dear friends,

*A few weeks ago, after months of going to doctors and hospitals,
I was diagnosed with late-stage Lyme disease—either a relapse of
a condition I believed I was treated for in 2009 or a brand-new
infection (nature-lovers never learn!). I was hospitalized in Germany
for several days in March (where I had been a guest professor) and
then at Cedars-Sinai in May and nobody could figure out what was
wrong with me.*

*After going on all sorts of medication regimens for the wrong
diagnoses, a very specialized test revealed I have Lyme (these
Lyme tests alone cost $2,000). I have been mostly bedridden for
the last months (though been fighting this) and things are rapidly
advancing—I am now having extreme trouble with my digestive
system (can't swallow solid foods properly) on top of other problems.
I'm trying to afford the type of IV antibiotic therapy that this
condition now warrants and to move to a city where I can be properly
treated by an LLMD (the one recommended is $280 an hour). Right
now, I am most worried about my old hospital costs—the bills are
pouring in and the financial departments are not sympathetic.*

I have nearly $20,000 of bills from ER visits and hospitalizations

and alternative therapies and we've JUST begun to understand my
diagnosis, meaning the costs won't end soon. As I've been unable to
take full-time work—and unable to lean on my family to fund this—
I would greatly appreciate if you and yours would consider donating
and letting others know, too. I desperately want to make it past this
and get back to the swing of things—but I currently don't know how
to afford recovery.

It went off to the internet. Within minutes, there was activity apparently—
I could not look at it!—and some friends went so far as to send it to the
media. One day after it launched, Carolyn Kellogg wrote about it in the
Los Angeles Times. I'll never forget this line: "A novelist starting out is
a peripatetic creature, moving from one short-term position to another
while trying to complete her own creative work. And as such, healthcare
options are often intermittent and expensive." It almost made me believe
in me. I was still astounded when the campaign grew to 243 shares and
raised $15,901. It seemed the more people donated, the more people
wanted to donate. Within weeks, with renewed confidence in my future, I
was off to Santa Fe for a grueling six months of medical treatment.

For six more years, I was in what you would call "remission," thanks
to that crowdfund. I never imagined I would need to go there again.

In November 2014, I was assigned to review Amanda Palmer's book *The
Art of Asking* for the website Refinery29. The memoir, among other things,
details her many approaches to crowdfunding—from her roots performing as a living statue in a wedding dress, to sleeping on fans' couches while
touring, to ultimately launching the world's most successful Kickstarter.

I concluded my essayistic review by describing my own experiences
with crowdfunding and the aftermath—a few unfortunate encounters
with strangers and friends in the months after, where they criticized my
social media posts whenever it appeared as if I had money. (New boots:
were they designer? A lunch at an upscale hotel: who was paying? A trip
abroad: work or play?!) It made me wonder if people felt they were owed

their money back. After all, this was a new age of crowdfunding—the etiquette was not yet established, one could assume. Maybe I owed them indeed? After all, health had come back to me. I had gotten a job with health insurance back in New York and felt sure my crowdfunding days were long over. "Remission" had begun to look like complete "recovery."

It must have been something like confidence or arrogance that got me to write the final line in that review, on crowdfunding: ". . . and I, unlike Amanda Palmer, will probably not do it again."

And yet, I am doing it again: in 2018 it began, and more than halfway through 2019, it lived.

Just the other night, another donation of $100 came in. This time, 784 people raised $57,865 dollars in twelve months on GoFundMe, plus $27,000 on YouCaring, before it merged with GoFundMe. This time, the text and many updates were written by my friend, the writer Janice Lee, who with the help of another friend urged me to do this again at a time when there seemed little hope of survival without.

After four years of remission, what I thought was a simple Lyme relapse turned out to be severe mold toxicity and mycotoxin illness, which threatened my ability to breathe and even to get out of bed. The roof of my Harlem apartment had collapsed after renovations, and every room was overtaken by mold and toxins. Treatment after treatment proved ineffective, and on top of it all, I no longer had a stable place to live.

The difference between this campaign and the one in 2012 was my three books, the third of which was titled *Sick* and sold better than the other two combined—money I never saw, of course, as publishing goes. But a more prominent profile seemed to equal more funds.

All sorts of people from all over the world donated. A secret woman's advocacy group. One of the world's most famous novelists. A right-wing troll of mine. Another cyber-harasser of mine. Friends who made no money at all. A few relatives whom I had not heard from in ages. My mother, on occasion.

Money has never equated affection for me, but these donations had the feeling of hugs from afar. It had been so long since I had been in contact with my world, and seeing the names pop up in my inbox, regardless of how much they were putting in the pot, meant the world to me. They were tokens that translated to my existence, that told me I was still there, even as I felt like I was disappearing. The world of chronic illness is a world of numbers, but even as I saw my red and white blood cell counts and my weight drop, I watched my bank account grow. I became bolder with treatments. I ordered the supplements I needed. I contacted the doctors that people swore could help me. I dared myself to get better and very slowly I did.

I am not well yet, but there are some days, even through my daily pain, I can see a way out.

It astounds me to admit a part of my wellness has come from the psychological effect of crowdfunding. At a time when I felt so detached from my communities—literally, as illness keeps many bedbound, or me in this case certainly—love was the last thing on my mind. I felt unlovable in every way, every single day. But then there was this online self that told a different story: that I am loved and there is a testament to it, that others can witness it, too. That I can say yet again, once—or twice—upon a time, some friends and family and a whole lot of strangers put their resources together to save my life.

There is one stranger who stood out. In the late fall of 2018, I began to notice a name that popped up quite often—and quite often attached to the larger sums of money. It seemed he was one of my biggest donors, but I had no idea who he was. I googled him, imagining someone vaguely famous in some big-money industry that I was unfamiliar with. His name was not entirely uncommon, but out of all possible internet-listed incarnations, it seemed an employee of a famous Silicon Valley organization was most likely. I wondered if this was him.

A few days before Christmas, I decided that it might be nice to send him a personal message. But I could not find his email address anywhere. There was a Facebook profile with a picture that seemed to be his, but it also appeared to belong to someone way too young to be him. I wrote: "Are you the person who has been donating to my crowdfund? I feel weird trying to seek you out like this but I thought to tell you, you have been saving my life in very concrete ways, so if this is you, thank you so much. I wish I had better words. Too sick for them right now but just so thankful."

He wrote back nearly immediately. "Oh my gosh, yes that is me. I read your book recently and was really moved and am in the financial position to be able to donate this amount, so I really wanted to help. thank you for reaching out. it is really nice to know the funds are reaching you and helping. i don't want you to feel obligated or to have to say anything. your writing and continued living is enough. i know it can be a lot of effort to respond so do not worry on it."

But I did write him back, just as he kept sending me money. This went on and on. It was astounding. Sometimes I would ignore my email inbox for days and I'd miss his donation and there it would be and I'd rush to his Facebook Messenger inbox and send him effusive thanks that were often just a word salad of "OMG HUGEST THX U R SAVING MY LIFE OMG" because I knew he'd somehow understand that I was not well enough to write like I had when he first encountered my words—my memoir *Sick*—and that he'd also understand that there were no words you could put on a thing like this: the very concrete saving of a life.

In 1713, Alexander Pope was trying his hand at an English translation of *The Iliad* but still was not well known so he didn't know how to come up with the money to publish it. He came up with a "subscription method," where he promised donors a copy when he was done. The name of his 750 backers appeared on another volume of his work that came out just before this. Mozart had a similar predicament in 1783, when he did not have the money to perform at a Viennese concert hall he had his eyes on. He wrote to potential donors with the promise of a manuscript of the concert. The subscription method worked again, and after two tries, he had 176 backers.

The Statue of Liberty even has crowdfunding to thank for its existence as we know it. It was a diplomatic gift from France and was in crisis when it was delivered to the US—in 1885 it sat in pieces, unassembled, its future unknown. The US was unable to raise $250,000 for the statue's granite pedestal, and New York governor Grover Cleveland refused to let city funds pay for it. As other states began to offer to have it relocated, Joseph Pulitzer put an ad in the newspaper the *New York World*. The campaign eventually attracted 160,000 donors and brought in just enough money to pay for the pedestal and erect the statue where it now stands.

Some basic internet research told me my patron, my tech-savior, was only twenty-six years old. He had started college when I had crowdfunded the first time. I wonder if he'd learned about this millennia-old tradition of crowdfunding in a seminar or lecture on patronage—I wonder if he knew it was a tradition that artists had relied upon throughout history.

While the first credit unions can be traced back to nineteenth-century Western Europe, the first instance of modern crowdfunding happened in 1997. The British band Marillion was about to cancel its US reunion tour when donations from fans began to pour in. The lead singer's personal mailing list reached around one thousand fans, and in a newsletter he mentioned it would cost the band $60,000 to do the tour. Fans responded with a successful internet campaign.

Three years later, Marillion inspired "the father of crowdfunding," Brian Camelio, to launch ArtistShare—the first crowdfunding platform for artists. The platform ended up mainly backing musical projects, including ten Grammy-winning albums. It wasn't until 2009 that our modern-day crowdfunding giants, Indiegogo and Kickstarter, collectively launched around half a million projects.

Yet even today, the disdain my trolls have for me as a writer is mild compared to the disdain they have for my crowdfund. One Reddit thread that pulled my name as a potential "fake chronically ill person" (they singled out many women with chronic illness, until chronically ill activists pushed them to delete it), featured irate posts about me "financially profiting off of illness." They were in awe of my donations. I had apparently robbed so many, so brilliantly.

I wondered if just knowing these facts, this history, would mean the difference between asking for money or not asking for money when someone really needed it.

What would they do if their own lives were at stake?

While writing this essay, Valerie Harper died, just a few days after her eightieth birthday. She had been a constant fixture on sitcom television in the '70s and '80s, when I was glued to watching as a young immigrant studying my new country. In reading her obituaries, it shocked me that a GoFundMe campaign had recently been made for her, reaching $66,181. "Valerie has been grateful over the years for the medical breakthroughs along this difficult journey but insurance doesn't cover everything. There are unrelenting medical costs on a continuous basis. Valerie is currently taking a multitude of medications and chemotherapy drugs as well as going through extreme physical and painful challenges now with around the clock, 24/7 care immediately needed, which is not covered by insurance. This is just part of the daily cost that is without a doubt a financial burden that could never be met alone. This GoFundMe initiative from Tony is to ensure she receives the best care possible."

In 2018, another childhood favorite of mine, Dawn Wells—Mary Ann of *Gilligan's Island*—had a GoFundMe set up without her knowing. Her close friend set it up after she had broken her knee and was recovering from a major surgery where she suffered complications. After being rejected from an assisted living facility due to her large amounts of debt, and having lost her home, and being without any family support, her friend felt this was the only route. She raised over $200,000.

Wells was apparently upset when she first found out her friend did this. "The whole idea of asking for help took me by surprise. I soon realized it was an action taken out of pure love for me by my dear friend. You just can't stay mad at someone for acting out of love for you." To another news outlet, she stated, "A dear, dear friend of mine with a big heart was trying to help me with some common issues we all understand and some may face. I don't know how this happened. I thought I was taking all the proper steps to ensure my golden years. Now, here I am, no family, no husband, no kids, and no money. I'm grateful that God has given me so many friends and fans who care, or it would all be too . . . overwhelming." She was seventy-nine.

And then there are countless stories of non-famous people surviving because of this new world. Recently, I ran across the case of Eliana Cohen, who was diagnosed with a rare and fatal disorder called spinal muscular atrophy. A treatment protocol existed—the drug Zolgensma—but would have to be taken before her second birthday. The cost of the onetime dose? $2.2 million, which of course insurance would not cover. The family turned to a crowdfunding site that specializes in funding Jewish-related causes, the Chesed Fund, and in four days $2,202,364 from 23,353 donors was raised. Eliana is now reportedly doing well.

I look these stories up all the time. We live in dark times, and the idea that strangers can help other strangers seems like an impossible platitude. America feels more divided than ever; the whole world feels more divided than ever, truly. A lot of it has to do with money and that no matter what, there seems never to be enough of it to go around. That at a time when most of the world, including those countries we consider highly "developed," seems to be experiencing economic turmoil, people who don't know each other could, through the power of stories, give from what little they have still amazes me. That's the part that makes me understand why I did this.

Because this is what crowdfunding is: words that create stories that move us, and by moving us, inspire us to act. These actions represent what almost every writer of every story I know hopes for: transformation, a change in the reader's psyche, a new impulse to connect, reach out, make a difference—to fund a life.

I wouldn't be here without stories—being a writer was my only calling. Now I can also say it was, quite literally, my story that saved my life.

YOUR MONEY, MY BODY

SONALEE RASHATWAR

IN MY family, money always came with strings attached. From the time I was a child, my parents used monetary reward to control my body size, my gender expression, and my sexual orientation. Today—free from their cycles of threat and reward—I am a superfat, bisexual, nonbinary Indian American cat dad. My favorite foods right now are the Boston cream donut and barbacoa tacos. On Instagram, to an audience of nearly one hundred and twenty-five thousand people seeking the same kinds of freedoms, I'm popularly known as The Fat Sex Therapist.

Since separating from my family a year ago, my relationship with money is stressful but improving. Now in my thirties, I am a clinical social worker, a business owner, and a leaseholder of a lovely apartment. I offer these reflections to help others, because often we don't know when we're trapped inside warped, unequal relationships.

Looking back, while my parents were acting from a place of love, I know my family was asking for too much.

South Asian family systems rely on a particularly strict code of child obedience, and immigrant kids often cover up our parents' emotional abuse by mythologizing them. It makes the pain bearable. Being born into a South Asian family is committing to a life of pseudo indentured servitude, whereby our life is mapped out from birth to death, based on our assigned gender. This plan involves a high-risk, high-return investment scheme, in which our parents' investment in our future—through career and marriage pressure—ensures a long-term payout in the form of their care through old age.

This is often why South Asian families will pay for their children's education and pressure children to only take on high-paying careers. The initial investment also allows for the eventual benefits of grandchildren, seasonal visitation schedules, and a continuation of the family life cycle. My dad arrived in the States from India ten years after my mother, equipped with a thick Maharashtrian accent, maybe a few words of English, and less than twenty dollars in his pocket. He was desperate to make a better life in the US, after growing up with ten siblings on one salary. It didn't help that my *ajoba* was also an alcoholic and compulsive gambler. But my father's grit was abetted by a system held together with anti-Black racism, exploitative immigration policies, and the model minority myth.

My story of financial independence has as much to do with my body size as it does my bank account, and with my family's dedication to South Asian cisheteropatriarchy as well as their desire to assimilate to normative life in the US. I knew early on that my role as an eldest daughter was shaped with the sole purpose of training me to become a wife. My training began at age ten when I was placed on a cascade of nonconsensual diets lasting up until my mid-twenties.

By most conservative estimates, my parents spent almost $100,000 to tame my unruly, fat, disobedient, growing, feminine body.

When I was twelve, Mom took me to Jenny Craig for the first time. I weighed 160 pounds, which felt like a lot to my mom because I weighed more than she did as a thirtysomething woman. At first, I liked Jenny Craig because it felt nice to have snacks, dinners, and desserts I could prepare myself when I was hungry. Sweets and snack foods were strictly prohibited in our home, so it was amazing to have permission to eat them.

At the same time, I was embarrassed to be seen leaving the Jenny Craig in our suburban South Jersey strip mall carrying plastic bags overflowing with frozen health food as my thin peers enjoyed cheeseburgers, fries, and shakes with their mothers at a restaurant next door. For my mother, my body became a project of constant vigilance. For me, the daily shame of being fat, trying to be less fat, and still being fat was immobilizing.

It wasn't always that way. When I was younger, we lived in a blue-collar town, and both my parents worked so much that we only saw each other on the weekends. Every Friday, we shared quality time over steamed pork dumplings—still a comforting food for me—and a movie rented from the mom-and-pop video store next door. My food wasn't policed, monitored, or restricted yet, and I could eat to fullness.

But once we moved to an upper-middle-class town in another part of South Jersey when I was nine, things changed. With class ascension came a stronger pressure to control my body size. Thinness and fatphobia became markers of class and status, and even casual dinner parties were accompanied by constant food policing. I can still feel the pit in my stomach from the signals my father would send me throughout the night. When I'd head over to the buffet to make my plate, he'd often make a hand signal to tell me he was upset about how much food I was taking. Staring across the buffet table with a stern, disapproving look, he would pump his flat palm to encourage me to eat less food. I was mortified, afraid that our friends and family were watching the exchange.

At nine years old, I was still a growing child, and this restriction felt cruel—especially since I would only gain more weight (as I was supposed to) while going through puberty. At the same time, my siblings were having radically different food experiences from mine. My thin younger sister was treated as delicate and feminine because of her body size. And despite being almost identical in size and shape to me, my baby brother was never considered fat, nor was he food-policed: his gender allowed his body the space to exist.

This was how I lived with food insecurity in a food-abundant home.

On countless nights during my adolescence, long after my siblings were put to bed, my parents would lecture me for hours, telling me that my body was worth less because it was fat. They told me that my unacceptable body would make it harder for me to get married, be seen as feminine, or advance in my career. If I cried, I was told I was being too emotional. My mom actually once told my sister that it was her goal to make me cry, because once I'd cried, it meant I was broken down enough to be willing to try a new diet.

Though they believed they were doing what was necessary to make my life easier in the long run, they were actually doing the opposite. Instead of challenging normative desirability, weight, and health standards in order to make the world a safer place for a fat kid to grow up in, they were forcing me to change my fat kid body.

My parents did, in fact, have a firm grasp of the impacts of structural fatphobia; they did know exactly how immigrants were expected to assimilate into white supremacist cisheteropatriarchy. But instead of working to dismantle it, they chose to assimilate into the existing power structure. Assimilation means a willingness to step on others who are unable or unwilling to assimilate. It means leaving others behind. In my family, it was me. I was left behind.

When I was twenty, my mother pressured me to have weight-loss surgery (WLS) for the first time. I was working with a registered dietitian named Lynne, who changed my life forever as the first person to tell me I did not have to lose weight. Her words felt like a lightning strike inside my body. For the previous decade, I had assumed that all fat people everywhere utilized every second of every day to pursue constant weight loss. I lived a pretty sheltered life and had not been exposed to any anti-diet language or body positivity.

One day my mom sent Lynne an email to ask how I could become eligible for WLS in order to prepare for a potential arranged marriage after college. Lynne immediately began bcc'ing me on every email with my mom. She would also check in with me during our appointments, which were designed for nutrition counseling but had essentially become therapy. Lynne was the only adult who ever stood up for me to my mother, telling her that I'd never mentioned an interest in WLS. To this day, Lynne still checks in with me by email every few years.

When this avenue was shut down for Mom, she decided to try alternative medicine. One Saturday morning, I drove us to Manhattan to take my mom to see a famous Ayurvedic doctor she was excited to meet. But when we arrived, it was clear I was the patient. A phony shaman diagnosed me with a metabolic disorder simply by reading my pulse by hand and visually surveying my fat body. He then prescribed an assortment of herbal, non-FDA-approved supplements that were supposed to cure my "metabolic disorder" and get me to lose weight.

Every time Mom thought I was following a new diet, I would experience a lull in my surveillance. During the times when my parents believed I was complying with a diet, I was permitted to eat what I wanted, spend time with friends, and even ask for small amounts of spending money. But once Mom noticed my body was not changing in size, it became a police-style interrogation: Why didn't I want to consume these expensive pills? Why wouldn't I give it a fair chance? You'd think after the tenth failed solution, she'd begin to wonder if we both were on the same page about the perceived problem. I had started to wonder if my weight was not as big a problem as my parents thought it was.

Nonetheless, a few months later, Mom managed to get in my head again and convinced me to join her for a monthlong retreat. She said it cost $10,000 and was a rare opportunity to try new, improved weight-loss methods that even included therapy. I wasted a month of my winter break at this "cutting-edge" weight-loss facility in Durham, North Carolina. While there, I had outrageous mood swings due to salt and sugar withdrawal. But I also met incredible people going through similar challenges, people who suggested that my mom was there to exercise control over me, and bolstered my growing sense of sovereignty. But by the fourth week, I was being wildly congratulated for losing seventeen pounds in a single month—all while suffering from even more insidious patterns of disordered eating.

Flash forward four years. I was in graduate school learning to become the clinical social worker I am today. This was the year I decided I would never again allow my parents to bully me into feeling bad about my body size.

It was the summer between semesters, and I cut my hair super short to make a statement and play with gender in a way that felt experimental but authentic to me. I had just broken up with my boyfriend of three years, and he had outed me to my mother on his way through the door. He told her he was "concerned" about me because I thought I was gay, and he felt it was very important my mother know that he thought it was a phase. It's been five years since then, and my mother still clings to this bi-phobic understanding of my bisexuality.

That December, my family was slated to visit India for a few family weddings. Indian weddings are like family reunions, except it's a pissing contest over whose family looks the most outwardly successful. My parents decided they'd try again to convince me to have WLS in preparation for the trip, in the hopes that no one would notice how much weight I'd gained since our last trip six years ago.

I had no interest in WLS, but at twenty-six, I had just lost my health insurance coverage under my parents and was on Obamacare. It was working fine for my minimal medical needs, but my parents lured me with the promise of paying for better health insurance. And they'd chosen a plan that specifically covered all comprehensive costs related to WLS.

They were offering more than insurance: I was promised a sports car, a new wardrobe, and plastic surgery for all the excess skin I'd have once I'd lost enough weight. I could've asked for a polar bear if I'd wanted one. I was granted unlimited access to my parent's wealth if I allowed them to remove healthy gut tissue from my healthy, functioning body.

The process I went through to become eligible for WLS was shockingly easy, though time consuming. There was a rush of doctors' visits with a circus of physicians, from a pulmonologist, a cardiologist, and a gastroenterologist to a bariatric surgeon, a psychologist, and a dietitian. Each of these doctors would perform ultrasounds, electrocardiograms, endoscopies, colonoscopies, barium swallows, blood panels, mental status exams, and fasting glucose tests.

And each would give a resounding head nod of approval, affirming that my insides were super healthy. I was thoroughly scanned and deemed healthy enough to have this surgery. Which made me wonder why, for all these years, my parents were scamming me into thinking the fat on the outside of my body was an indicator of what was going on inside. They had bought into fatphobia, which conflates thinness and health and gives non-fat people permission to treat fat people like shit.

But it was only when I met the dietitian who showed me what my eating life would be like post-op that I was able to firmly hear the record scratch. I would only be able to eat one-quarter to one-third of a cup of food in one sitting, on a good day. My entire life would revolve around packing snacks and planning my day around my meals so I could be sure I was getting adequate nutrition. I would have to mix protein powder and vitamin supplements into all of my food for the rest of my life, because my stomach and intestines couldn't possibly digest and absorb the amount of nutrients I'd need to meet basic nutrition standards.

In other words: I'd have to devote my entire life post-op to thinking *even more* about food and my body than I already did. I'd have to agree to surgically induced malnutrition. At the same time, my sister began doing research on the danger of WLS. She came to me deeply concerned for my life and shared that one in two hundred patients die on the table during surgery. Unconcerned by the statistics, my parents were happy to foot the bill.

When it came time to say no to them, I was too chicken to do it in person—mostly because I knew I'd break down and cry, and they'd be able to sweet-talk me into agreeing again. By that time, my parents' lack of concern about my physical safety had become a great emotional weight, and the saddest part of the experience was realizing that they would rather have a child who died while attempting to become thin than a fat one. That's the understanding that changed everything. It's the knowing that puts anger in my chest and reminds me why I set the boundaries with them that I have. The boundaries that have given me space to be free to eat and be and love whoever I want. Space to be happy.

I called them over the phone to say I was not going to voluntarily amputate my healthy gut tissue and that this was the healthiest decision I could make for myself.

For two decades, I had allowed people to make decisions about my body without my fully informed consent because I did not have the money, power, or control to decide otherwise. I realized this pattern of control, dieting, and shaming was actually a form of body image abuse. Body image abuse should be considered any pressure from a romantic or intimate partner, family member, or significant others to manipulate body size using tactics of power and control.

Now in my thirties, I am finally learning how it feels to be financially independent. I know I cannot ask my parents for money the way my siblings do, and it's extraordinarily stressful. My parents have plenty to share, but accepting money from them comes at too high a price. Whether the length of my hair, the fatness of my belly, or the gender of my partner, to them, money is a tool to control and demand obedience. This is not a legacy I desire to carry on. I want to share freely with others, from a place of generosity and abundance.

Today, my business partner and I co-own Radical Therapy Center in Philadelphia. We have hopes to franchise and create new passive revenue streams. My journey to financial freedom has come from a painful understanding of what can happen when I cannot support myself independently. My story is not written out of spite. I am currently in therapy, and actively processing the rage I carry from years of body image abuse, health concern trolling, and diet trauma.

It's devastating to realize that the people who raised me are just human beings—and that these regular humans may not always have my best interest in mind. One of the hardest parts of my healing process was letting go of the myth of the incredible, indefatigable immigrant. I had to accept that I was raised by people, not superheroes.

While I will always love and have respect for my parents, I survived those years through the blessings of my own good humor and resilience. Right now, they don't take much interest in my work, but I hope to someday tell them the full truth of how I survived.

I learned to love my body without changing it first.

SHOULD I BE SELLING THIS?

CAMERON RUSSELL

THE DAY I got my first test photos back for my modeling portfolio, I stared at them like I'd just found oil in our backyard: *Maybe I'm going to be a millionaire*, I thought. And then, immediately: *I really shouldn't be selling this.*

I remember thinking that I looked sexy, like a person from a magazine, or a movie, or one of those hairstyle books I flipped through when Dad got his haircut. It wasn't until years later that I remembered what made me feel so guilty. I overheard my fourteen-year-old cousins scrolling through Instagram. One said, about a girl in a photo I couldn't see, "She's the most beautiful girl at school." The other snapped back, "You can't say that! Everyone is beautiful in their own way." I knew no one should be more valuable because of how they look, and yet I was about to exploit that I might be.

I can't logically explain how I ended up selling my face and body over and over, for nearly two decades. Instead, I have a hoarder's collection of footnotes, feelings, gossip, and research. I return to these in private, late at night, making notes in a book next to my bed, trying to make sense of what I have sold and why. Taken together over the past sixteen years of my working life, it appears I made a choice—but often I felt I was not choosing. I made money in single days and occasionally in contracts of ten, twenty, or even thirty days, but I was never required to make a long-term commitment. Every time I asked myself, *Should I take this job? Should I sell this?*, it seemed my agent needed an answer right away. I do not know what will happen if I sit down and try to account for all my decisions on paper, in public.

My first big paycheck was $5,000, for an advertisement shot in a single day that ran for a few weeks in the *New York Times* (and maybe elsewhere, I now forget). I was sixteen, and Mom told me not to tell anyone how much I made, because it might make people feel bad. "How would your hardworking friends feel if they found out?" During the first summer I spent modeling, my friends all got jobs to save for college, mostly waitressing or babysitting for tips or minimum wage. I divided $5,000 by $5.15 and figured out it would take them six months of full-time work to make what I had earned that day.

My parents said I should save: "You'll never make money like this again." So, I tried to ignore making money and treat modeling like a chore to accomplish responsibly. Dad did my taxes and was a joint owner of my bank account and I didn't pay much attention to the specifics. I tried to act, as Mom instructed, like this was a fluke and any job could be my last. "Easy come, easy go," she reminded me every time a shoot confirmed. And each time a check arrived, she said, "You won a genetic lottery. You happen to look this way. You did nothing to earn it." She was right, of course.

I continued to be frugal: I only took public transportation and never bought food out except for the occasional large fries at Burger King with my friends. I bought all my clothes from Goodwill, Clothes by the Pound, or the basement sale rack at Urban Outfitters. When H&M opened in Boston, I bought a couple of new shirts for work, all under ten dollars. In 2003, I wrote a letter to myself, signing and dating below the entry in my blue Mickey Mouse diary: *You do not need any more luck. You will give away any money you have after paying for college.*

There were moments when earning money was emotionally, undeniably, more than a chore. To be worth something other than "student" was a thrill, an escape from long days of studying and academic pressure. The job afforded me freedom. Not just because I missed school to fly to Paris or London for forty-eight hours, but because it meant school was no longer the only important measure in my life: I had value beyond grades, SAT scores, and teacher approval.

Other times the job made me feel like crying. I missed my grandfather's celebration of life, a gathering of our family a year after he passed. It was too much money, my parents and I reasoned, to turn down. I missed friends' birthdays and sleepovers. I missed the first house party without parents. I missed the school vacation when my family camped in the Grand Canyon. I missed seventy days of senior year of high school. I missed my seventeenth and eighteenth birthdays. Ten thousand dollars a day. Twelve thousand dollars. More. I missed sleeping. I was doing homework way past midnight. I used red-eye flights to write essays due when I landed. How could I be so silly and spoiled as to ever feel sorry for myself? I kept my feelings secret. I knew I should be grateful and had nothing to complain about.

I was being paid fifteen thousand dollars to shoot from nine to five: one light setting, thirty outfits, five minutes each. Front. Side. Back. Front. Portrait. Close-up. Full-length. Hand on hip. Hand in hair. Chin left, chin right, chin up, chin down. Slight smile, full laugh. Lunch and coffee breaks included.

I forgot about trying to answer *Should I be selling this?* because I always felt that I just didn't have enough information to understand the situation, that I was too young and too lucky to question what was happening. I focused on doing what was right: taking a one-in-a-million opportunity with grace and perseverance.

If they asked me to put on a corset and howl like a wolf, I did it, no questions asked. If they handed me a mask that would cover my face, I knew not to whine, *But I'm missing school and flew myself here to shoot this editorial for free, to advertise my face.* If they told me to stand in the back behind the other models, of course I did. If I stayed up all night getting fit for a show only to be canceled in the morning, I knew to say, politely, thank you, and then cry when I was back out on the street alone, or better yet, back in the hotel or models' apartment.

If they asked me to jump into the ocean on a cold day, or stand in painful heels because the clothes might wrinkle if I sat down, or sit for hours getting my hair curled in a hot back room, with no window for cigarette smoke to escape, only to have them decide it would really look better flat-ironed, I just smiled and said no problem.

When they told me I'd be making out with a male model for a commercial I said okay, even though I'd never kissed anyone. When photographers told me I was jailbait, or watched me undress, or turned a European double kiss into a real kiss, or photographed me in a way that made me look nude even though I was in a strapless bra and had asked not to look naked, I told myself to act professional, to be confident and easygoing, amenable to whatever request they made. I didn't understand yet that confidence also included standing up for myself, not just quiet resilience. The sticks-and-stones rhyme played in my head, and I counted my blessings and kept going.

I was on set the day I learned that the big online retailers actually knew exactly how well I sold clothes. How well all the girls sold, and specifically what worked best for each of us. On me, they said it was hair down with a middle part for lingerie; up in a ponytail or messy bun for sportswear. Half smiles. Cutlets in the bra for evening wear. For a brief moment when I heard they crunched such specific numbers, a weight was lifted: *Yes*, I thought, *I am worth this much, I should be paid this much, I should be selling this.*

I missed my college graduation.

When the diploma came in the mail, it struck me: I was no longer a student with a part-time job—I was a full-time model. And I began to notice that somehow, every day, while getting paid an extraordinary amount, the industry found ways to remind me of my disposability: clients moved on, looking for younger girls or newer faces; I was consistently excluded from creative conversations and often pressured to do things explicitly off-limits in my contracts (nudity, cultural appropriation, fur). The highest praise for a model is "she'll do anything," which leaves little room for self-determination or authentic collaboration beyond the superficial.

By then all of my friends had, or were in pursuit of, "real" jobs, full-time work that would support them. They worked as nurses, baristas, bartenders, teachers, tutors, lawyers, waitresses, and Uber drivers. Some went to grad school, and most went into debt. They went to work every day and told me about long hours, difficult bosses, depression, and anxiety. They told me about new cancer drugs they were learning to administer, legislation they helped pass, archives they got to access for research, clients they fought for in court. And sometimes I thought privately that their grass was much greener because instead of doing anything useful, I was making money. Week by week I accidentally picked a career that didn't matter. As a kid I had dreamed of becoming a teacher, a writer, a stand-up comedian, a community organizer, a state senator, or maybe even the president. Instead, it turned out I was pretty.

I imagined alternatives. I was in New York City and networked: joining a young entrepreneur's community, going to panels and meetups. But when I fantasized about job interviews at nonprofits, I guessed that they would want my most valuable assets—access to media and donor dollars—putting me right back where I already was. Everyone I met was always most interested in my background as a model. And when I really thought about it, modeling money was wild, and I'd put nearly a decade into this career; did it really make sense to walk away?

Fashion was my full-time job and I was a full-fledged participant. I felt, for the first time since I started, like I had a choice to make. At night, after being paid to sell earrings that broke when we opened the package, made of a metal that caused my earlobes to swell and turn red, and shooting new collections so quickly I wore clothes that weren't even made yet, clothes by designers the client planned to knock off later, shirts that tore in the armpits when I pulled them over head and pants that split when I bent down to tie shoes, I began my own industry audit. *What exactly was I selling?*

Haphazard research commenced. I saved PDF articles from JSTOR, and downloaded NGO reports. I went to the library and checked out the entire section on fashion critique, six or so academic books that were difficult to wade through.

I learned fashion is responsible for 8 percent of all greenhouse gas emissions (putting it right behind the transportation sector, which accounts for 14 percent of all emissions), and if the industry continues business as usual, it will use a full quarter of the world's carbon budget by 2050. I learned that the textile dyeing and finishing industry is the second largest polluter of clean water after agriculture. That three-fifths of all clothing ends up in a landfill or incinerator within a year of being produced.

I learned the minimum pay for an entry-level garment worker in Bangladesh is 8,000 taka, or $95 US per month. I divided $15,000 by $95 and learned it would take thirteen years to make my day rate. And I learned garment workers weren't the only ones who didn't make a livable wage. In fact, 80 percent of the fashion workforce—everyone from garment workers to retail workers to models and creatives—were women, and the majority didn't make a living wage. Even most models in New York were barely making it: according to the Department of Labor, models had a median income of $22,000 a year, $14,000 below livable. How did it make sense, then, that I could earn more in a single day?

How could my income be explained in an industry and economy that undervalued women? Modeling is one of the few jobs where women outearn men. Perhaps it reinforced that a woman's highest value is superficial and out of her control. How did it make sense in an industry and economy that particularly undervalued women of color and exploited their "invisibility?" My success was in large part due to my whiteness: in 2018, 66 percent of advertisements, 67.5 percent of runways, and 68.6 percent of magazine covers featured white models, and those numbers reflect a vastly more inclusive casting than when I started working eighteen years ago. My success reinforced white supremacy.

I was on set the day of the Rana Plaza factory collapse. Sitting in hair and makeup, with the blow-dryer going too loud to make conversation,

I read the day's headline stories. More than a thousand people lost their lives and two thousand and five hundred more were injured in the collapse of a factory that made clothes like the ones we were selling. "Smile with the eyes," the photographer said to me after I left the chair and stood before the camera. I apologized and grinned, silly and big, trying to put on a lighthearted mask. But the truth was that I felt sick: my toes pressed into the plastic shoes, my earlobes burning, the beaded acrylic sweater, the kind I knew required a human to do the handiwork, brutally hot in the July sun. And then the question, again, ringing like a siren in my mind: *Should I be selling this?*

I continued to model, but at night I became an activist. I went to Occupy Wall Street and Black Lives Matter protests. I organized artists and for a few years edited an indie publication aimed at bringing media resources to marginalized storytellers. Rarely did my activism and fashion careers intersect.

When I was asked to speak at the launch of a fashion development initiative, an effort to invest in burgeoning garment industries in ten different countries, I was conflicted. They wanted me to talk about how fashion empowers women. I spoke but privately felt increasingly certain that what modeling actually models is the way an industry can exploit a lack of labor and environmental regulation.

I knew the development narratives tout the garment industry's wages for women as a success, but while fashion supply chain workers might make more than two dollars a day, this still isn't a living wage, and women are more likely to be harassed or abused at work. To compound matters, their air and water are polluted by the very industry that provides them jobs, and their homes are at risk from the climate crisis that fashion plays no small part in furthering.

I began to turn down jobs. I spent my days alone, writing and researching fashion, or doing work unrelated to fashion, where I didn't talk about my day job. I continued to support indie publishing, organized a hackathon with a group of artists and techies for campaign finance reform, participated in movements for climate justice and civil rights, and showed up wherever else I could. I tried to understand what I should do with myself, with my new understanding of systemic problems.

To continue to participate in fashion made me an accomplice, didn't it? The vast inequality and the sheer silliness of my well-paid job: two ends of a seesaw tilted in my favor. When I told Mom some of the unsavory details, she said, "You're a spy." "A spy for whom?" I asked. "For us. Report back," she said.

But how can there be us versus them when I am a them?

Nonetheless, I tried to follow her advice. She introduced me to the organizer of a TEDx event in DC, and I gave a talk about fashion, privilege, and white supremacy. I said nothing particularly new, but I said it as a model. I said it in a way that was rehearsed, with short soundbite stories, the kind you learn to tell when you work in pop culture, and newsworthy means entertaining.

When the talk went viral, I was surprised that my success did not disgust people, as if it was an achievement and not the product of the broken system I had described. Instead, I was introduced at the UN, the DNC, on CNN and ABC, in the *New York Times*, on various stages in multiple countries as a successful model. I was speechless. What should I say to them? What should I tell myself? Looking for language, I binge read every model autobiography I could get my hands on.

In *I Am Iman*, I discovered a supermodel who acknowledged not only that she has been racially fetishized and objectified by the industry responsible for her success, but that her silence made her an accomplice. Her words felt like company, gifting me space to recognize the complexity of my own experience.

In an interview entitled "Can a Supermodel Be a Feminist?," published in Rebecca Walker's seminal Third Wave anthology *To Be Real: Telling the Truth and Changing the Face of Feminism*, supermodel Veronica Webb tells Walker, "I . . . think that if you are a woman, any way that you can amass power and money you have to do it . . . because it's just something that we don't have . . . [and] we've become phenomenally empowered by trading off our looks." And I found examples of women who were acting on that power: Waris Dirie shared the story of her circumcision in order to end the practice. Alek Wek redirected media attention to the genocide in the Sudan.

These models described moments of finding themselves—no longer fourteen and doe-eyed like the day they were scouted, but as young women navigating access to wealth and mainstream media. Looking around they saw very few women at the table, and even fewer people of color, queer people, disabled people, people born in the global south, people born into working-class families, and rarest of all: people who were ready to challenge the status quo. I saw myself in their stories. Like them, I found myself in exclusive rooms, with the feeling that this was the opportunity we had been waiting for. And I started to see that there was not only space but an imperative to be an activist at work, to go beyond being an anonymous body at a march or a young person building new community. I had to bring the work into fashion, where I had more influence, more connections, and more at stake.

Wondering whether it was right or wrong to "sell this," I had mistakenly framed this moral quandary as the most important choice I could make in my life. In doing so, I had missed a much larger question: Was individualistic morality inside this current system part of a false dichotomy to begin with? How could it not be in a system whose success was predicated on extraction, subjugation, objectification, and, inevitably, participation? What did it feel like to accept not only the inescapability but also the necessity of working within the system?

As I stopped framing the situation as us and them, I could see my coworkers, and myself, more clearly. Working for success, for the access it sometimes granted to power and money, was a drive rooted in more human motivations. We shared an ambition not for money, power, and access, but to be of use: to care for ourselves, our families, our communities, and the earth. As I began to consider what it might look like to respect and invest in ourselves and one another, I started having these conversations, not just in my head, but with fellow models.

As a result, in 2016 Áine Campbell and I founded the Model Mafia, an active group of hundreds of models committed to a more just and sustainable industry and world, finding the frontlines near us and building change. This has looked like bringing the #MeToo movement to fashion, supporting model-leaders in Los Angeles, the Bahamas, Polynesia, Sudan, Rwanda, Iceland, and beyond as they call for our industry to lead on the climate crisis, to raise rapid response funds and visibility for frontline movements, to build solidarity across the supply chain, and find kinship with those working in retail, export processing zones, and garment factories.

At times, modeling felt to me like acting the role of the accommodating mindless mannequin, except more humiliating, because there was no script. I delivered lines I did not believe but I wrote. I played a character that made me uncomfortable, and yet I chose how to perform. But organizing in my own industry has given me the opportunity to bring more of who I am to this job. To find it is neither a costume I can take off nor the full measure of myself or my colleagues. It has been to find, within a system we did not build, ways to own harm done, marshal our agency to make change, and cultivate the parts of our work that we like and want to grow.

As a model I have been able to experience the pleasure in being a body observed, a body speaking. I know how liberating it can feel to be valued even as I express vulnerability, sensuality, femininity, masculinity, joy, seriousness, silliness, eccentricity, and more. When I have made work as an equal, a collaborator, creating images is a powerful, if small, act that says: this body is part of a whole. How sublime it can feel to be seen. But these moments, these exhilarating partnerships, are rare enough to be reminders that they aren't the norm.

It is clear to me that money is no measure of success. Reminding myself of this and acknowledging how my participation reinforces the extractive and oppressive parts of our system helps me have the clarity and confidence to find different ways to measure the worth of a job, the value of my time spent. I ask for mood boards, casting, and certification of feminist, environmental, or activist claims. When the jobs are big, with people I genuinely enjoy or admire and the opportunity to do things just a little bit differently, I sell.

And I balance paid work with unpaid efforts that feel valuable: time with my children, organizing in fashion and beyond, writing. Most of this other work is caring work: caring for myself, my family, my friends, my community. I wonder daily how it is that the most important and fulfilling labor in my life has little to no monetary value.

My height, weight, skin color, hair texture, the slope of my nose, and the shape of my chin should not make my body worth more than anyone else's. As an adult I want to be able to fully own my decision to continue to participate in an industry that explicitly pays for these superficial characteristics. I want to make sure I can explain it to my children.

When they are old enough to understand, I think I will tell them that asking *Should I be selling this?* made me think like an outsider and encouraged me to imagine a blanket condemnation was possible, and even useful. But when I stopped imagining an invisible opt-out button, I was released from an us-versus-them trap that made me feel either entirely guilty or smug and superior, entirely powerless or carrying the weight of the world. I could see that what is beautiful and worth keeping coexists with what urgently needs to change.

I will tell them that I am trying on a new question, one they will no doubt have to ask themselves many times as they move out into the world: *I am selling this—now what?*

THE PRICE OF FABULOUSNESS

TRESSIE McMILLAN COTTOM

> Fabulousness doesn't take a lot of money. It requires high levels of creativity, imagination and originality; it's dangerous, political, risky, and largely practiced by queer, trans, trans-feminine people of color or other marginalized groups; it's about making a spectacle of oneself in a world that seeks to suppress and undervalue fabulous people.
>
> —madison moore, "Fabulousness"

> What do you call an educated negro with a BA or an MA, with a BS, or a PhD? You call him a nigger.
>
> —Malcolm X

EVERY TIME there is a national news story about a Black shopper harassed in a store, there is a predictable backlash to the miscarriage of justice. We tend to move quickly from being outraged that it happened to critiquing why a Black person was shopping there at all. Much as we interrogate what a woman was wearing when she was raped, we look for ways to assign personal responsibility for structural injustices to bodies we collectively do not value. If you are poor, why do you spend money on useless status symbols like handbags and belts and clothes and shoes and televisions and cars? One thing I've learned is that one person's illogical belief is another person's survival skill. And nothing is more logical than trying to survive.

My family is a classic Black American migration family. We have rural Southern roots, moved North, and almost all have returned. I grew up watching my great-grandmother, and later my grandmother and mother, use our minimal resources to help other people make ends meet. We were those good poors, the kind who live mostly within our means. We had a little luck when a male relative got extra military pay when he came home a paraplegic or used the VA to buy a Jim Walter house. If you were really blessed, when a relative died with a paid-up insurance policy, you might be gifted a lump sum to buy the land that Jim Walter used as collateral to secure your home lease.

That is how generational wealth happens where I am from: lose a leg, a part of your spine, die right, and maybe you can lease-to-own a modular home. We had a little of that kind of rural Black wealth, so we were often in a position to help folks less fortunate. But perhaps the greatest resource we had was a bit more education.

We were big readers and we encouraged the girl children, especially, to go to some kind of college. Consequently, my grandmother and mother had a particular set of social resources that helped us navigate mostly white bureaucracies to our benefit. We could, as my grandfather would say, talk like white folks. We loaned that privilege out a lot. I remember my mother taking a next-door neighbor down to the social service agency. The elderly woman had been denied benefits to care for the granddaughter she was raising. Her denial had come in the genteel bureaucratic way—lots of waiting, forms, and deadlines she could not quite navigate. I watched my mother put on her best Diana Ross *Mahogany* outfit: a camel-colored cape with matching slacks and knee-high boots. I was miffed, as only an only child could be, about sharing my mother's time with the neighbor girl. I must have said something about why we had to do this. The Vivian fixed me with a stare as she was slipping on her pearl earrings and told me that people who can do, must do.

It took half a day, but something about my mother's performance of "respectable Black person"—her Queen's English, her *Mahogany* outfit, her straight bob and pearl earrings—got done what the elderly lady next door had not been able to get done in over a year. I learned, watching my mother, that there was a price we had to pay to signal to gatekeepers that we were worthy of engaging. It meant dressing well and speaking well. It might not work. It likely wouldn't work, but on the off chance that it would, you had to try. It was unfair, but, as The Vivian always said, "Life isn't fair, little girl."

I internalized that lesson and I think it has worked out for me, if unevenly. A woman at Belk once refused to show me the Dooney & Bourke purse I was interested in buying. The Vivian once made a salesgirl cry after she ignored us in an empty store. I have walked away from many a hotly desired purchase, like the impractical off-white winter coat I desperately wanted, after some bigot at the counter insulted me and my mother. But I have a PhD and I support myself by aping the white male privileged life of the mind. It's a mixed bag. Of course, the trick is you can never know the counterfactual of your life. There is no evidence of access denied. Who knows what I was not granted for not enacting the right status behaviors or symbols at the right time for an agreeable authority?

Respectability rewards are a crapshoot, but we do what we can within the limits imposed by a complex set of structural and social interactions designed to stifle access to status, wealth, and power. I do not know how much my mother spent on her camel-colored cape or knee-high boots, but I know that whatever she paid was returned in hard-to-measure dividends. How do you put a price on the double take of a clerk at the welfare office who decides you might not be like those other trifling women in the waiting room and provides an extra bit of information about completing a form that you would not have known to ask about? What is the retail value of a school principal who defers a bit more to your child, because your presentation signals that you unleash the bureaucratic savvy of middle-class parents to advocate for them? I didn't know the price of these critical engagements with organizations and gatekeepers relative to our poverty when I was growing up. But I am living proof of its investment yield.

Why do poor people make stupid, illogical decisions to buy status symbols? For the same reason all but only the most wealthy buy status symbols, I suppose. We want to belong. And not just for the psychic rewards, but because belonging to one group at the right time can mean the difference between unemployment and employment, a good job as opposed to a bad job, housing or a shelter, and so on. Someone mentioned on Twitter that poor people can be presentable with affordable options from Kmart. But the issue is not about being presentable.

Presentable is the bare minimum of social civility. It means being clean, not smelling, wearing shirts and shoes for service, and the like. Presentable as a sufficient condition for gainful, dignified work or successful social interactions is a privilege. It's the aging white hippie who can cut off the ponytail of his youthful rebellion and walk into senior management, while aging Black Panthers can never completely outrun the effects of stigmatization against which they were courting a revolution. Presentable is relative and, like life, it ain't fair. In contrast, "acceptable" is about gaining access to a limited set of rewards granted upon group membership. A manager at the apartment complex where I worked while in college told me, repeatedly, that she knew I was "okay" because my little Nissan was clean. That I had worn a Jones New York suit to the interview really sealed the deal. She could call the suit by name because she asked me about the label in the interview. Another hiring manager, at my first professional job, looked me up and down in the waiting room, cataloging my outfit, and later told me that she had decided I was too classy to be on the call center floor. I was hired as a trainer instead. The difference meant no shift work, greater prestige, better pay, and a baseline salary for all my future employment.

I have about a half dozen similar stories. What is remarkable is not that this happened. There is empirical evidence that women and people of color are judged by their appearances differently and more harshly than are white men. What is remarkable is that these gatekeepers, in one way or another, actually told me why I was deemed acceptable. They wanted me to know how I had properly signaled that I was not a typical Black or a typical woman, two identities that in combination are almost always conflated with being poor.

I sat in on an interview for a new administrative assistant once. My regional vice president was doing the hiring. A long line of mostly Black and brown women applied because we were a cosmetology school. Trade schools at the margins of skilled labor in a gendered field are necessarily classed and raced. I found one candidate particularly charming. She was trying to get out of a salon because ten hours on her feet cutting hair would average out to an hourly rate below minimum wage. A desk job with forty set hours and medical benefits represented mobility for her. When she left, my VP turned to me and said, "Did you see that tank top she had on under her blouse?! OMG, you wear a silk shell, not a tank top!" Both of the women were Black. The VP had constructed her job as senior management. She drove a brand-new BMW because she "should treat herself" and liked to tell us that ours was an image business. A girl wearing a cotton tank top as a shell was incompatible with BMW-driving VPs in the image business.

Gatekeeping is a complex job of managing boundaries that do not just define others but also define ourselves. Status symbols—silk shells, designer shoes, luxury handbags—become keys to unlock these gates. If I need a job that will save my lower back and move my baby from Medicaid to an HMO, how much should I spend signaling to people like my former VP that I will not compromise her status by opening the door to me? Maybe that candidate could not afford a proper shell. I will never know. But I do know that had she gone hungry for two days to pay for it or missed wages for a trip to the store to buy it, she may have been rewarded a job that could have lifted her above minimum wage. Shells aren't designer handbags, perhaps. But a cosmetology school in a strip mall isn't a job at Bank of America, either.

At the heart of incredulous statements about the poor decisions poor people make is a belief that we, the hardworking, sensible not-poor, would never be like them. We would know better. We would know to save our money, eschew status symbols, cut coupons, practice puritanical sacrifice to amass a million dollars. There is a regular news story of a lunch lady who, unbeknownst to all who knew her, dies rich and leaves it all to a cat or a charity or some such. Books about the modest lives of the rich like to tell us how they drive Buicks instead of BMWs. What we forget, if we ever knew, is that what we know now about status and wealth creation and sacrifice are predicated on who we are—that is, not poor.

If you change the conditions of your not-poor status, you change everything you know as a result of being not-poor. You have no idea what you would do if you were poor until you are poor. And not intermittently poor or formerly not-poor, but born poor, expected to be poor, and treated by bureaucracies, gatekeepers, and well-meaning respectability authorities as inherently poor. Then, and only then, will you understand the relative value of a ridiculous status symbol to someone who intuits that they cannot afford not to have it.

(SEX) WORK

MELISSA PETRO

AT NINETEEN years old, I found myself in Oaxaca, Mexico, living as a student abroad. One day at the grocery store, about a month into my stay, my credit card hit its limit and I made a decision that would define me for the rest of my life: rather than go back to the claustrophobic suburbs I had worked so hard to escape, I became a sex worker at a strip club called La Sirena.

Becoming a sex worker hadn't been the plan. I'd worked in fast food. I'd worked in retail. I'd been a checkout girl at the grocery store. I stuffed envelopes, then worked a switchboard, and later was an attendant at the child-care facility where my mother worked as a secretary. One summer in high school, I even sold singing telegrams.

My first job was at Marvin's Diner. My best friend, Lisa, and I worked the Sunday morning shift, starting at five-thirty. Our first task was to turn potatoes into hash browns. The potatoes were boiled in enormous cast-iron pots on oversized commercial gas stoves—no easy task for two ninety-pound girls. Once boiled, they went straight into the freezer to cool while we peeled and grated potatoes, cold as clumps of ice, from the day before. We worked all morning, unsupervised, in the drafty bowels of the diner. When the potatoes were done, it was time to start the dishes, which had been piling up all morning. Marvin, the owner, sat all day at the counter, drinking black coffee, chain-smoking, and ordering us around. He was a decrepit old man with crooked yellow teeth and foul breath. At the end of our first shift, he told us to wear skirts next time, "the shorter the better." We held out our hands, red and raw from the dish sanitizing solution, for our cash.

We did it because we were paid in cash under the table and because no one else would hire us: we were twelve.

At Marvin's, Lisa and I found ways to make the day go by faster. We'd crank up the radio and steal cigarette breaks, often ashing those cigarettes straight into the hash. While enjoying endless cups of coffee (the job's only perk), we fantasized aloud what we'd tell Marvin, if only we could.

Had you asked me as a teenager my ideas of "work," I would've said that work sucked and I would've been half-right: the jobs available to me at that time did. The environments I worked in were highly restrictive. The tasks were repetitive. Work required more strength than skill. You couldn't go fast enough, and there was always more to do. The money was barely enough to make it seem worth it, but you did it anyway. Why? In the community where I grew up, everyone worked, but most people were poor. It was just the way things were. I worked because I wasn't given an allowance, and I needed cash. What was the alternative?

For some women, the alternative is sex work.

I learned this during my very first semester at Antioch College, when Lisa called me long-distance to let me know she'd started working at the Crazy Horse, a strip joint in a row of strip joints in a part of town known only for its strip joints. That semester, I had enrolled in my first women's studies course. Everything I learned about sex work contradicted what I knew about my best friend.

I was taught that sex work is humiliating, brutal, and dehumanizing. In my women's studies class, we read that radical feminists define pornography as rape and torture as a form of entertainment. From Catharine MacKinnon's book *Only Words*, I learned that "empirically, all pornography is made under conditions of inequality based on sex, overwhelmingly by poor, desperate, homeless, pimped women who were sexually abused as children."* Many of these same theorists described marriage as "rape as a practice" and heterosexual sex as "an act of invasion and ownership undertaken in a mode of predation." Prostitution was seen as the cornerstone of patriarchal domination and sexual subjugation of women. It was described as modern slavery and considered inherently traumatic and tantamount to abuse. To this day, individuals working in the sex trades are commonly thought to be victims of sex trafficking.

Prior to Lisa's confession, these arguments had me convinced. Like most people, I'd grown up with no knowledge of the industry short of *Dateline* specials and made-for-TV movies, cautionary tales about girls without families or backstories, girls with fake names like "Candy" or "Mercedes." Prostitutes existed only from the waist down. Girls who sold sex were fishnet-stockinged legs leaning into tinted windows idling at red lights. They were girls—never women—foolish, desperate: the butts of jokes.

I pictured Lisa working in the kind of place that decent women, girls like her and me, would picket to shut down. When I said as much to Lisa, she told me to fuck off.

"What the hell do you know?" she said, and she was right: I'd never so much as been in a strip club.

I hung up and cried. Of everything I had been led to believe that a sex worker could be, Lisa was none of it. She was smart and funny, beautiful inside and out—the toughest bitch I'd ever met. She was my best friend, and I didn't want to lose her.

And so, that winter break, my then-boyfriend, Rick, and I visited Lisa at work. We walked in to find Lisa onstage in the spotlight, exactly as I remembered her. Beautiful Lisa, bedazzled in a rhinestone choker, hot-pink halter top, and matching thong.

Rick and I took seats at a table in the back. The place looked like a normal bar, not at all how I thought a strip club would look. I guess I'd expected guys going crazy, hooting and hollering while sad, vulnerable-looking girls

*Catharine A. MacKinnon, *Only Words* (Cambridge, MA: Harvard University Press, 1993).

walked around, demeaned and exposed. Instead, average-looking guys sat
civilly at fancy little tables talking politely to above-average-looking girls.
Everyone looked like they were having a great time, and why not? It was
like all the clubs Lisa and I weren't old enough to get into. Here, not only
were girls our age allowed in, they were getting paid.

When Lisa came over, she explained how it worked. She answered
all my questions: Can the guys touch? No. Do you have to take off your
bottoms? Yes. What do you do if you have your period? You stick in a
tampon and you cut off the string. What if a guy's being an asshole? You
walk away.

In the car on the way home, Rick and I made fun of Lisa. I told my mom
the place was gross. I wanted my mother's approval. I wanted to make her
proud. But at the end of that night, I had been convinced. I saw the attention
Lisa was getting and the money she made, and I wanted it, too.

A month or so later, I found myself in Mexico. For the first month, I
worked at a preschool as an assistant teacher. Alongside the preschoolers,
I learned Spanish words for colors and the seasons, and the way to tell
time. I liked the kids—the way they climbed all over me, even when they
pulled my hair. I liked the way we could communicate through smiles.
Tourists, I soon came to find out, were the organization's bread and but-
ter. When a group of tourists came in, we'd stop what we were doing and
parade the preschoolers out into the courtyard for the tourists to take pictures. They'd taught the kids the words to English songs and key phrases
in English such as "I love you" and "Give me peso."

There were no governmentally funded programs for the poor, so by
collecting money from tourists for items such as school uniforms to send
the children to school, the organization I worked for hoped to improve the
kids' lives. But it was humiliating. *What were these children being taught,*
I thought, *except how to beg?* In the evenings I'd see the same kids in the
zocalo, picking through the garbage, chasing after their little brothers and
sisters, running up to tourists and begging for change.

I'd arrived in Mexico with about nine hundred dollars in my bank account, which was rapidly depleting, and so I'd begun using my credit card

whenever I could. I wasn't sure of its balance, only that it had a $1,500 limit and that I'd put my airfare on it, too. I tried not to think about it. I couldn't get a paying job because I had a non–working student visa. Besides, I didn't speak Spanish.

After a month, I stopped going to work, bored by the monotony of caring for toddlers. I told myself I wouldn't be missed, and I probably wasn't. Without a job, I sat around my host family's house all day, bored still, watching *The Simpsons* dubbed into Spanish. When lunchtime came, my host mother would politely offer me a plate. My host brother teased me about how much I ate. *How unladylike,* he'd say. *How American.* After a month, they raised my rent to cover the unanticipated cost of food.

I was running out of money, and I was homesick, longing not so much for the actual place where I grew up as I was missing familiar things and wearied by the difficulties of living everyday life abroad, where everything, from using the toilet to making a phone call, was different and difficult.

I called Rick every day, sometimes two or three or four times a day, until I'd spent nearly all my cash on calling cards, and we'd both run out of things to say. "Melissa," he finally said, "I don't understand. You wanted so badly to be there, and now you sound miserable. Why don't you just come home?"

One day at a grocery store, my credit card was denied. It had reached its limit. I don't remember how I felt at the time, but it was probably relief. I had known the day was coming, and finally it was here. *I guess something's going to have to happen now,* and then something did. I met a tattoo artist at a parlor close to where I lived, who introduced me to La Sirena.

The rules of La Sirena were simple: Every dancer was called to stage three times nightly to perform three songs per set: the first fully dressed, the second topless, and the third fully nude. Girls made money in three ways: customers bought them drinks, they sold table dances, and they sold private dances, called *privados.* Prostitution is illegal in Mexico, and the sex industry is regulated.

All this was explained to me by Lila, the floor manager. Most likely an ex-dancer herself, Lila had a frizzy orange dye job and enormous sagging breasts. Everything Lila said, she repeated once and sometimes twice, as if she was used to dealing with foreigners, as if she'd given this same speech a hundred times before. I took it all in, overwhelmed but trying desperately to appear casual, more afraid that they wouldn't let me work.

That first night, I tagged behind Lila as she showed me the club. The tropical theme, which had begun with a mural on the outer wall, extended through the main room, where palm fronds decorated the ceiling and a hula skirt lined the deejay booth. A disco ball spun lazily above the stage. The TVs in the corner of the room were set to soft-core porn. Pamela Anderson rubbed her swimsuited body soundlessly in slow motion. Other than that, the place looked like a normal bar, like an American dance club. For the first time in Mexico, I felt at home.

It was early in the night, and the club was already filling up. A handful of dancers sat with clientele at tables, while large men in conspicuous blue jumpsuits watched the room. One waiter hurried past with three beers alongside a little neon drink topped off with an umbrella. He placed the drink before a young woman sitting with three men.

Instead of paying girls in cash, Lila explained, the customers bought tickets from the club. "Orange counts for a drink. Green is a table dance. Red indicates a *privado*."

"There's no touching anywhere," Lila assured me. "Not in the *privado*—not here on the floor. Absolutely no touching on the floor," Lila repeated. "That is the law. In the *privado*, you have privacy. It is private. *Privado*. Technically, in there, there is also no touching. But what happens in there is up to you."

The music changed as the deejay introduced a girl to the stage. Petite, in knee-high boots and a white Spandex slip, she appeared just as the up-beat *banda* faded into a Spanish ballad. The girl was slim with light skin. Her long, dark hair fell in buoyant waves down her back, curling around her breasts. Her curls stayed in perfect place as she took her first spin around the pole. Everything about her looked perfect. From her tight, proportioned body to the seemingly routine movements on the pole and around the stage, even the indifferent, somewhat absent look on her face.

At the end of the first song, she casually slipped out of her dress. The reaction from the clientele in Mexico was like nothing I had seen before, and nothing I've seen since. The room erupted with whistles and applause.

As the girl started her second song, Lila took me to where the *privados* took place and into the dressing room, where she introduced me to Paco, the housemother. A housemother's job is to take care of the dancers by applying makeup, fixing broken costumes, breaking up fights, and preventing theft.

"*Que bonita su mariposa!*" Paco said girlfriend-to-girlfriend, resting his hand on my shoulder just above the tattoo.

"Don't spend too much time in the dressing room." Lila threw a wary glance at Paco. "Time is money. Spend your time on the floor."

Before this moment, it felt as if I'd been bluffing. Now, there was no denying it was real. I pulled out a Spandex miniskirt, a velvet tube top, and a pair of strappy heels. Paco and Lila stood together behind me as I took off my T-shirt and jeans. I studied the reflection standing in the mirrored dressing room in a lace bra and cotton underwear. I put the heels on first.

I didn't look like a stripper—at least, not to me. I looked nothing like the girl I'd just seen onstage. Still, I saw how Lila and Paco were assessing me. I could tell they approved. I knew they would. I knew the way men in Mexico looked at me. They called out in the street and hissed when I walked past. I knew the way men at home looked at me. Even older men, friends' fathers, male teachers—even when I was a little girl. In grade school, I knew what it meant to be a woman, and I was no longer a little girl. At nineteen years old, I was well aware that my body had become a woman's body. Even as a child, I knew what that was worth.

Back on the main floor, the girl was just finishing her set. Totally nude, she gave one more spin around the pole before the deejay came back on, announcing her name one last time. The applause continued as she gathered her dress. As the lights went back to normal, a bouncer helped her off the stage and to a waiting customer.

Lila turned to me, "You're next."

From that night on, Paco called me "Mariposa." I went by Melissa.

This is my real name and I didn't bother to change it, even though most customers heard "Molesta," the Spanish word for "annoying." I kind of got a kick out of seeing the confusion on a customer's face, knowing that it didn't matter what my name was or if I had one at all. All that mattered was that I was white and American. They'd call me over and ask where I was from. In the beginning I'd say "Ohio," and they'd ask if Ohio was near California or New York until I began answering the question by saying I was from "Ohio, west of New York," to which they'd nod and smile. Then they'd ask about my family, how many brothers and sisters I had. Sort of a weird question to be asking in a strip club, I thought, but I'd tell them I had one brother and my mom. Next, they'd ask for a dance.

In the beginning, I took the assignment of "striptease" literally. In the *privado*, I made my customers sit on their hands. "If you want to touch," I'd say in broken Spanish before the start of a dance, "you'll have to take another girl." Rarely would I lose a customer. Most men wanted at least one dance from the white girl.

Standing two feet away, I'd pose coyly, removing articles of clothing bit by bit. If the guy tried to touch, I'd gently slap his hand away, waving a finger at him as if he were a child. If he tried it again, I'd stop the dance for a number of seconds, a punishment. A third time, I'd put my hand out the curtain to alert security and the man would be removed. The times I did this, I felt powerful and in control.

For the same number of pesos, my coworkers were downright acrobatic. Most of the girls who worked at La Sirena, I'd learn from Paco, were professionals, part of an organized cartel that traveled club to club as monthly features. They'd roll in one week, and the next week they'd be gone, another crew just as beautiful arriving in their high heels. I viewed the girls I worked alongside with a mix of awe, idealization, and fear. As I'd lead my client to the next available booth, I'd sometimes catch another girl's act. She'd straddle her customer, one leg catapulted over his shoulder, vagina inches from his face. Such displays brought looks of fear to young boys' faces, whereas the older men drooled like dogs.

I held myself apart from the others. At nineteen years old, I felt like an exception to every rule. I did it for the money, but it was also true I found the work exciting. Stripping gave me an opportunity to express a side of myself I had felt, until now, incapable of expressing—a part of myself I had been taught to be ashamed of and had learned to hide.

By becoming a sex worker, I was rejecting the role of *mujer abnegada*— the long-suffering woman who sacrifices her own desires and needs for the good and welfare of her husband and children. I was, in many ways, rejecting the life of my own mother. I was going to college (the first in my family), exploring my budding sexuality, and transgressing social norms, and it was all very exciting.

My coworkers, on the other hand, were not students abroad, here for three months, and then returning to college. The women I worked with had little formal education and had come from a surrounding area with few other opportunities and where low wages and patriarchal attitudes precluded them from substantial jobs. Sex work for them was considered an undesirable but viable way to support themselves and their families. Eighty percent of prostitutes in Mexico are mothers. Had they the opportunity, the women I worked with would have much preferred the life of the sanctified *mujer abnegada*.

There's a difference between doing a job to supplement your income and doing something in order to survive. There's a difference between doing something you don't particularly want to do and doing something you're forced to do, knowing you have no other choice.

On the way home that first night, the taxi driver put his hand on my knee and asked, politely, *cuánto?* How much? I pretended I couldn't understand. We were driving down an otherwise abandoned road, fields of dust on both sides. It was dawn. The sky turned pink. In the silence of the car, the night spun fuzzily in my head, music from the club still banging in my ears. My body ached with exhaustion, warm but for the cool, damp wad of bills tucked in my bra.

The next day I slept in. I awoke well past noon, the sun high and hot, the city noisy and congested. I went on the balcony and lit up a smoke. A week earlier, I'd moved out of my host family's house and into my own apartment in a hacienda closer to town. For the first time in my life I was living alone. It was a single room furnished with a bed. There was no kitchen, no heat, and as I discovered the first time I took a shower, no hot water. I'd rented the place on first sight, taken by the balcony where I imagined I would sit and smoke and write. It was all part of a romantic vision I held of myself: I was living fast, dying young, being wild in a state of paradise. With nobody monitoring me, no one to answer to, no one to whom I had to be polite, I could just be myself, I thought. Whoever that may be.

Finishing the cigarette, I reached for the journal Rick had given me as a going-away present. It was navy blue and decorated with a half-moon and stars. As I began to write, the night before came back to me like a crazy dream—dancing until I was drenched in sweat, heart pounding in my chest. For hours, I'd been sought after, the exact measure of how much I'd been desired counted out to me in cash at the end of my shift. I thought back to that moment the manager handed me my earnings. The greedy, fucked-up feeling of being paid in cash reminded me of the feeling I'd get as a kid when my mom would come home with groceries on the first of the month.

I went back inside, lifted up the mattress, pulled out the wad of money, and spread it over the bed. The bills were in all different colors, including denominations that I hadn't seen in the two months I'd been in Mexico. It felt unreal, like money belonging to a board game I didn't know how to play. I gathered the paper back into a pile, put it in order by denomination, and then counted it slowly. I counted it again. At La Sirena, I would become one of the highest earners, thanks to nothing but the fact that my race and nationality were prized. As a white woman working as a stripper in Mexico, in one night, I had earned more than triple my rent.

It wasn't a lot of money, I realize today, only a couple hundred US dollars a night, and it hadn't been easy. Dancing was hard work, but at nineteen years old, no other job in my life had offered such earning potential, and, more important, more than with any other job I'd had before it, I had enjoyed the work. I thought back to the humiliation, just days earlier, of asking my boyfriend to send me money and the guilt of putting him in a position of having to say no. He didn't have any money to give me. Neither did my mom. I hadn't even asked her.

Contemplating what I'd do with the rest of my afternoon, I felt suddenly free, as if a burden had been lifted, something so heavy but such a part of me I hadn't even known I'd been carrying.

While feminists endlessly debate the notion of "choice," they fail to acknowledge what is obvious to anyone who's ever been put in a difficult position: the decisions women make in life are sometimes less a choice and more a consequence of circumstances. Whereas some people tolerate their work, as Lisa and I tolerated working at Marvin's, some jobs are easier than others to tolerate, and some people have the privilege of working jobs they actually enjoy. Sex workers fall into every category, and as long as there is poverty, there will be individuals who would rather sell sex than be poor.

When I returned from Mexico, I worked as a stripper on and off through college as a way of making ends meet, transitioning out of the industry once I graduated from college and falling back into it, this time working as a call girl. Prostitution was not the job for me. What began as fun and freeing became increasingly fraught. The indignities added up, starting when I was walking through the club in Mexico and a customer grabbed my ass. Without thinking, I swung around and slapped him. He slapped me back, hard. Security stepped in and the issue was brought to management. I expected the man would be ejected; instead, I was dismissed for the night.

Another time, during a private dance, an old man pulled out his dick, and before I even knew what was happening, he'd come on me.

But many girls endured worse, and so I kept my humiliations to myself. I wanted to carry on doing what I felt I had to do, but to feel a sense of dignity while doing so, I couldn't admit to feeling disturbed, not even to myself, by what was clearly disturbing.

Then I was raped. And quit sex work for good. Much like my decision to start working in the sex industry, I did not allow myself to think very deeply about why I suddenly felt compelled to stop, admitting to myself only that I felt burned out and depressed. I knew I needed a major change, so I applied to the New York City Teaching Fellows and was chosen to be a public school teacher. I taught art and creative writing at an elementary school in the Bronx. And I started writing again. I have an MFA degree in creative nonfiction, and writing became a way of reconciling myself with the identity imposed upon me by my former profession.

After publishing a nine-hundred-word op-ed on the *Huffington Post* in which I disclosed my status as an ex–call girl, a reporter at the *New York Post* put two and two together. In September 2017, he and a photographer ambushed me on the front steps of the elementary school where I worked. Some days later, the photo they took of me ran on the cover of the paper under the headline "Bronx Teacher Admits: I'm an Ex-Hooker." That headline, and the media circus that followed, ultimately cost me my career as a public school teacher.

What was clear from the "Hooker Teacher" headlines, which went on for months, was that people still believe there are two kinds of women: the impudent, shameless, and morally unrestrained woman willing to have sex for money, and the virtuous, decent type of girl who would never even consider doing that kind of work. While scandalized men have a knack for bouncing back, emerging from self-imposed sabbaticals and returning to their former existences relatively unscathed, women whom society deems have behaved badly are branded for life. The loss of my career made clear the sad fact that, to many, "once a prostitute, always a whore."

Much of my writing tries to combat this stigma, as well as the false belief that all sex workers are victims. Fact is, sex workers do not deserve to be hurt or to suffer because they sell sex. But they do suffer. I suffered. I was hurt. And yet, so much of the legislation purporting to help victims does, in fact, the opposite: it further marginalizes what Amnesty International identifies as "one of the most disadvantaged groups of people in the world, often forced to live outside the law and denied their most basic human rights."

According to Tawanda Mutasah, Amnesty International's senior director for law and policy, "Sex workers are at heightened risk of a whole host of human rights abuses including rape, violence, extortion, and discrimination. Far too often they receive no, or very little, protection from the law or means for redress."

The reality is that many sex workers, even those with sad stories, even those who squarely qualify as victims of sex trafficking, do not have an immediate interest to leave the industry. Others express a desire but lack the means to do so. As in any profession, there are sex workers who love their work. There are also countless individuals currently relying on sex work as a means of survival. The stigma, shame, and rejection they experience as a result of working in the sex industry only exacerbates the rigors of the work.

In college, at the same time I was working in the sex industry, I interned at two domestic violence shelters as an advocate and as a rape crisis counselor. These were great jobs, but they paid poorly, hence the stripping. Between undergrad and grad school, I worked in nonprofit development as a grant writer, charitable event coordination, and cause-related marketing (a job requiring skills very similar to stripping). I worked a desk job for a while as a research assistant, another job that paid well but that I found terribly boring. My favorite job, by far, was teaching art and writing to children.

Which brings me to now: After I lost my career as a public school teacher, I hustled as a freelance writer until 2017, when I became a full-time mom. Becoming a stay-at-home mom was never my intention, but when my husband and I first got together, I made about a third of his salary, only a little more than what our then-hypothetical child care would cost. After Oscar was born, it made little financial sense for me to keep working, especially for as long as I wanted to breast-feed. As much as surrendering was my decision, it's definitely fair to say I was economically coerced, like with my choice nearly twenty years ago to become a sex worker.

Interestingly, I've learned in the last year that stay-at-home moms

242   WOMEN TALK MONEY

endure their own idealization, mockery, and belittlement. Stay-at-home moms, like sex workers, are similarly disparaged as antifeminist. Ten years after hanging up my six-inch heels, I've once again become the butt of jokes. But I am not a joke. I am a writer, a feminist, a wife and mother, and yes, a former sex worker. And I deserve respect.

THE REQUIREMENTS OF WEALTH

LEAH HUNT-HENDRIX

MONEY HAS been the defining part of my life for as long as I can remember. It has brought me opportunity, safety, and power in addition to conflict, confusion, isolation, and despair. As the legend goes my grandfather H. L. Hunt, a poor man from Oklahoma, won a tract of land in East Texas during a poker game, and under that land lay vast oil reserves the depths of which could hardly be imagined. From those beginnings, my grandfather became one of the richest tycoons of the mid-twentieth century. My family would grow oil companies, amass real estate, serve as ambassadors, buy football teams, and start sports leagues. They were the owners of tremendous capital and benefited mightily from its profits.

While the rest of the family focused on acquiring more and more wealth, my mother decided to use her part of the family fortune to propel the women's movement. From a young age, she had suffered the consequences of patriarchy. Her mother, my grandmother, was H. L.'s secretary and mistress, and for the first ten years of my mother's life, she didn't know who her father was, as they lived in relative isolation until his first wife passed away. Eventually, H. L. moved her family into the mansion. There was no explanation. When my mom and her sisters recount their childhood, they don't mention the sudden influx of material goods, new dresses, or jewelry. They mostly recount the ways that they dealt with the strangeness of this family, living under a right-wing mi-sogynist and his odd forms of demagoguery. They remember the mental illness of their half brother, their mother's fragility, and the secrets. Yes, there was money, but mostly there was silence and questions without answers.

My father was raised in a vastly different environment. He was born a sharecropper in rural Georgia in 1935. The youngest of nine children, he stayed home with the women and learned to cook black-eyed peas and collard greens, while the men picked cotton and peanuts in the fields. By the age of six, he had lost both of his parents—to a farming accident and a stroke—but he was taken in by his older sisters and worked his way through high school as a soda jerk and a Baptist preacher. He did well in speech and debate and was the first person in his family to go to col-lege. Ultimately, he made it to the University of Chicago for a PhD in reli-gion and psychology. He would go on to become a professor at Southern Methodist University in Dallas, where he met my mother while she was in graduate school.

Somehow, these two individuals found each other, despite their dif-ferences. They were both passionate about understanding the human psyche. They were both broken and longed to heal. While my mother had access to wealth, there were never any illusions in our family that money created happiness. She often talked about the "golden handcuffs" that wealthy women wore, usually forced into silence by their powerful fathers or husbands. Wealth was associated with trauma. And in response, my parents sought a simple life for us, one that wasn't based on material goods. We didn't take trips to Europe. Instead, we traveled around the United States in a motor home, fishing in lakes and ponds, boiling coffee on outdoor stoves.

There was an understanding in our family that the world wasn't as it should be. My father introduced us to philosophy at a young age, giving us *Sophie's World*, a children's introduction to Western Thought. For the Ancient Greeks, the quest was to live the good life. They pondered true happiness and concluded it was based on virtue and justice rather than fame and fortune. My parents seemed motivated by healing—healing themselves and others. I wanted to heal the brokenness, too.

I spent much of my teens and twenties investigating these divergent goals—fame and success or justice and virtue—trying to understand how I should live my life. I studied political philosophy, waited tables, learned Arabic and lived in the Middle East, and enrolled in a PhD program in philosophy of religion, seeking more guidance on who I should be . . . and how I should be.

It wasn't until the eruption of a movement in downtown Manhattan that I began to see the role I could play. It was 2011 and I was living in a tiny, shared apartment in Brooklyn, working on my PhD dissertation. I had been studying social change and social movements and had decided to write about the concept of solidarity, a key term in movement spaces, when I saw on the news that people had gathered to occupy Wall Street, demanding attention to the state of economic inequality in America and the corporate capture of our society. I decided to go see it. The experience would transform my life.

The streets were even more crowded than usual when I emerged from the subways. It was September, and still muggy in Zuccotti Park, a spot of green in the midst of skyscrapers, where financial advisors and wealth managers take their lunches, but now it was filled with the sound of chanting and drums. Tents blanketed the park, where people had been sleeping for several days. A kitchen had been erected and was serving free food to anyone who passed by. The energy was electric. People were angry but also joyous. There was a thrill in finding themselves together and discovering that more and more people from around the country were flooding in to join a shared outcry.

I would have left after that brief sighting, but on my way back to the subway, I ran into my friend Max, who had arrived a few days before me. He encouraged me to join him in the meetings that were taking place. It was clear that this wasn't simply an organic eruption—yes, it was growing far beyond what anyone had imagined, but it was in fact planned, and there were methods and processes in place to determine next steps.

I followed Max around for the next several weeks as I learned about the culture, theory, and politics of this movement, and got to know many powerful activists.

What was compelling about Occupy Wall Street was the clarity of its analysis. We are often broken into siloed issue areas—those who care about education, or health care, or housing. But Occupy made the case that all of these issues are tied together by the fact that 1 percent of American society has control over the vast majority of our resources. All of these issues are a result of disproportionate distribution of wealth—which is further entrenched by the hold that the wealthy and corporations have over our political institutions. Wealth is power, and money makes money. There was no way to win by taking these issues on one by one—they were part of one and the same problem.

The solution we called for was solidarity. We needed people from all these fields and backgrounds and sectors to come together and fight for some kind of deep restructuring of American society. The protestors knew, like I did, that the concentration of wealth and power wasn't working for anyone—even those at the top. I wanted to be part of creating that kind of change.

Sustaining an occupation outdoors in wind, rain, and snow became untenable. The police and the city were also constantly threatening to evict the protestors. Finally, the day came when the park was cleared. It was a decisive blow to the momentum that Occupy Wall Street had created, but many were thinking about how to continue the work in new and different ways. I was asking this question of myself, too. What should my role be going forward?

One day, Max and I were walking down Broadway, trying to figure out what to do next. It was March 2012. We'd made it through a dramatic winter, and now the spring air was calling us to new things. I was still working on my PhD dissertation, but I knew I didn't want to stay in academia. I thought, perhaps, I should become an organizer—someone who works in communities and helps them fight for improvements in their lives. Max shook his head. "No, Leah," he said. "You should go organize your community. Organize wealthy people." I remember my physical re-action to that idea. It took me aback. It was distasteful at first. Was my community "the wealthy"? Is that who I was? I had been trying so hard, living deep in Brooklyn, dressing in inexpensive jeans and T-shirts, to hide that background. But Max saw the potential of being honest about who I was and where I came from. I had access to rooms that others didn't. I could be a bridge from these visionary movement spaces to the rooms of power and wealth.

By this point, I had begun to develop an understanding of the role that money could play in building movements. Movements can begin without money, but over time, food, materials, supplies, housing—basic human needs—require financial resources. Occupiers tried to resist these monetary exigencies. They lived together or squatted in empty locales. They survived off of donated pizza and leftovers from restaurants at the end of the day. But this was not sustainable.

In the midst of all of this, I purchased an apartment in Fort Greene, Brooklyn. My hope was to create a refuge in the middle of bustling New York City that could be used for gatherings and meaningful conversa-tions. Every month, I would roast a chicken and vegetables and people would huddle around the kitchen table, or sometimes spill over onto the couches and pillows on the floor, to discuss how to transform our eco-nomic system, how to redistribute wealth, and how to support people who were risking their lives for social change. I began to invite young people with wealth to talk about the role of philanthropy in particular. It was four of us, to start. But soon the group grew to eight, to ten, to twenty-five, to fifty.

We became a body through this heartbeat of monthly meals and daily emails. We named the community Solidaire—the French word for solidarity—to denote our commitment to getting to the root of what it means to stand with, and be led by, social movements. Most of us hadn't experienced the fear of not being able to pay your health care bill. Or the sensation of a cop pulling you over because of the color of your skin. Or the feelings of powerlessness in the face of incarceration. It was clear to us that we couldn't solve economic injustice, racial profiling, or mass incarceration on our own. But we could do our part.

Solidarity, it seemed to us, was based on an understanding of interconnection. It was based on the admission that my wealth is partly tied to your poverty. It was scary and guilt-provoking to admit, but we were forced to recognize that our families made their wealth by extracting the labor of workers or refining the raw materials of the earth. Our accumulated wealth did not take place in a vacuum—it was at the expense of someone else. Mark Zuckerberg made his billions by selling the data of Facebook users to advertising companies. Jeff Bezos made his billions by putting innumerable independent stores out of business. There is always a component of exploitation behind massive accumulation. My family's accumulation was no different, and my role was to begin to undo this.

When #BlackLivesMatter went viral after the shooting of Michael Brown in Ferguson, Missouri, we were ready to support. We didn't ask for grant proposals or reports but instead we tried to stay in a close and real relationship with movement activists so we could understand their needs and move resources quickly. We used our email LISTSERV to share what we were hearing in real time and to collaborate to get the resources where they needed to go. We sent money for protest supplies, plane tickets, bail funds, housing. Five years later, our email list is still active, and we have moved millions and millions of dollars quickly and seamlessly to movements like Standing Rock, #MeToo, and many others.

Money is like oxygen—it is necessary in our world. To hoard that oxygen when others need it to breathe is a crime. But it is not enough to simply give it away—especially in ways that serve to sustain the status quo. The vast majority of philanthropy serves to soften the hard blows that characterize our society; it does little to challenge the ongoing role of white supremacy, patriarchy, or class domination—the daily realities of American life. Getting to the root cause of inequality is uncomfortable and often requires a disruption that shakes us out of the trance that tells us this is a normal and inevitable way to live. But we have the power to change our world. We have the power to make history. And philanthropy should be in service of those who are courageously stepping into that fight.

Philanthropy is not an altruistic, generous act. It is the bare minimum moral requirement for those who have too much. When done poorly, it simply solidifies social inequalities. But we had—have—hope that, when done well, it has the potential to be part of healing the brokenness of a society confused about where to find happiness. Social movements are going to happen, with or without the support of people with wealth. Philanthropists will not save our society. But if they are willing to let go of some of their privileges and become part of something bigger and more meaningful, they might finally know what it means to be in real community. They might discover that in letting go, they might find true happiness.

SHARKS IN THE *BANYA*

GABRIELLE BELLOT

THE GIRL in the *banya*'s dressing room already has her top off, her small, compact, beige breasts half-moon-ringed with long black hair. Before I know it, she is naked, her swimsuit at her feet, body by her brown locker. It is a sudden nudity, at once unremarkable and astonishing: a quick tuft of black hair, a glimpse of genitalia. In a few moments, my girlfriend, too, has stepped out of the Merlot-red bottom of her ruched bikini while she chats with me, a sudden vision of soft brown against her light skin. I don't say anything. None of the other women do. We've all been bathing in the Brooklyn bathhouse a floor below for a few hours—I came with my girlfriend for a quite literally steamy Valentine's Day event—and we need to change.

But on the inside, I'm freaking out. I've never actually changed in public like this; for some reason, I hadn't expected the suddenness of these naked bodies. They're just our bodies, yet the quick sight reminds me, with a sharp twitch of fear, of how my body is different, how my body makes mundane moments like these either magical or mortifying. It is like the sudden leap into the blue as a scuba diver off the side of a boat, when you must get your bearings as you enter the sea, hoping you have not missed the shadow of a shark, the shadow of some quiet deadly thing, and then you are just there, floating, part of a new world, yet different from it all the same.

As a pre-op trans woman, I know I cannot undress like them, not unless I want the stares and glares and up-flares of eyebrows and anger and voices. No one in here, as far as I know, knows I'm trans, aside from my partner. I "pass." But if I take off my swimsuit, something else will be there. I do not want to be branded an intruder. A voyeur. A pervert. A rapist. A freak—not in the good, faintly punk sense of the word, as I am happily both freak and geek, but in the dangerous definition that gets the cops called on you. Even in liberal, trans-friendly worlds, there is always someone who thinks you do not belong, who will cause chaos once they realize what you are. The sharks are always there, even if you can't see them.

I tell my partner I want to take a shower first. It's true, as I reek of chlorine, but it's an excuse to take my floral blue-white one-piece off without anyone else seeing me. In the little shower, as she turns on the nozzle and tilts her head back so the water hits her blond-brown curls, I make sure the white curtain is pulled all the way closed. I keep on the black panty I wore under my swimsuit for precaution—I didn't absolutely need it, but I wanted to make sure no one would see a little bulge down there. It's wet, but I consider leaving it on even under the shower's spray for precaution, in case someone peeks in. Instead, I leave it close by. My girlfriend nibbles my nipples; I stifle my voice so no one will laughingly or indignantly decide to take a look through our curtain. She finishes her bath before me, leaving the curtain open by mistake; I yank it back, heart pounding for a moment. It is both beautiful and terrifying that she sees me so totally as female that she is able to forget, for a moment, the danger I can be in from something as mundane as nakedness in a public shower or changing room.

I put my damp panty back on and walk into the locker room to get my bra and dress; I have learned, at least, not to be afraid of baring the small, cuppable breasts I have acquired, over years, from hormone replacement therapy, and no one gives me a second glance as I return. Still, I dress as quickly as I can, trying not to show my trepidation as other cis women wander in and strip out of their swimsuits to change.

This moment, in some ways, is money, in that money has made it possible. Being trans is an identity, like having a switch marked Girl always flipped in your mind, even when people, confoundingly, tell you that you cannot be one. Transitioning, by contrast, is a financial privilege, and those of us who cannot "pass" as the gender we see ourselves as may never feel welcome in spaces like this changing room, no matter how liberal a state one may live in. I am shielded, I realize, by my ability to, for the most part, "pass" as a cis woman if I do not fully undress—and that ability to "pass" is partly a roll of the genetic dice, such that I have always been androgynous, and partly, scarily, because of another shield: money, which pays for the little and big things that allow me to "pass." The truth is, the "I" I am now and have always wanted to be is, quite literally, the product of money—and that is as mundane as it is frightening.

Sometimes, I imagine my life as an interview, a series of questions proffered to me by a stony-faced woman in a dark blue robe, her face flanked by blue ringlets. She looks, somewhat alarmingly, like how I often envision Death, but without her trademark disarming smile. This woman, instead, offers neither smile nor glare.

Q: What is the financial cost of being trans? How much does it cost to become someone?
A: More than most of us can afford—and we don't stop paying until we die.

At this point, the tone morphs, incredulously, into something more chiding.

Q: Why would you do this? And how can you authentically become anything, anyway, if you pay for it? You can't buy a self, can you?
A: No, but you can buy something that helps you become the you that you see inside. *[There's no why, I think, a little defensively.]* It's just me. The compass of me just points this way, and because I don't have magic, money has to help me orient my body so that it aligns with who I've always seen myself as.

Q. Very philosophical. How much does that cost?
A. A lot, from my wallet, and from my soul. It's not fun.

Q. So why?
A. Because the alternative is dying.

Death is a thing that circles many of us trans people, like a silent shark, waiting, waiting. Feeling comfortable about who we are and getting help if we have suicidal thoughts may keep it at bay, somewhat—but getting that help, and that comfort, so often costs us financially and emotionally.

Each day, I follow a regimen: three light-blue oval pills, and two round white pills that taste, when they touch my tongue, like mint, all five taken over the course of the day. They are a simple magic, alchemizing my body from boy to girl, if we understood these terms reductively, over time, by softening my skin, shifting the distribution of fat in my face and thighs and butt, thinning the hairs on my body. Perhaps most notably, they enlarge the breasts they helped create, first as sore buds, then as little mango-shaped emanations on my chest, new pieces of me that hurt, at first, when I walked or jumped, from the unexpected sensation of gravity on them. After some years, my breasts became simply a part of my shape, my silhouette, my sexuality, my sense of self.

I have taken these pills—the blue ones estrogen, the white ones anti-androgens that reduce testosterone—for many years now, and my body and mind feel closer to being right, finally. I have always had a somewhat androgynous form, even in the fat distribution on my waist, which was always like a plump hourglass even when I was a teen, but the hormone therapy has helped me feel content in my body.

If this regimen helps me feel more in tune with my womanhood, it also is a quiet, constant reminder that my womanhood costs money— a lot of it. You can't get hormone therapy medication, in the first place, without jumping through a series of financial hoops. First, you have to find a therapist who, after an indeterminate number of sessions, will write a letter confirming that you have gender dysphoria and are a candidate for hormone replacement therapy. My therapist, who I was also seeing to try to deal with my depression, cost $100 a session and wanted to see me once a week. From there, you have to find an endocrinologist who will accept your therapist's letter and who will agree to start you on HRT—and you'll pay for these evaluative visits, of course. My hormone therapy, each month, comes to a little over thirty dollars—affordable for me, inaccessible for someone poorer, and not covered by all insurance plans if you get HRT in the form of pills. If a doctor were administering injections, it would cost more. I will never stop being on HRT; this is money I must pay for the rest of my life.

If I stop taking my hormones, first, I get menopausal symptoms as my levels shift: hot flashes, dizziness, nausea, pain. Then, ugly old aspects of my body reassert themselves. My body hair will grow thicker and darker; my underarms, which smell like onions if I don't use deodorant, will take on a thick musk; my fat will redistribute, subtly yet saliently, in my face and legs and waist. I will hurt, too, in my head. I want none of this. My ability to keep being myself, to keep this old darkness at bay, is contingent upon having enough money each month when I go to my pharmacy.

When I put my latest containers of hormone pills into my purse, I feel a sense of relief. I get to have another month of me, as me. The regimen will go on—and, with it, the alignment of my body and brain.

There are more costs to transitioning, of course. I started life with a very non-androgynous name, which I wanted to change; it hurts to be called your old name when your old name is very masculine-sounding, because it feels as if you're misgendered, and it causes chaos when someone perceives you, at a glance, as female, and then sees a male name on your ID. At worst someone may think you are a peculiar sort of identity thief, trying to get by with someone else's ID. If nothing else, it forces you to out yourself as trans to the stranger examining your ID, and that is always a risky revelation. There are countless trans women, predominantly trans women of color, who have been beaten up, even killed, when someone realized, through an ID or otherwise, that they were not cisgender.

So, I changed my legal name, and, later, the gender on my documentation—for a set of hefty fees. In America, these processes can easily run to hundreds of dollars, depending on where you live. Then, because I still was uncomfortable with a certain aspect of how I looked, I decided to remove the thick black hairs on my cheeks, chin, and upper lip. I tried lots of things: buying an epilator that left my face pulsing red and made me cry from the pain; purchasing orange blush and lipstick that I could apply over where I would get a five o'clock shadow, the orange neutralizing the green tint when overlaid with heavy foundation. Finally, frustrated and desperate, I decided to try laser hair removal. I ended up going to well over twenty sessions of lasers being shot into my face, each like a little snap of a rubber band, which I was able to afford through, of all things, a student discount. The sessions all together still came, however, to hundreds of dollars. In the future, I will probably have to do touch-ups, which will come to hundreds once more.

Being trans is damn expensive—and this isn't counting the price of surgeries. I haven't had any surgeries; the most extreme, a vaginoplasty, is something I've yearned for, but the procedure is so expensive, especially if your insurance provider does not cover it (and only a few do), that it might as well be impossible. Many other surgeries that trans people consider are costly, too: facial feminization, top surgery for trans men, vocal feminization surgeries for trans women.

Of course, these are just the bills for the cosmetic and internal aspects of transitioning. Being trans in the workplace—where, conceivably, you might make the money you would use to pay for your transition—can feel financially perilous, particularly when a number of states still allow employers to fire you simply for being LGBTQ. And when you work, as I do, as a freelance writer and editor in an industry where many publications pay very little per piece and take weeks to send off a check at all, it's even harder. Reveal what you are, and certain employers won't hire you, even if they loved your experience and credentials before learning that you're transgender. Reveal what you are, and certain parents will kick you out of your home or tell you, as mine did, it would be safer not to return to your home country, given how anti-queer it is, given how shameful you are by being, as my mother frequently termed me, such a freak.

I try to push my mother's words down into some gray place in me, where I can't hear them, where they can't hurt so much. But I still do hear them, often, when I place those blue and white tablets on my tongue. I want to prove her wrong, to show her that I can find success in this world as an openly trans woman. But her guilting is heavy, and I feel it as I look at myself in the mirror, wondering, as I run my fingers across the curve of my jaw to feel for stray hairs, if I can really afford another session of laser, or if I can really afford these magical little tablets all my life, and how long that life will be, under all the pressure of her unhappiness and all the heaviness of living in a country where trans people are still the easiest political targets.

Unlike in that interview of the soul, I don't have an answer.

Just being trans, my mother has often suggested, is a financial death sentence, and fatal in other ways, as well: in terms of my love life, my mental and spiritual well-being. Please reconsider, she tells me often even now, a sea away in Dominica, trying to convince me, through the witchcraft of pleading and gaslighting, that being trans is unsightly, untenable, unlivable. No one will want you like this, this thing. You will end up homeless and begging on the sidewalk. No one will love you. Why must you do this to me? To yourself? To everyone? You should forget you had a mother if this is what you will do to me. I have become accustomed to it, even as her words still make me cry sometimes; I have become accustomed to her begging that I change back, like Circe's pigs transforming back into Odysseus's sailors.

Her words are emotionally taxing, like the language of transphobic government policies—the endless proposed bathroom bills that posit trans people as monstrous would-be rapists who want to use the women's bathroom solely to commit assault; the Trump administration's military ban of trans people that claimed trans people are mentally ill and thus unfit to serve. When you hear this kind of thing over and over, it becomes a painful, poignant mantra you begin to internalize, a hateful rhythm you start to live by without even realizing. You begin, in other words, to actually believe that these absurd, propagandistic tropes of transphobia are true, not because you have any evidence that they are, but because when you're lonely and vulnerable—as unaccepting societies often render us— it's easier to internalize these self-loathing ideas.

Womanhood is so often heavy already, even without being trans. It is taxing on brain and body alike to be crudely catcalled, followed, hunted by men. It is taxing to so often be told that our stories of such harassment and abuse are lies or exaggerations. It is taxing to know, immediately, the way that certain men will look down upon you the moment they see you, simply because they perceive you as female.

When you're trans, and people doubt or outright deny your womanhood, it's even harder and heavier to bear. It becomes a Sisyphean struggle when you have all of this and still have to bear being told by others, or even by yourself, that you aren't really worthy of being a woman. It hurts. And when it hurts too much, you sink, all the way down to the place where the sharks wait.

They almost got me, twice. The first was before I came out as trans, when I was in so much pain about being perceived as a male that I considered drinking poison to kill myself; coming out saved my life. The second time was after I'd come out, and the weight of all the damnations and claims that I would die loveless and lonely that my mother and others put upon me became too much to bear, and I came close to jumping in front of a C train in the NYC subway.

Being trans is expensive in this way, too: when it aches, it really, really aches. It costs a lot, metaphorically and mentally, to deal with dysphoria when it's at its worst—and though not all trans people experience dysphoria to the same degree, for me, at least, it has been traumatizing. On my worst days, I was sometimes so afraid of being misgendered and followed by angry men that I avoided going out altogether and just sat on my bed, trembling and crying, wishing I were more confident and wishing that transitioning to the point of being accepted as female, in nearly all situations, was easier.

I will never understand the people who think that anyone transitions on a whim, or that being trans is some trendy, "fun" thing to identify as, when I would never wish the pain it's brought me upon anyone I know. To be sure, I love myself; it's just hard, when the world doesn't love you back, but sees you, instead, in its nightmares.

I've stood naked in front of my mirror, sometimes, often when the light is fading, or in an artificial semidarkness. My body is never quite right, but I try to pose in such a way that I can believe, for a moment, I don't look as bad as I fear. I tuck what lies between my legs in between my thighs, then stand in such a way that it almost looks like those genitals aren't there. I imagine what my life would have been like if I had been born with a vagina. I imagine how so many scenes would play out differently if I could afford the surgery to have one. I imagine walking through the TSA's body-scanning machines without having to fear, for once, that my genitalia will appear on the scanner as an "anomaly" that forces a woman to pat me down near my crotch. I imagine not being afraid to undress with other women. I imagine not being afraid a bathroom stall door will swing open, by mistake, as I am urinating and that someone will catch a glimpse of the "wrong" anatomy. I imagine feeling freer to be naked during sex, without my dysphoria overwhelming me.

It's a toll to preserve one's mental health with this stress. Transitioning while counting dollars is harder still. I want to save enough to have a family, a home, kids, but I need to pay rent in the present, too. And yet I always feel lucky, knowing how many of my trans sisters cannot do any of these things at all, be it walking into a *banya* or paying for the little and big things that help us survive, inside and out, in a world that rarely seems to desire such survival.

I still fear, some nights when I stay up into the wee hours from stress, that I won't make it, and will sink, like some girl made of iron, through the blue to where the sharks are waiting. I take the sleeping pills I also must budget for each month, to try to ward off those shadows. And then I snuggle against the partner I feel so lucky to have, the one who sees nothing incongruous about me being in the women's room of a *banya* with her, and, despite all that heaviness, all those glimpses of fins, I smile, and I let myself feel at ease, for a bit.

INHERITANCE

RACHEL M. HARPER

FOR THE first half of my life, I lived with the knowledge of a single inheritance: when my parents died, I would inherit our lake house—a small, musty cabin under a canopy of burly oak trees beside a mud-colored lake in central Minnesota. Throughout my childhood, we spent our summers there, but to call it a summer house is to inflate it in both size and stature. Yes, it was a *house*, and we lived in it for several weeks in the *summer*, but it was not grand or fancy or desirable—words I associate with people who summered on the Cape or the Vineyard, people who used the word *summer* as a verb. Our cabin was a two-bedroom, one-bath house with an unfinished attic and a shower that never worked. Beneath its small, square shape was a basement that was perpetually damp; no matter how often we aired it out, it held a permanent stench of wet rags and spilled oil. I was convinced that several ghosts lived down there, characters who'd escaped from books I'd been forced to read on rainy days: Boo Radley, Beloved, Mr. Rochester's wife.

Each June we packed the car and drove 1,500 miles in four days, the five of us squished into an overburdened Volvo station wagon, a car with spotty air-conditioning and wide strips of rust over the wheel beds, the radio dial permanently stuck on NPR. We crossed the country from Northeast to Midwest, staying in motels along the way or on the pull-out couches of my father's faculty friends, newly tenured professors who taught in small towns like Ann Arbor and Hamilton, or large sweltering cities like Chicago. They welcomed us with trays of hamburgers and pitchers of ice-cold lemonade when we arrived, mosquito-bitten and sweat-stained after hours in the car.

We needed it to be understood: we were not spoiled like many of our private school classmates, who flew first-class or went to expensive overnight camps, who owned houses by the beach and had paid staff making their meals; our cabin was in Minnesota, one hundred miles from a real city, and our beloved little lake was far from impressive in a state known for ten thousand of them. My father drove three miles to town to pick up our mail each day. The house didn't have a telephone, a television, a toaster, or air-conditioning. Every night after dinner, my mother burned our trash in a small dirt firepit behind the compost pile outside the kitchen window.

Our closest neighbors were family: my grandparents lived next door, on the other side of a hedge of chokecherries; one aunt and uncle lived in an old farmhouse by the main road, while another owned a strip of land behind us, driving a camper down on the weekends to escape the Twin Cities. My uncles worked for themselves or other men they knew: renovating barns, restoring tractors, growing marijuana on foreclosed farms on the edge of the county line. My aunts worked all day long but never got paid: they fed the children and pets, raised livestock, mucked out barns, weeded gardens, sewed dresses and darned socks, ironed patches over worn-out overalls, developed photographs and organized slide shows, made scrapbooks, washed dishes, and ran endless loads of laundry, hanging the clothes to dry on the lines behind the house.

By the time I was ten, my family had turned a dozen acres of flat, unremarkable land in Kandiyohi County into our version of the Kennedy compound. But in our minds, we were roughing it: we ate directly from the garden, pulled carrots straight out of the earth, still covered with a dusting of dirt; we picked blackberries by the side of gravel roads; fried sunfish we caught in the lake with handmade fishing poles like Huck

Finn. We washed our hair once a week in the lake. We reread the same books left behind from the summer before: *The Old Man and the Sea*, *A Prayer for Owen Meany*, *The Bluest Eye*. We lived in our bathing suits. We misplaced our shoes for weeks at a time, only needing them for trips to the $2 movie theater on Wednesday nights, or the annual All You Can Eat farewell dinner we had every August, hosted by the bar that sponsored my cousin's Little League team from a few towns over. We flattened pennies on the railroad tracks, collecting them later to use as poker chips.

My father, the only one with a real job, which is to say a retirement account, sat at the typewriter all day, writing postcards and poems at a desk he made by placing an old door on top of four wooden crates, one still holding an errant glass bottle, long empty of milk. He wore shorts, sunglasses, and sandals; it was the only time all year I ever saw his bare feet. How powerful his brown legs looked under that desk, muscles twitching like a thoroughbred at the gate. He had the whole day to himself: no students, no classes, no committee meetings. I thought that was an achievement beyond measure—to have the freedom to dictate your days, and that's exactly what he did.

I wasn't raised to believe in God or heaven or Santa Claus, but I was taught to believe in the permanence of objects, to worship land that our ancestors had tamed, to value homes their hands had built. I loved our house as if I had dreamt it into being. The cabin had the best well water I've ever tasted, which came out of the faucet as cold as a mountain stream and with such force it was like turning on a hose, the flood of water as solid and thick as a pipe, shimmering like mercury. So, when my parents told us, my two older brothers and me, that the cabin would one day belong to us, when we were grown up and responsible, I felt a sense of pride settle into my bones. They were entrusting us with not only our home but with our shared past. We would own it together, and like our DNA, it would bind us and make us one.

But my inheritance gave me something else: a safety net. I understood that if something terrible happened to me, like poverty or illness, or even something less dire, like the need to take a break from the grind of regular life, the cabin would always be there. No one could close the door on me; I would always have a place to take me in. This gave me a sense of freedom I might not otherwise have known. I felt free—to become an artist, a musician, a writer; to follow my passions. I was free to fail. With the cabin to fall back on, I took risks others didn't have the luxury to take. I traveled abroad, took jobs with no benefits, decided to become a novelist; I moved with a sense of security, a quiet confidence. I lived like I was unafraid.

When my parents divorced, during my first year of graduate school, my mother called to tell me the news. She said it was what they both wanted, that she had already moved out. Her voice was strained and she sounded nervous, upset. I knew there was something else. I asked about her health, if she was sleeping, and how my middle brother—the most vulnerable of us all—had taken it. Everything was fine, she said. The real reason for her upset didn't become clear until the end of the phone call: they were selling the cabin. I felt my face get hot as my palms started to sweat. *No, that's not possible.* I slumped down on a stool, leaned against the wall for support. I could barely hear my mother's voice as she went on, saying she needed money to live on before the divorce settlement came through, that my father had agreed to split the proceeds. Just like that: I lost my inheritance.

She said other things I didn't want to hear and can't remember, perhaps even that she was sorry. I hung up the phone, too shocked to cry, and didn't move for a long time. The room was soon dark, and the cat circled my ankles, begging for food. I was filled with a vague sense of unease, an unfamiliar loneliness. That night I went to bed late, and for the first time I could remember, woke with a feeling of dread. I noticed a crack in the plaster that ran along my ceiling, a remnant of the '94 earthquake, and felt a certain kinship with the building: the structures of my world had also shifted. I had been altered.

I was the baby of the family, the easy favorite, yet no one thought to ask how I felt. My older brothers—one still in college after eight years, no degree in sight, the other working full-time as a librarian and part-time cutting hair—weren't that upset. They hadn't been to the cabin in several years, and when they did come, the visits were short and devoid of the intimacy we had once shared. The lake water was too warm, they complained, no longer refreshing, and the neighbors had built bigger houses along the opposite shore, ruining our once idyllic view. Our childhood was over, they said; it's time to move on.

But I was living in a one-room apartment in LA, with an unpaid internship and thousands of dollars of student debt, and the lake house was part of my backup plan. If rents got too steep and I couldn't find a real job, I could always go there to reset. Without it, the pressure to succeed increased exponentially. But beneath the worldly concerns was the unbearable pull of nostalgia, the ache I suddenly felt for the innocence and ease of childhood. The memories that seemed to coalesce under that single, distant roof, etched into the rafters of a cabin to which I could no longer return.

I had been betrayed. It was as if my parents had taken out all of our family photo albums, covered them with kerosene, and lit a match, committing all of our memories—past and future—to ash. The cabin was the only home we had owned for my entire life, purchased from my grandparents the summer after I was born. I didn't have memories of moving into or out of it; it simply existed, as permanent and steady as the oak trees in our front yard. I had come to see my life as the time that existed between visits; each year, I needed to go there to see who I was—or rather, who I had become. Without it, who would I be?

When they sold the cabin, to my mother's cousin for a ridiculously small sum, I vowed I would never return. I didn't want to see anyone else enjoying the view of the lake from our living room windows; I couldn't bear to hear the slap of the screen doors banging against their crooked frames as visitors stopped in on another family. I didn't want to see our home filled with someone else's furniture, to smell their dinner in our kitchen, to hear the sounds of other voices filling the rooms. And God forbid they make any improvements—I knew I couldn't live through that. So, I stayed away, despite the invitations to weddings and funerals, despite the hole it opened in my summers, empty weeks I tried to fill with extra work, love affairs, and travel to more interesting, exotic locations; places that, unlike our lake house, were visible on maps.

In time, I finished my master's degree, but lacked enough publications to secure a good teaching job. Instead, I worked security, temp jobs, and moved in with friends to save money. I contemplated law school or a PhD, stayed up nights working on a novel, and drank too much; I amassed credit card debt to rival my student loans and wrestled with thoughts of futility. Eventually I left California and moved back to my hometown, got a regular job, and finished the novel I'd been working on for five years. I submitted stories to literary journals and got a few published. I became a mother.

I was still heartbroken over the loss of the lake house, but when my daughter was a year old, I decided to go back. I wanted to give her something else I had found in Minnesota: time to be with her cousins, to make memories on the land my grandparents farmed, to know the untamed countryside I spent many hours exploring; to swim in the lake where I learned to dive, where I water-skied for the first time and had my first kiss. I couldn't give her the actual cabin, but I wanted her to have a sliver of the freedom I had enjoyed there, even if it was only a taste. Otherwise, I feared I might run forever.

My daughter and I stayed in my aunt's house at the top of the hill, and for two days I managed to avoid going down to the lake to see our old cabin. But on the third day, I knew I had to face it. My daughter was newly walking, and I held her hand as we set off, neither one of us wearing shoes. I looked down at her bare feet, amazed that she seemed to handle the gravel path much better than I could, the soles of my feet soft now, unaccustomed to the contours of stone. She pointed at the dragonflies and wanted to stop to pick raspberries from the thicket beside the barn. There was no rush, so I let her dawdle, buying time before I had to face what I had lost. I had survived without the cabin for ten years but still hadn't fully accepted that it was gone, that I was living without the security I'd grown up with, and that by extension, my daughter would have to live without it, too.

My heart galloped in my chest as we stepped back on the path and resumed our walk. My daughter's small plastic bucket was half-filled with raspberries, which she dragged along the ground between us. "Look," she said, "tree," pointing at the crab apple tree, beside the patch of worn grass where we used to park our car. I forced myself to follow her finger, staring at the canopy of oaks that were always tall but now seemed to cover the cabin completely, as if in a show of solidarity. As I walked closer, knowing the lake house, *my lake house*, was about to reveal itself to me, I relished my last seconds of ignorance, imagining the small, square structure as it always was, the faded green paint trimmed in burgundy and white, the front door propped open with a five-gallon bucket of sweet corn my uncle had just picked.

I still couldn't see it, but everything surrounding it was the same, and for a few moments I could almost convince myself that nothing had changed, that it all still belonged to me. And then I saw the cabin. Or rather, the house that now stood in its place. Our cabin had been demolished, and a new structure—long and bright, with shining glass windows and a gray shingled roof—stood in its place. It was twice the size of our cabin, and though it wasn't ugly, I hated it instantly. As we walked by, I willed myself not to look at it, focusing only on the lake as it came into view. We arrived at our old beach and I picked my daughter up; holding on to her soft, warm body, I waded into the shallow water, afraid to look back.

But my daughter wasn't afraid. She peeked around my shoulder and pointed at the oaks. "Look," she said, "trees," and I knew I had to look. Together we turned back to the land, taking in the sight of the new house, the half-dozen oaks towering overhead, the treehouse we built from old railroad ties and pallets when I was ten. "Look," I said, pointing to the treehouse, "a house." She laughed then, and even though I had tears in my eyes, I laughed, too.

A few seconds later she pointed at the house. "Look," she said, and I held my breath as I waited for her to speak again, expecting her to say something that would make me have to acknowledge it. But instead she said, "A bird." I didn't notice it at first, but soon I saw the fluttering of the bird's black wings, which seemed to disappear into its body as the bird came to rest on the chimney. "Yes," I said, looking at the house, "a bird."

It has taken me years to get over the loss of my inheritance, and sometimes I think I'm deluding myself to say I have. But on my best days, when I'm aware of the freedom my creative life has afforded me, despite the sacrifice of security, when I feel at peace with who I am, regardless of what I lack in material comforts, I realize how lucky I was that day with my daughter, when we walked down to the lake and saw that the cabin was gone. The structure we called our home, the one we had lived and loved in, no longer existed, and by being erased, had become permanently fixed in our memories.

Like a time capsule, it was forever locked in an earlier time—the days and weeks of a now endless childhood, when we were young and fearless and full of hope; when we were still a family, living under the same small roof, safe in the knowledge that we had a home, a place to gather in a storm that would always take us in—and we could live there always, in the only landscape that could not be destroyed.

The lake house was my inheritance, and even though it no longer exists, I still carry the story of what it meant to me. In the end, that is the inheritance I will pass down to my daughter—not simply the story of its loss, but the memory of our walk to the lake, of her small hands filled with raspberries, of standing in the shadows of ancient trees and wading into the warm waters of our lake, of seeing a bird come to rest on a rooftop, and of her voice telling me to look, showing me what it's like to be unafraid.

WHAT MY MOTHER TAUGHT ME

HELEN ZIA

MY MOTHER never said much to me about money at any time of my growing-up years in New Jersey. Mom was an immigrant from China with a limited ability to speak English; her education had stopped after the third grade. It was wartime, and there wasn't money to spend on educating girls, she'd say. She was a twenty-one-year-old widow in a foreign country—America—with an infant son to care for; she remarried in short order and by the time she was twenty-five, she had three more kids and a difficult second husband—my father—whose sporadic income came from selling items that we, as a family, made in our home.

I know that Mom was an exhausted young mother. When I was about three, her health deteriorated to the point that she was diagnosed with tuberculosis and had to be quarantined in a state TB sanitarium. With no health insurance, the state stepped in and placed my brothers and me in foster care for a time, while our mother convalesced. Mom shared little of that time, except to say that when she was released for a home visit and came to check on us, my infant brother was covered with mosquito bites and cried in discomfort. She was so heartbroken that she checked herself out of the facility and brought us all home.

This was during the anti-communist witch hunts of the McCarthy period, with intense xenophobia, homophobia, and American nativism.

People of Chinese descent were special targets of government surveillance and racism, under the constant threat of arrest and deportation. My parents had separately fled to the US in the 1940s as part of the exodus from civil war and revolution. In those days, Chinese weren't hired for well-paying "American" jobs at the post office or union-wage factories, and certainly not for professional white-collar work. Thinking that his children would face less discrimination if we could speak perfect American English, my father decided that it would be better to speak only English to us, even if it made life even more difficult for our mother.

Truth is, I can't recall talking with my mom about much of anything when I was a youngster. Language is a common barrier between children and parents in immigrant families from non–English-speaking countries, especially for the mothers who are often isolated at home with little chance to practice speaking the new foreign language.

Instead, Mom taught by example. My first lesson about money from my mother came when I was about eight years old. I learned the hard way that my mom always knew exactly how much money she had on hand. She kept her handbag on a shelf near our dining table; with the help of a nearby chair, it was easily within reach of an errant child. Once, I took a few quarters from her change purse. I can only guess that I wanted to be ready when the Good Humor ice cream truck came, ringing its bell down our street.

Before that could happen, my mom summoned her four children, ages six to ten, and asked each of us, in her Chinglish accent, "Who took money from my bag?" I have repressed the details of how my guilt came to light, though I strongly suspect one of my brothers ratted on me. Mom didn't tell my father, the family enforcer, but I couldn't forget how disappointed she was with me.

Mom taught me some important lessons that day: first, pay attention to what money is coming in and going out, and, second, there's no money to be had at the expense of others. That honest money is earned, and stealing by any name is wrong.

Early on, I also learned how my mother made every penny count. Going food shopping with Mom was a painful exercise in patience for a kid, as, when we were small, she often took the four of us along with her, rather than leave us at home. Once a week, our dad scraped together an allowance for my mother; our food, clothing, doctors if we got sick, all had to come from that allowance, even after two more kids were eventually born and the total brood numbered six.

No matter how many kids she had in tow at the market, Mom carefully picked through string beans, apples, oranges, every bit of produce, one by one. She was determined to provide only the freshest, most perfect foodstuff for her family—at a bargain price, of course, if possible. I didn't appreciate then how well my mother was able to calculate the total purchases as she went along, mentally itemizing and stretching her household budget while choosing the best produce and cuts of meat that she could afford. Now I realize that her meticulous selections were not only about getting the best value for money, but that her care was also an expression of her love for her children.

Sometimes Mom would let us wait in the breakfast cereal aisle, where we entertained ourselves by perusing the colorful boxes, with their funny cartoons and fascinating tidbits, all aimed at children. That ended after a white store manager hustled us to wherever the one Asian-looking woman—our mom—was shopping and accused us kids of opening cereal boxes. We told Mom that we didn't do it—we really hadn't! She angrily defended us to the store manager as best she could in English. We stomped out of the market together, shopping day ruined.

I remember, too, the feeling of humiliation and shame that tinged my mother's anger, her helplessness at seeing her children falsely accused and not having the American words to tell him to fuck off. That offered another lesson years later, when stories emerged of Asian American shopkeepers racially profiling their Black customers. Such racist indignities—the thousands of cuts by microaggressions—inflict deep wounds and trigger justifiable rage that can be channeled into mass action. Seeing the racism that my mother and father endured just trying to get by, I absorbed the imperative of calling out and working to end systemic racism and all oppressions.

My mom didn't have to tell me how precious each cent was to our family. I saw how hard she worked. After a long day of caring for her six kids, she stayed up late every night to make the things we called "baby novelties" that my father sold to flower shops, which added floral arrangements to our novelties to be sold as gifts for families with new babies.

As my siblings and I grew older, we, too, worked in the family business that occupied part of our home. On weekends or after school, I'd make a few dozen baby novelties. Following the example of my mom, I'd keep an account of my work, for which I was paid a nickel or a dime a piece, depending on the item. It wasn't much money; I'd earn a dollar or so if I was lucky. Mom took me to the local bank and helped me open up a savings account. I don't think I ever saved more than $100, but at some point, I used that account to pay for my own expenses for school. I kept track of my expenditures and savings the way my mom did, in simple lists, trying to keep something aside, just in case.

I never knew how much my mother could squirrel away from her household allowance; it was another thing we never talked about. Yet somehow she managed to give her kids a small gift on birthdays and Christmas. New shoes and winter coats had to be paid for from the allowance; credit cards weren't common then, and Mom didn't even have a checking account. Of course, it was rarely enough for six growing kids; I remember the fights my parents would have over money, a lot of shouting in their Chinese dialect. Even though I was a monolingual ABC (American-born Chinese) kid, I could decipher well enough. Why do the kids need winter coats at all? Can't they keep wearing the same shoes?

Mom was the lioness, fighting for her cubs, and she always managed to find a way. We'd end up shopping at the bargain stores for what we needed; my mom never shopped "brand" names and I grew up unaware of what brands were "in." As the children of immigrants, we knew it was pointless to be fussy. To my mom, material things are not important; rather, taking care of those you love is.

Being a daughter, I also gleaned some lessons that my brothers may have missed: I was going to grow up to be an independent woman, so I wouldn't ever be dependent on a man for finances the way my mother was, having to fight for her kids' shoes. Mom eventually shared that my dad was a good provider, because he always gave her the food money first, no matter how little he had earned. But from watching my mother, I could see that an independent life, financially and otherwise, was the more liberating path for women. I remember realizing this as a middle schooler and concluding that college would have to be my ticket out. I also understood that my family couldn't pay for my college education and was determined to make myself competitive enough to get a full scholarship package for college—and I did.

A path to independence opened for my mom as we, her kids, graduated from high school and were no longer around to make baby novelties and our dad grew too old to drive to flower shops. To make some money, Mom started working outside the home. At first she was a part-time school aide, then was hired as a packer at a cake factory in a nearby town. Her coworkers were Black, white, Latinx; she loved their friendship and camaraderie—and they adored her. As Mom's English vocabulary grew, so did her own sense of self and freedom. Mom had been working there for a few years when, during one of my visits home, she suggested, "Let's take a break and chat." I was so surprised. Growing up, Mom worked constantly, no such thing a break. And *chat*? I had never chatted about anything with my mom, let alone about money. I loved seeing my mother reach for her own independence, helping to plan holiday parties with her coworkers, and to see her *chat* with all kinds of people. And to have her own money to spend, using her own checking account.

But Mom's job in the cake factory wasn't enough. As my siblings and I began working, we took what we had learned from our parents about living within our means and setting a bit of money aside. We each sent some of that money home to help out our parents, who, like many immigrants, didn't have jobs with retirement income. We, like so many grown children of immigrants, had always known that we were the pension plans for our elders. They had taught us, by their examples, about money, sacrifice, and taking responsibility for others.

As Mom grew older and bolder in managing her money, she paid bills with her checking account and even wrote checks for $10 and $20 to Hillary Clinton's presidential campaign. She still kept track of money the way she had when I pinched some quarters from her change purse. After Mom passed away, I found notebooks in her careful hand that tracked every cent she earned—and every dollar she received from each of her kids. I wondered if that bit of recordkeeping might sow discord among us. But no one begrudged that some had given more at different times, others less. No matter how much or how little we sent home, Mom always showered us with her deep appreciation and love with a generosity that was greater than any amount of money.

Having reached my seventh decade, I still find myself keeping lists of what I spend so that I know what's come in and what's gone out. I can't say that I can track every quarter in my purse, the way my mom did, but I try my best to be aware. I can look back and see the wisdom of what my mother taught me by example: that a woman needs to have some money of her own. No matter how much or how little, each quarter contributes to a woman's sense of security, confidence, independence, and ultimately, empowerment.

Although Mom rarely talked about money with me, she taught me what is important to know about money, and life. For this and much more from my mother, I have unending gratitude.

THE KIND OF MONEY THAT CAN CHANGE YOUR LIFE

MANDY LEN CATRON

WHEN SHE was thirty-six—the same age I was when I published my first book—Lucy Catron's husband died in a farming accident, leaving her alone with four boys, a mother-in-law, a herd of dairy cows, no driver's license, and $26,000 in debt.

Lucy—whose real name, you should know, was Luzilla—was my grandmother. And, over the past few months, I haven't been able to stop thinking about all the ways the choices she made during her life have shaped mine.

This obsession with Lucy began at a retreat in Palm Springs last May. It was a small gathering where women and nonbinary folks met in the desert to eat and dance and talk about things that matter: from sex and parenthood to the opioid crisis and climate change. I'd been to the retreat once before, and everyone I met was so smart and warm and curious that I promised myself I would go back. But when the invitation arrived, I wavered.

Spending a thousand dollars for three days in the California desert felt wildly self-indulgent. I'd just turned thirty-eight and, after two years of deliberating, I'd finally decided to quit my job. I'd spent the previous decade teaching English at a large university—a job I loved—but I wanted to try working full-time as a writer. In the end, I decided I could go to California if I used up my credit card points and skipped the retreat hotel in favor of the Motel 6 next door.

That first morning, a woman named Anita led us in a simple meditation. "As you close your eyes and focus on your breath, I want you to think about all the people who made it possible for you to be here in this room, on this land today," she said. "With each inhale, try to focus on one of those people. And with each exhale, offer that person your gratitude."

I took a deep breath and thought of Lucy. Lucy, whom I called Granny until she died when I was thirteen. Lucy, from whom I inherited my chin and my cowlick, but whose life looked so different from mine.

It was 1962 when a beam fell from a loft in the barn and hit my grandfather on the head, killing him instantly. When I was thirty-six and leaving for a book tour I had fantasized about for years, it felt like my life was just beginning. But at that same age, the only life my grandmother had known was ending.

What would she think of this—of me sitting next to a turquoise pool with my eyes closed? What would she think of my life, which, unlike hers, was not constrained by caretaking and obligation? Or of my days, which were often spent reading books and taking the dog on long walks and immersing myself in ideas? How luxurious this would all seem to her. How indulgent. It still felt that way to me.

In my MFA program, we were thoroughly disabused of the idea that one could make a living as a writer. Sure, there was a time when such a life was possible, but by then—the early 2000s—this career was nothing more than an illusion harbored by young men who read too much Hunter S. Thompson. We could blame Amazon, or giant publishing conglomerates, or the death of print, or perhaps, even, a general decline in literacy. The reasons didn't matter. The important thing was that we wrote—and published—because it was inherently rewarding, because saying something true was a meaningful way to spend one's time. We weren't there to become Famous Authors; we were learning to be writers—to make a sentence that sliced like a scalpel or clanged like a cowbell, to see both praise and criticism as tools, not currency.

I have always been a dutiful student, so I took this to heart. I didn't need money or fame, just time, a cup of coffee, a working laptop. I would find a job that paid the bills and, in whatever time remained, I would write. And this is what I did. I taught enough classes to get by, I lived as cheaply as I could, and I wrote.

I was okay with the terms of this agreement. But then, somehow, after a decade of writing for small literary journals and a few hundred blog readers, the terms of the agreement changed.

In 2015, I sold my first book—a collection of essays about love and love stories—for what was, by all accounts, a lot of money. It was, as my agent Sam put it, "the kind of money that can change your life." And it changed mine.

I was on my way to a friend's house in the suburbs when Sam called to say that a publisher was interested in the book.

"Are you driving?" he asked. "You might want to pull over for this."

I parked on the side of a steep hill and sat down on the curb.

"So." He paused. "Simon and Schuster made an offer."

I was silent, terrified that saying anything would somehow break the spell.

"Do you want to know how much?"

"I think so . . . ," I said.

"They're offering three hundred fifty thousand dollars. But I think we can ask for more."

I genuinely do not remember what I said in response, though it was probably something like "Holy shit." I only remember a moment of shock, followed quickly by the thought that $350,000 could buy an enormous amount of writing time. I immediately understood that my life as a writer, which had, up to that point, been shaped by a careful toggle between earning money and making time, could become a different thing entirely.

I could take a year off from teaching to finish writing the book. I could buy a keyboard and a mouse and a laptop stand and sit at my dining room table every day transforming words into sentences. When my neck got sore from too many hours at the computer, I could pay to see a chiropractor. If my fifteen-year-old car died, I could replace it. If I decided to have a kid, I could afford child care. I could do all of this and still write. The future changed shape in an instant.

What does it mean to look to the future and know that it will be different from the thing you imagined for yourself? For my grandmother, it meant simply doing what needed to be done to get by.

"Dad died at two in the afternoon, and we were out milking the cows at five," my dad told me. "We didn't have time to grieve. We had to run a farm."

Lucy and her boys managed to keep the farm for a few more years. Eventually, the older boys wanted to leave home, so she sold the place and got a job in the high school cafeteria.

When I was a kid, Granny was the woman who made green beans and chicken and dumplings for Sunday supper. In the evenings, she drove out of town to the community college, where she learned bookkeeping and typing. She never dated again, and my dad doesn't remember her having any real social life. She cooked and studied and went to church and raised my dad, her only son still at home.

Eventually, Lucy worked her way up to a job as the school's secretary.

I grew up in a corner of Appalachia that was shaped by generations of poverty. And yet I believed that, with dedicated effort, one could work their way out of it. It was easy to buy into this version of the American Dream because, when I looked at my own family, that's what I saw: the daughter of a coal miner and the son of a farmer who'd grown up to be the IT manager and the high school principal.

None of us could see that we were living in a particular historical moment when coal and tobacco were still reliable ways to earn a living and opiate addiction had yet to ravage the region. Social mobility seemed possible. And when my parents told me that if I worked hard, I could do whatever I wanted with my life, I believed them. It never occurred to me that things didn't—or couldn't—always work this way.

Because no one talked about privilege. Perhaps we were reluctant to reckon with the fact that hard work *wasn't* always rewarded and that some of us got more than we deserved. Or perhaps it was because some communities, like the town where Lucy lived, were so small and so homogenous that it was hard to see how anyone had an advantage over anyone else. Lucy was offered a job in the high school cafeteria because the principal knew that she needed one. In a town of only five hundred people, and with limited resources to go around, success was often communal and collaborative.

In the end my book sold for $400,000. Sam explained that the payment would be divided over roughly four years. I'd get one quarter at signing, another when the manuscript was submitted, the third when the hardcover was published, and the final one when the paperback came out. Sam would take 15 percent off the top of each payment and the rest, $85,000, would appear in my bank account. I know that for some people this might not seem like much, but in the literary world, it was extraordinary.

When the first payment arrived, I bought a mail-order mattress, which I hoped would soothe my chronic pain, and a thin gold necklace. The necklace cost one hundred dollars—an amount I would have never spent on a single piece of jewelry for myself. But I wanted something I could see in the mirror each day, a testament to the fact that, whatever else happened in my life, I had once gotten the thing I wanted most in the world: a book contract with my name on it.

In the weeks after the first payment arrived, I was surprised to find that, once the initial shock wore off, I didn't feel the complete and total joy I expected. Instead, I felt embarrassed. It was such a relief—a thrill, really—to sit down in front of my computer and write every single day. But I couldn't bear the thought of anyone—especially other writers—knowing the dollar figure on that book contract.

I could just picture them thinking to themselves—or worse, saying to each other—"but Mandy's not even that good." And they wouldn't be totally wrong. It wasn't that I thought I was a bad writer; I didn't. I knew that I was skilled. But I also knew that lots of other people were just as capable as me—and many of them were struggling to pay the bills. I knew I didn't deserve financial success any more than they did.

When I tried to explain this to friends who weren't writers, they assured me that I just had impostor syndrome. I needed to embrace my success. "You worked hard for this," they would say.

"But lots of people work hard and don't get this," I countered.

Sometimes I wondered if, as a woman, I should be leaning into my successes. After all, how many male writers went around feeling embarrassed by their six-figure book advances? Still, I couldn't shake the feeling that I had gotten away with something, that I had cheated the system somehow.

When it came time for the book's publication, I worked hard to prove that I could play the role of a successful writer. I wrote pieces to promote the book. I did one interview after another after another. I was so nervous and excited that I stopped eating much or sleeping more than a few hours. But I went on live national television like a real six-figure writer is supposed to, and I tried my best to be charming. I wanted to show my publishers that they hadn't made a mistake hiring me for this job.

While I went from airport to airport, hotel to hotel, I worried over every post on Facebook and Instagram. Did my life seem glamorous or exhausting? Was I supposed to position myself as a success or just a regular person having a weird experience? And which one of those people was I?

After three weeks of book tour, I came home, sick and exhausted, and curled up on the couch with the dog. Despite the publicity and the kind reviews, the book's sales dropped off quickly. Within just a few weeks, it was clear my publishers would be losing money on me.

For months after, I felt like I had failed. The whole experience seemed so arbitrary, both that I had gotten such a generous advance in the first place and that, despite putting everything I had into the book, it fell so far short of success.

I had spent my life dreaming about answering the question "What do you do?" by simply saying, "I'm a writer."

But, now, when I introduce myself that way, I feel the weight of everything I do not say that has made such a life possible. It is easy to invoke the social prestige of the job and imply that my successes are mine alone. Yes, I worked hard, and no, I'm still not sure if I can support myself this way in the long run. But my life has been shaped far more by circumstance and the hard work of others than by anything I have done.

As I sat beneath towering California palm trees thinking of Lucy, I felt an immense sense of gratitude and clarity. The choices she had made during the most unimaginably difficult part of her life had opened up so many possibilities for me.

I'm a writer because I earned enough money from the sale of my first book to support myself for a few years.

I was able to sell that book because I had a flexible teaching job that allowed me to make time to write.

I had a flexible job because I had a graduate degree. And I was able to toggle between teaching and writing because my living expenses were so low.

My living expenses were low because my parents bought me a car when I was twenty. Because I didn't have student loans. Because I live in British Columbia and spend $37 a month on provincial health care.

I didn't have student loans because, after my grandmother died when I was thirteen, my parents invested the small inheritance from the sale of her house so I could pay for my education. I used that money for grad school. I didn't have undergraduate debt because I'd gotten a good scholarship.

I got a good scholarship because I had high grades and SAT scores. Because my parents put me in an SAT prep class. Because SAT questions are designed for white middle-class kids. Because my dad was a school principal, and he taught me how to succeed in the public education system. Because I was the kind of person who liked being liked by teachers and other adults, and I went out of my way to please them.

My dad was a school principal—not a farmer—because his mom insisted he go to college. She knew how to offer him this other future because she worked as the secretary at his high school. Before school began, she found my dad's schedule and, without saying a word, changed his agriculture class to chorus.

My grandmother was a high school secretary because her husband died in a farming accident. She worked a day job, took night classes, and sold tickets at the varsity basketball games in exchange for five dollars a night, all so her youngest son could be the first in his family to go to college.

I could keep going, but my point is this: so many things shape our access to opportunity, and our hard work is only one of them. I haven't even mentioned the fact that my race and sexual orientation and any number of other demographic factors work in my favor in visible and invisible ways every day. Ignoring those things makes it easier to imagine that you are not merely lucky or privileged but deserving.

And I get it: it's a nice story. But it can also be a relief to ourselves and those around us to let it go.

We tell ourselves so many stories about money: that it is the reward for our hard work, that it signals what is valuable, that it cannot buy things that will give our lives meaning, that we will never have equality until women assess their worth in the same ways men do. But none of these stories feel completely true to me.

When I got my book advance, I did all the things you're supposed to do when suddenly presented with an abundance of money and time: I donated to organizations that mattered to me and volunteered in my community. I taught myself to think of time and money not as social currency, or resources to hoard, but as tools. I wanted to use these tools however I could to amplify the voices of other women and nonbinary writers, especially those with fewer resources than me. I wanted this priority to seep into my life, influencing what I read and what I recommended, which books I bought and where I bought them. I let it shape how I teach and how I write and how I live. Because what is privilege if not an opportunity to decide exactly how you want to be in the world?

The one thing I didn't do, though, the thing I couldn't do, was talk openly about money. In Palm Springs, as I sat thinking of Lucy, I could see how much energy, how much potential value, I'd wasted feeling embarrassed about my own successes. Maybe I was worried that other writers would resent me. Or maybe some part of me was clinging to the possibility that I was especially deserving after all. But the truth is that when writers don't talk about money, and specifically how we got it, we obscure the various paths to success and perpetuate the myths of hard work and meritocracy. We don't help to alleviate inequality, we perpetuate it.

When I was eight or nine, I would go to Granny's house for a few days every summer. It would be just the two of us, and she would do whatever I wanted. She was the best cook I knew, but I wanted frozen chicken nuggets in the shape of dinosaurs, so that's what we ate. She would always find an excuse for us to go to the drugstore on Main Street, where she'd let me pick out a cheap plastic toy from the shelves. I was oblivious to how little she had and how much she offered.

Now that I'm an adult, I can see that what she offered was more than toys and snacks. She made me feel valued and interesting. More than that, she gave up so much of her own life so that her children and grandchildren could live lives that were shaped not by circumstance but by possibility. This is what intergenerational privilege can do.

Being a writer is no more important or necessary than being a lunch lady or a farmer's wife. But it comes with luxuries that generations of women before me never had—not just time and flexibility but a sense of self-determination and the assurance that my voice carries some weight in the world. I won't presume that this is exactly what Lucy imagined for me, but it is a profound thing to have been given.

HOW TO MAKE A LOT OF MONEY

TRACY McMILLAN

YEARS AGO, I encountered a woman who changed my life. She was a friend of a friend of a friend, and we were standing in a parking lot in Beverly Hills—not a place I wanted to be, then or now—after a birthday lunch. I happened to be in a life moment where I was particularly scared about money. And she happened to tell me she was a financial planner who considered it her highest spiritual calling to help women know the truth about money. Did I want to know the truth about money?

Not really, tbh.

Because I already knew the truth about money. *Money is hard to come by.* (If you add a *girrrl* on the end of that, it would capture the approximate tone of my inner voice.) Money takes work—a lot of work, so much work, Rhianna-song levels of *work work work work work*—and if you get some, you need to hang on to it, because you might not get any more anytime soon. Furthermore, other people can have money—they can have a lot of it, tons really—and you know many of those people, they were your friends growing up, they're your friends now, and they're your son's friends, too, but you've never been one of those people, and you never will be. To summarize, the truth about money would go something like this: *There might be enough. (Just barely.) But there will never be a lot.*

At the time I was a thirty-six-year-old single mom, living with my preschooler in a tidy but also hot and noisy apartment situated above a dog groomer. I had been freelancing three or four days a week as a writer in television news, a decently paying job that I couldn't say I loved, but I definitely didn't hate—but I had hit a dry spell. I drove a cute banana-colored 1984 Volvo station wagon that I paid $1,600 for and wore thrift-store clothing because I actually preferred it. I had purposely chosen not to work full-time because I valued hanging out with my son more than I minded having a car with Swedish air-conditioning. I also loved pursuing my many creative projects: my mom-friendships, knitting, gardening, spiritual growth, and yes, my band. I was happy. But I sure as hell didn't have a lot of money.

Eighteen years later, I kind of do. Little Tracy totally thinks I have a lot of money. Even Big Tracy is starting to think so. I go to Europe. Sleep on fancy sheets. Own my own small but lovely home. Paid cash for my kid's private liberal arts college. I even (this is almost embarrassing) fly first-class sometimes. I also have a will, a trust, an S corp, and some other white-man money thing called a Cash Balance Plan. If I had to, I could probably retire right now—in Grand Forks. I don't say all this to brag. I say it because my mom was a prostitute and my dad was a drug dealer and the fact that I just paid cash for my kid's private liberal arts college blows my fucking mind.

And it all began the minute I looked at the Beverly Hills Money Lady (BHML) and said: Okay, fine. What is the truth about money? Here's what she told me, and the journey it took me on:

1. THERE IS A LOT OF MONEY OUT THERE. JUST BREATHE IT IN.

I know, I know. It sounds so California, right? But BHML was really clear. She said: "You know how you just breathe in and fully expect air? You don't say to yourself, *Oh, God—I hope there's enough air when I go for this next breath!* And when you go to the beach, you're not worried they're going to run out of waves. You just *know*. It's there. You don't even think about it." And then she uttered the life-changing words: "That's how you can be about money."

2. MAKING MONEY STARTS WITH MAKING MONEY. ANY MONEY.

BHML told me to come up with a list of every single thing I could do for money. *Every single thing.* At the time I was really into knitting these long patchwork scarves. Reader, damned if I didn't go into the long patchwork scarves business. I started knitting my ass off. I gave every scarf a cute little handmade tag, branded with my band name. It turns out People With Money wanted to pay me eighty-five 2002 dollars apiece for those bad boys! Two weeks later, I took my scarves to a local cool-mom craft fair—and hauled in my *rent.*

3. CHANGE YOUR DAMN MIND.

Your mind runs your whole money show, whether you know it or not. Everyone has a belief system around money, and if you want to know what yours is, look at your bank account. Let me be clear: I am not saying how much money you have equals your *value.* I'm saying it's a reflection of what you believe to be true about money. My belief was that I could have enough (just barely), but I could never have a lot. I needed to change my mind about that. *Wayyyy* easier said than done.

4. DEAL WITH YOUR TRAUMA.

Is your mind telling you that making/getting/having a lot of money is fine for someone else, but you are *permanently* broke (or broke-ish) for all sorts of really real reasons—like structural racism, sexism, generational poverty, history of abuse, you name it? There's a reason for that: *trauma.* Which sears itself into your brain, body, and emotions and limits what you believe is possible. But you can heal! There are sliding-scale therapists, books at the library, twelve-step groups, community yoga classes, spiritual centers, abuse survivor support groups, and prayer and meditation, to name some resources. If you are determined, the help is out there. I promise. But you gotta want it like your life depends on it. Because it does. And you might find the biggest resistance comes from a surprising place.

5. THE CALL IS COMING FROM INSIDE THE HOUSE.

There's a famous horror film where the police trace the bad guy's call, and it turns out to be coming from inside the very same house where the main character has barricaded herself for safety. This is a pretty great metaphor for what we're talking about here. Changing your whole way of life—because that's what it takes to get a lot of money: you have to change your beliefs, and your actions, and in the process everything gets reorganized—is terrifying. Not because money is scary. Because letting go of everything you think you know is a form of annihilation. The old you has to die to make room for the new you.

6. START SEEING MONEY EVERYWHERE. WRITE YOUR NAME ON IT.

Selling the scarves was a powerful experience. Eighty-five dollars apiece for doing something I would have done for free? That's three hours at my TV-news day job laboring over sentences like: "There's a big fire burning in Whittier. Jane Doe is there with the story. Jane?" Even more crucially, knitting scarves was easy! And fun! Maybe there was even more money out there with my name on it, and maybe it could be a joy to earn.

7. IT'S NOT ABOUT HOW MUCH MONEY. IT'S ABOUT HOW MUCH ENERGY.

I expanded my scarves hustle to handbags. I found new places to sell them. I started writing fashion website blogs for $12 per post. I wrote a couple of (bad) screenplays. Then I wrote a couple of (better) screenplays. I used my band's Myspace page (yup) to tell a cool serialized story, one post each day. I stopped being interested in *how much money* I was making for doing something, and I started getting interested in *how much energy* I was creating and circulating. I knew the money would follow. And I was right. One morning I woke up to find a direct message from an editor at a small publishing house who had been following my story and offered me a $15,000 book deal. You guys, from Myspace! The old ideas were crashing down around me in the best possible way.

9. IT'S NOT ABOUT ODDS. IT'S ABOUT WILLINGNESS.

I was now five years past my encounter with the BHML. All my therapy, meditation, mind changing, and scarves (not to mention another marriage and divorce) had rearranged my belief system. To the point where I finally understood that having good things—and a lot of money is simply one of *many* possible good things—doesn't come down to odds. It comes down to *willingness*. And willingness isn't about deserving something, or even earning something. It's just about saying "yes" to it, instead of "no." Because all good things begin with "yes." And "yes" is a practice.

10. YOUR SPOT ISN'T TAKEN. BECAUSE YOU HAVEN'T TAKEN IT YET.

Eventually, my cumulative yesses led me to my second biggest childhood dream: becoming a television writer. (The first biggest was becoming Cher.) It was a dream I had given up on before even starting, because I "knew" that all the TV writer jobs were taken by people who are white, male, Ivy League grads (actually, any two out of three will do) with loads of industry contacts and/or a parental safety net the size of Nebraska. Also, they're like twenty-seven. And I was a forty-two-year-old biracial single mom with a ten-year-old son, no health insurance, and a degree from the University of an Unimportant State, whose dad was doing twenty years in federal prison. But my willingness practice led me to give one of those better scripts I had written to the one TV writer I knew—a mom-friend who'd gone back to work—and she generously passed it along to her agent. Eight months later, he called me. And a year after that, I got my first job. So, was I right? Do I work with a shocking number of people who have doctors for parents and/or went to Harvard? *Yes, I do.* But you know where I was wrong? *That didn't mean there was no room for me.*

11. MAKING MONEY IS AN ACT OF SELF-CARE.

So, you are almost there. You still with me? Great. There is one last thing to do. One last spiritual practice that will transform your relationship to the almighty dollar. *You're going to have to love yourself.* Yup. Getting a lot of money—then growing what you have and using it wisely—ultimately has come down to my deep and abiding commitment to take care of Little Tracy. I wanted to do for her what no one had ever done for me. I wanted her to feel safe! I wanted her needs to be met! And not just barely. I wanted her to see the world, and be comfortable, and have great health care, and maybe even a car with German air-conditioning. I wanted her to move through life knowing that I was here for her—with a safety net the size of Nebraska. Nothing made me more willing to get money than wanting to take care of that little girl. *My* little girl.

12. ONE LAST THING.

It's been eighteen years since that random parking lot encounter. I've never seen the BHML again. I doubt I would even recognize her if I had. But I don't need to see her again—I need to *be* her. So, I talk about money. All the time. Except instead of going to Beverly Hills, and being a professional Money Lady, I'm just trying to turn the world into my parking lot—running around telling any woman who will listen to nominate herself to get a lot of money because it's out there, with her name on it. My goal is to empower you the same way the BHML empowered me. I want you to get in touch with the actual reasons why money is important to you. Because that's when the Get Money doors fling themselves open and you come to know the truth: Money isn't hard to come by. It's not for other people. It's right here. All you have to do is breathe it in.

Notes

5   *. . . the wealth of twenty-two men*: Clare Coffey et al., "Time to Care:
    Unpaid and Underpaid Care Work and the Global Inequality Cri-
    sis," Oxfam (Oxford, UK, January 19, 2020), https://webassets.oxfam
    america.org/media/documents/FINAL_bp-time-to-care-inequality
    -200120-en.pdf?_gl=1*c5c8ee*_ga*MTY3NzIyNDczMS4xNjE4OD
    g3NTU1*_ga_R58YETD6XK*MTYxODg4NzU1NC4xLjEuMTYx
    ODg4NzgxMC4w.

5   *Women's domestic labor*: Sarah Coury et al., "Women in the Work-
    place 2020," McKinsey & Company, September 30, 2020, https://
    www.mckinsey.com/featured-insights/diversity-and-inclusion
    /women-in-the-workplace.

Acknowledgments

EDITING AN ANTHOLOGY—this is my sixth—takes an inordinate amount of faith, energy, curiosity, and care. Because each voice in the book speaks to the others to elevate the whole, a successful anthology is a collaboration that epitomizes the American Dream: out of many, one. My job is to envision, curate, harmonize, and attempt to realize that dream.

From the moment I decide a subject is worthy of a deep dive of this sort to the final days of proofing galleys and editing ARC copy, I carry both a vision for what I want the work to be, do, and mean in the world; plus a sense of responsibility to, and gratitude for, the writers who excavate daunting personal truths in order to illuminate the critical themes of the subject at hand. But beyond the writers, there are many collaborators who must be acknowledged, and to whom I send bushels of lilies and lilacs, peonies and poetry.

Gratitude to my adored agent, Richard Abate, who loves my voice as much as I need and admire his. A deep bow to my first editor and dear comrade in publishing, Dawn Davis, who acquired this book and shepherded it until she could no longer. Many thanks to Chelcee Johns, who picked it up where Dawn left off and made sure it ended up in the exacting hands of Hana Park, who skillfully brought the book home through the various twists and turns of production. Thank you to Simon & Schuster's supportive publisher, Dana Canedy, editorial director Priscilla Painton; and the many people at the house whom I will never meet, but have given some of their precious energy to bring this work to life.

It is impossible to imagine getting anything done, especially an anthology of this intensity and depth, without my team, whom I treasure more with each passing day. Nat Moon and Lily Diamond, words fail. You are true blessings in my life. Hope Leigh and Melanie Abrams, thank you for attending to your respective responsibilities with grace, goodwill, and competence. Heather Scott, artist and designer extraordinaire, you stepped in to give me a cover I will be proud to live with for the rest of my life. Thanks to Danzy Senna, my stealth support, who consistently cheered me on and up even when the rainbow felt like enuf.

And then there is my family. My parents, sister, Jessica, and my children—all of whom have suffered my lapses in attention and heightened moods—will always have my gratitude for supporting me and this book even when they didn't quite understand my long-winded attempts to describe it, or why it was taking so long to complete. My wife, Rachel, as she well knows, will always have my heart. Without her, I would not, ever, have been able to meet the demands of this book, and so much more. She is a partner par excellence, and for this I am exceedingly fortunate. I have chosen the perfect color with which to paint my life.

Finally, I could not have edited this book without the writers who make it sing, or the readers who listen for its song. I thank each and every one of you, and am so moved that you have appeared to mingle your stories, insights, and hearts, with ours.

May we all, together, be free.

GABRIELLE BELLOT

Gabrielle Bellot is a staff writer for Literary Hub and a contributing editor at Catapult, where she also works as head instructor. Her work has appeared in the *New York Times*, the *Guardian*, the *New Yorker*, the *Atlantic*, the *Cut*, *Guernica*, *Bookforum*, and many other places. She lives in Queens, New York.

adrienne maree brown

adrienne maree brown is the writer in residence at the Emergent Strategy Ideation Institute and the author of *Holding Change: The Way of Emergent Strategy Facilitation and Mediation*; *We Will Not Cancel Us and Other Dreams of Transformative Justice*; *Pleasure Activism: The Politics of Feeling Good*; and *Emergent Strategy: Shaping Change, Changing Worlds* and the co-editor of *Octavia's Brood: Science Fiction from Social Justice Movements* and *How to Get Stupid White Men Out of Office*. She is the cohost of the *How to Survive the End of the World*, *Octavia's Parables*, and *Emergent Strategy* podcasts.

RACHEL CARGLE

Rachel Cargle is an Akron, Ohio–born public academic, writer, and philanthropic innovator. Her book with The Dial Press/Penguin Random

House, *I Don't Want Your Love and Light*, examines the intersection of race, feminism, and womanhood and how we are in relationship with ourselves and one another. Rachel is the founder and president of The Loveland Foundation, Inc., her nonprofit offering free therapy to Black women and girls. Rachel recently launched The Great Unlearn, a self-paced, self-priced community utilizing Rachel's monthly curated social syllabi. As a gift to her younger self, Rachel created Elizabeth's Bookshop & Writing Centre, currently an online independent bookstore and innovative literacy center designed to amplify, celebrate, and honor the work of writers who are often excluded from traditional cultural, social, and academic canons. Rachel has been featured on TEDx and *Red Table Talk*, is a regular contributor to *Harper's Bazaar*, and has been featured in the *Washington Post*, *Glamour UK*, *Essence*, Refinery29, *Forbes*, and the *New Yorker*.

MANDY LEN CATRON

Mandy Len Catron is the author of the critically acclaimed essay collection *How to Fall in Love with Anyone*. The book was listed for the 2018 RBC Taylor Prize and the Kobo Emerging Writer Prize. Her writing can be found in the *New York Times*, the *Atlantic*, the *Guardian*, the Rumpus, Catapult, and the Walrus, as well as other newspapers, literary journals, and anthologies. Her essays and talks have been translated into more than thirty languages.

Mandy's article "To Fall in Love with Anyone, Do This" is one of the most popular articles published in the *New York Times*'s Modern Love column. You can find her two TEDx talks at TED.com and her blog on love and love stories at The Love Story Project, thelovestoryproject.org. She's currently working on a book about loneliness, which you can read more about in her newsletter. She teaches creative writing at the University of British Columbia and at the Downtown Eastside Women's Centre in Vancouver. She is originally from Appalachian Virginia.

TRESSIE McMILLAN COTTOM

Tressie McMillan Cottom is an assistant professor of sociology at Virginia Commonwealth University and the author of *Lower Ed* and *Thick* (The New Press). Her work has been featured by the *The Daily Show*, the *New York Times*, the *Washington Post*, PBS, NPR, *Fresh Air*, and the *Atlantic*, among others. She lives in Richmond, Virginia.

LILY DIAMOND

Lily Diamond is a writer, educator, and advocate working to democratize wellness through storytelling, accessible practices for inner and outer nourishment, and revolutionary acts of self-care in relationship to our earth and human communities. Lily is the author of the bestselling memoir-cookbook *Kale & Caramel: Recipes for Body, Heart, and Table* and coauthor of *What's Your Story? A Journal for Everyday Evolution*. Her work has been featured in the *New York Times*, VICE, Healthyish, *Women's Review of Books*, Refinery29, and more. She lives in Maui, Hawai'i, where she grew up, on occupied native Hawaiian land.

THE FRASIER-JONESES

Helena Frasier-Jones is a Caribbean writer of the African diaspora. She has worked in art galleries, cofounded a literary salon, and published interviews and articles in various magazines, on topics ranging from art and culture to ecological revolution. She believes that attending to Black consciousness in its entirety is the only means for Black survival, and continues to be astonished by the determination of white supremacy to destroy Black joy. She uses her writing to expose, resist, and document the ongoing project of colonization in all of its guises.

RACHEL M. HARPER

Rachel M. Harper is the author of three novels: *The Other Mother*, upcoming from Counterpoint Press; *This Side of Providence*, which was shortlisted for the 2016 Ernest J. Gaines Award; and *Brass Ankle Blues*, a Borders Original Voices Award finalist and Target Breakout Book. Her short fiction has been nominated for a Pushcart Prize, and her poems and essays have appeared in numerous journals and anthologies, including *Chicago Review*, *African American Review*, and *Black Cool: One Thousand Streams of Blackness*. She has received fellowships from Yaddo and MacDowell, and is on the faculty at Spalding University's School of Creative and Professional Writing. She lives in Los Angeles.

DAISY HERNÁNDEZ

Daisy Hernández is the author of *The Kissing Bug: A True Story of a Family, an Insect, and a Nation's Neglect of a Deadly Disease* (Tin House). She's also the author of the award-winning memoir *A Cup of Water Under My Bed* (Beacon Press) and coeditor of the anthology *Colonize This! Young Women of Color on Today's Feminism* (Seal Press). A journalist, she has reported for *National Geographic*, the *Atlantic*, the *New York Times*, and *Slate*, and her writing has been aired on NPR's *All Things Considered*. She is an associate professor in the Creative Writing Program at Miami University in Ohio.

JEN/ELEANA HOFER

Jen/Eleana Hofer (they/ellx/she) is a poet, translator, social justice interpreter, teacher, facilitator, urban cyclist, and cofounder of the language justice and language experimentation collaborative Antena Aire (2010 to 2020) and the language justice collective Antena Los Ángeles (2014 to 2021). They identify as a queer white Latinx (Argentinean) Jewish BDS supporter who grew up mostly monolingual in a bilingual/bicultural family. Jen/Eleana lives on unceded Tongva land at the confluence of the Los Angeles River and the Arroyo Seco in Northeast Los Angeles, where they teach writing, DIY bookmaking, and literary translation and support community groups in building equitable communication. They have received support in many forms from many entities, including CantoMundo, the Academy of American Poets, the City of Los Angeles, the NEA, and the PEN American Center. They publish poems, translations, and visual-textual works with numerous small presses, including Action Books, Atelos, Counterpath Press, Kenning Editions, and Ugly Duckling Presse, and in various DIY/DIT incarnations. Their translations of Uruguayan poet Virginia Lucas published in 2021 by Litmus Press. *Between Language and Justice: Selected Writings from Antena Aire* published in 2021 by The Operating System.

LEAH HUNT-HENDRIX

Leah Hunt-Hendrix is a writer and organizer whose work has focused on social movements and building progressive political power. She has a PhD from Princeton University, where she studied political theory and philosophy of religion. In 2012, she founded Solidaire, a network of philanthropists dedicated to funding progressive movements, which contributed to a shift in the philanthropic field toward "movement philanthropy." In 2017, building on that work, she cofounded Way to Win, a community where high-net-worth political donors can coordinate their electoral funding strategies. She has served on numerous boards, which now include the Solutions Project and the Quincy Institute for Responsible Statecraft. Her writings have been featured in the *New Republic*, the *Nation*, *Huffington Post*, the *Guardian*, and *Politico*, and she has been profiled by Salon, *Avenue* magazine, and *San Francisco* magazine. Leah was born and raised in New York City and has lived in Egypt, Syria, and the West Bank.

POROCHISTA KHAKPOUR

Porochista Khakpour was born in Tehran in 1978 and raised in the greater Los Angeles area. Her debut novel, *Sons and Other Flammable Objects* (Grove/Atlantic, 2007), was a *New York Times* "Editor's Choice," *Chicago Tribune* "Fall's Best," and 2007 California Book Award winner. In 2014, Khakpour was one of *Dazed*'s "Top 10 American Writers You Need to Read This Year." Her first memoir, *Sick*, a memoir of chronic illness, misdiagnosis, addiction, and the myth of full recovery, chronicling the long, arduous discovery of her late-stage Lyme disease, was published by the Harper Perennial imprint of HarperCollins on June 5, 2018. She lives in New York City.

TERESE MARIE MAILHOT

Terese Marie Mailhot is from Seabird Island Band. Her work has appeared in *Guernica*, *Pacific Standard*, *Granta*, *Mother Jones*, *Medium*, *Best American Essays*, and elsewhere. She is the *New York Times* bestselling author of *Heart Berries: A Memoir*. She is the recipient of a 2019 Whiting Award. She teaches creative writing at Purdue University.

MARNIE MASUDA

Marnie Masuda writes about art, entertainment, education, and the complex language and culture of grief. As executive director of The Creative Core, she helps teachers and students cultivate and expand the most essential habits of mind: curiosity, imagination, creativity, and questioning. She lives on Maui with her family and is working on a darkly sparkly memoir about living through the unimaginable. Her blog, *Where You Stay*, explores the "full catastrophe" of love, home, and joy that manages to get through and grow, even in the darkest and bleakest of times.

NANCY McCABE

Nancy McCabe is the author of six books, most recently *Can This Marriage Be Saved? A Memoir* (University of Missouri Press, 2020). Her creative nonfiction has appeared in *Prairie Schooner*, the *Massachusetts Review*, *Newsweek*, *Michigan Quarterly Review*, *Fourth Genre*, *Los Angeles Review of Books*, the anthology *Oh Baby: True Stories About Conception, Adoption, Surrogacy, Pregnancy, Labor, and Love* (In Fact Books, 2015) and the anthology *Every Father's Daughter: Twenty-Four Women Writers Remember Their Fathers* (McPherson, 2015). She is a recipient of the Pushcart Prize and eight recognitions in the "notable" sections of *Best American Essays* and *Best American Nonrequired Reading*.

TRACY McMILLAN

Tracy McMillan is a television writer, relationship expert, and author whose credits include *Mad Men*, *Good Girls Revolt*, Marvel's *Runaways*, and *United States of Tara*. She's the author of three books: a memoir, *I Love You and I'm Leaving You Anyway*; a novel, *Multiple Listings*; and a relationship book, *Why You're Not Married . . . Yet*. The latter is based on the viral blog *Why You're Not Married*, which for more than two years was the most-viewed article in the history of the *Huffington Post*. Tracy's television appearances include Oprah Winfrey's *Super Soul Sunday*, the *Today* show, *Access Hollywood Live*, *Katie*, and more. Her Tedx talk, "The Person You Really Need to Marry," has more than 15 million views.

VICTORIA PATTERSON

Victoria Patterson's latest story collection, *The Secret Habit of Sorrow*, was published in 2018. The critic Michael Schaub wrote: "There's not a story in the book that's less than great; it's a stunningly beautiful collection by a writer working at the top of her game." Her novel *The Little Brother*, which *Vanity Fair* called "a brutal, deeply empathetic, and emotionally wrenching examination of American male privilege and rape culture," was published in 2015. She is also the author of the novels *The Peerless Four* and *This Vacant Paradise*, a 2011 *New York Times Book Review* "Editors' Choice." Her story collection, *Drift*, was a finalist for a California Book Award and the Story Prize and was selected as one of the best books of 2009 by the *San Francisco Chronicle*. She lives in South Pasadena, California, with her family.

MELISSA PETRO

Melissa Petro is a freelance writer and stay-at-home mom living in New York. Her work has appeared in *Marie Claire*, *Real Simple*, and *Pacific Standard* magazine, and on *Cosmopolitan*, *Redbook*, *Good Housekeeping*, *Esquire*, the *Guardian*, *Washington Post*, and elsewhere on the web. Follow her on Twitter @melissapetro.

SONALEE RASHATWAR, LCSW MED

Sonalee Rashatwar (she/they) is an award-winning clinical social worker, sex therapist, adjunct lecturer, and grassroots organizer. Based in Philadelphia (licensed in New Jersey and Pennsylvania), she is a superfat queer bisexual nonbinary therapist and co-owner of Radical Therapy Center, specializing in treating sexual trauma, body image issues, racial or immigrant identity issues, and South Asian family systems while offering fat- and body-positive sexual health care. Popularly known as TheFatSexTherapist on Instagram, their notoriety first peaked when they were featured on Breitbart in March 2018 for naming thinness as a white supremacist beauty ideal. Sonalee is a sought-after speaker who travels internationally to curate custom visual workshops that whisper to our change-making spirit and nourish our vision for a more just future. Sonalee received their Master of Social Work and Master of Education in Human Sexuality from Widener University in 2016 and has been working in the field of anti-violence for eight-plus years.

SAM REGAL

Sam Regal is a writer, artist, and librarian-in-training living in Los Angeles. Her translation of Macanese poet Yao Feng's *One Love Only Until Death* was published by Vagabond Press, and her poems, plays, and stories have appeared in Grub Street, Santa Ana River Review, The Wild Word, and elsewhere. She has performed at MoMA PS1 and Le Poisson Rouge in New York City, and her exhibition *Turbulent Femme*, in collaboration with artist Alex McClay, was staged by the University of Georgia galleries in 2019. She earned an MFA in Poetry from Hunter College, and she's working toward an MLIS at UCLA, where she also serves as project manager of California Rare Book School (CalRBS). She thinks a lot about empathic professional praxis, abolition, and her tuxedo cat, Tomato.

NINA REVOYR

Nina Revoyr is the author of six novels, including *Southland*, a *Los Angeles Times* bestseller and "Best Book" of the year and a 2021 pick for the California Book Club; *The Age of Dreaming*, a *Los Angeles Times* Book Award finalist; *Wingshooters*, an *O, The Oprah Magazine* "Book to Watch For" and winner of the Indie Booksellers' Choice Award; and *Lost Canyon*, a *San Francisco Chronicle* "Recommended Book." Her most recent novel is *A Student of History*. Nina was a longtime executive at a nonprofit organization serving children affected by violence and poverty. She now works as part of a philanthropic effort to improve economic mobility for low-income children and families. Nina has been an associate faculty member at Antioch College and a visiting professor at Cornell University, Occidental College, Pitzer College, and Pomona College. She lives in Southern California with her wife and their dog.

CAMERON RUSSELL

Cameron Russell is a model, organizer, and writer whose work leverages creative collaboration and collective storytelling to facilitate evolution. She has spent the last seventeen years working as a model for clients like Prada, Calvin Klein, Victoria's Secret, H&M, *Vogue*, and *Elle*. With more than 37 million views and counting, she gave one of the top ten most popular TED talks of all time, on the power of image. She's currently finishing work on a book about fashion, intuition, and power. In 2012, she graduated with honors from Columbia University with a degree in economics and political science and wrote a thesis about grassroots cultural workers and political power. After graduating, she organized a collective of artist activists based in Brooklyn. In 2016, she cofounded the Model Mafia, a growing network of hundreds of fashion models committed to building a more equitable, just, and sustainable industry and world.

SONYA RENEE TAYLOR

Sonya Renee Taylor is a world-renowned activist, award-winning artist, transformational thought leader, author of six books including the *New York Times* bestselling *The Body is Not an Apology*, and founder of the movement and digital media and education company of the same name. Her work has reached millions of people by exploring the intersections of identity, healing, and social justice using a radical self-love framework. She continues to speak, teach, write, create, and transform lives globally.

LATHAM THOMAS

After giving birth to her son, Fulano, in 2003, Latham Thomas set out on a mission to help women reclaim birth. A graduate of Columbia University and the Institute for Integrative Nutrition, Latham is a maternity lifestyle maven, world-renowned wellness leader, and master birth doula on the vanguard of transforming the wellness movement. Named one of Oprah

Winfrey's "Super Soul 100," Latham is bridging the gap between optimal wellness, spiritual growth, and radical self-care and is the go-to guru for the modern holistic lifestyle for women. She authored the bestselling book *Mama Glow: A Hip Guide to Your Fabulous and Abundant Pregnancy* with a foreword by Dr. Christiane Northrup in 2012 and most recently published the bestseller *Own Your Glow: A Soulful Guide to Luminous Living and Crowning the Queen Within*. Latham serves on the Tufts University Nutrition Council and is also a member of the Well+Good Council, where she provides expertise in women's wellness, pregnancy, and self-care. In March of 2018, Latham released the meditation audio program *Beditations: Guided Meditations and Rituals for Rest and Renewal*. She teaches at universities and teaching hospitals around the country, helping to improve the patient labor and delivery experience.

NEELA VASWANI

Neela Vaswani is the author of the short story collection *Where the Long Grass Bends*, the mixed-genre memoir *You Have Given Me a Country*, the middle-grade novel *Same Sun Here* (cowritten with Silas House), and the picture book *This Is My Eye* (author and photographer). She is the recipient of the American Book Award, a PEN/O. Henry Prize, the ForeWord Book of the Year Gold Medal, the Italo Calvino Prize for Emerging Writers, and other literary honors. Also an audio book narrator, she received a Grammy for her narration of *I Am Malala: How One Girl Stood Up for Education and Changed the World* and multiple Audies for other narration work. Vaswani has a PhD in American Cultural Studies and an MFA in Writing. She lives in New York City with her family and teaches at Spalding University's brief-residency MFA in Writing program.

ALICE WALKER

Alice Walker is an internationally celebrated writer, poet, and activist whose books include seven novels, four collections of short stories, four children's books, and several volumes of essays and poetry. She won the Pulitzer Prize in Fiction in 1983 and the National Book Award, and has been honored with the O. Henry Award, the Lillian Smith Award, and the Mahmoud Darwish Literary Prize for Fiction. She was inducted into the California Hall of Fame in 2006 and received the LennonOno Grant for Peace in 2010. Her work is published in more than two dozen languages around the world.

REBECCA WALKER

Rebecca Walker has contributed to the global conversation about race, gender, power, and the evolution of the human family for more than two decades. The author of several bestselling books, she is a popular speaker who has appeared at more than four hundred universities, literary conferences, and corporate campuses and served as a DEI consultant for several Fortune 500 companies. She is active in the film and television space, and cofounded the Third Wave Fund, an organization that gives grants to women and transgender youth working for social justice. Walker was named by *Time* magazine as one of the most influential leaders of her generation. She lives in Los Angeles.

JAMIE WONG

Jamie is an entrepreneur, adviser, and investor. She founded Vayable, an early pioneer in the local experiences segment of travel, where she was CEO for seven years. She then founded Project Empathy, a virtual reality series and social justice initiative to help the prison population. As a founder, she was backed by top Silicon Valley investors and built partnerships with some of the world's largest technology, travel, and media companies. Jamie has been named a *Forbes* "Up-and-Comer," a *Business Insider* "Top Founder to Watch," and a *Huffington Post* "Top 50 Non-Technical Founder in Technology." As a thought leader in social justice, impact investing, and entrepreneurship, Jamie has appeared on major networks, such as CBS, BBC, CNN, and Bloomberg, and her writing has appeared in several publications, including *Fast Company*, *Entrepreneur*, and *The End of The Golden Gate*, an anthology published by Chronicle Books. Jamie was a producer for *The Daily Show with Jon Stewart*, Michael Moore, Sundance Channel, and PBS's *Frontline* and has worked for leading social justice organizations, including the NAACP Legal Defense and Educational Fund, Dream Corps, American Jewish World Service, and Action Against Hunger. Jamie holds a bachelor's degree with honors in History from Wesleyan University, where she received the Butterfield Prize, and a master's in Science from Columbia Journalism School, where she was awarded the Chancellor Scholarship.

HELEN ZIA

Helen Zia is an award-winning activist, author, and journalist; her most recent book is *Last Boat Out of Shanghai: The Epic Story of the Chinese Who Fled Mao's Revolution*.